Home Fires
and Foreign Fields

British Social and
Military Experience in the
First World War

Other Brassey's titles of interest

BARNETT *et al.*
Old Battles and New Defences: Can We Learn from Military History

GODDEN
Harrier: Ski-jump to Victory

LIDDLE
Gallipoli 1915: Pens, Pencils and Cameras at War

McNAUGHT
Nuclear Weapons and Their Effects

SCHULTZ & GODSON
Dezinformatsia: Active Measures in Soviet Strategy

WINDASS
Avoiding Nuclear War: Common Security as a Strategy for the
Defence of the West

Home Fires and Foreign Fields

British Social and
Military Experience in the
First World War

Edited by

PETER H. LIDDLE
Sunderland Polytechnic, U.K.

BRASSEY'S DEFENCE PUBLISHERS
a Member of the Pergamon Group

LONDON · OXFORD · WASHINGTON D.C.
NEW YORK · TORONTO · SYDNEY · FRANKFURT

U.K. (Editorial)	Brassey's Defence Publishers Ltd., Maxwell House, 74 Worship Street, London EC2A 2EN
(Orders)	Brassey's Defence Publishers Ltd., Headington Hill Hall, Oxford OX3 0BW, England
U.S.A. (Editorial)	Pergamon-Brassey's International Defense Publishers, 1340 Old Chain Bridge Road, McLean, Virginia 22101, U.S.A.
(Orders)	Pergamon Press Inc., Maxwell House, Fairview Park, Elmsford, New York 10523, U.S.A.
CANADA	Pergamon Press Canada Ltd., Suite 104, 150 Consumers Road, Willowdale, Ontario M2J 1P9, Canada
AUSTRALIA	Pergamon Press (Aust.) Pty. Ltd., P.O. Box 544, Potts Point, N.S.W. 2011, Australia
FEDERAL REPUBLIC OF GERMANY	Pergamon Press GmbH, Hammerweg 6, D-6242 Kronberg-Taunus, Federal Republic of Germany

First edition 1985

Library of Congress Cataloguing in Publication Data
Main entry under title:
Home fires and foreign fields.
1. World War, 1914–1918 – Great Britain – Addresses, essays, lectures. 2. World War, 1914–1918 – Addresses, essays, lectures. I. Liddle, Peter.
D546.H66 1985   940.3'41   85-7723

British Library Cataloguing in Publication Data
Home fires and foreign fields: British social and military experience in the First World War. 1. World War, 1914–1918 – George V, 1910–1936
I. Liddle, Peter, *1934–*
941.083   DA577

ISBN 0-08-031171-7

Printed in Great Britain by A. Wheaton & Co. Ltd., Exeter

The Soldier

If I should die, think only this of me:
   That there's some corner of a foreign field
That is for ever England. There shall be
   in that rich earth a richer dust concealed;
A dust whom England bore, shaped, made aware,
   Gave, once, her flowers to love, her ways to roam,
A body of England's, breathing English air,
   Washed by the rivers, blest by suns of home.

RUPERT BROOKE

Keep the Home Fires Burning

They were summoned from the hill-side
They were called in from the glen,
And the country found them ready
At the stirring call for men.
Let no tears add to their hardship,
As the soldiers pass along,
And although your heart is breaking,
Make it sing this cheery song.

Keep the home fires burning while your hearts are yearning.
Though your lads are far away, they dream of home.
There's a silver lining through the dark clouds shining,
turn the dark cloud inside out, till the boys come home.

IVOR NOVELLO

Acknowledgements

In several areas *Home Fires and Foreign Fields* displays an indebtedness to the Public Record Office. The Editor filled his own particular pitcher from this seemingly bottomless well and joins with those who worked in Chancery Lane or at Kew in acknowledging a substantial debt to the institution and to its staff.

Contents

By Way of Introduction

In January 1984, conscious of the year being the 70th anniversary of the outbreak of the First World War, it seemed to me highly appropriate that a Conference should be held which would commemorate that anniversary. Authorities at Sunderland Polytechnic, where my 1914–18 Personal Experience Archives are housed, willingly gave their approval and I embarked upon the task of inviting historians to give papers. There was such a readiness to support the venture that I was fortunate in being able to get almost without exception the men I particularly hoped to see in Sunderland and also to ensure the handling of a range of topics which would include both the popular themes as well as a number of highly significant, but less well known, subjects of research investigation.

That the Conference, when it was held in September, was such a success must be attributed in large measure to the quality of the papers produced and the contribution in personal terms made by the speakers who showed a degree of involvement in the full proceedings which so much lessened the natural anxieties of those whose responsibility it was to plan for an intellectually stimulating but also a socially agreeable occasion.

There were other factors too accounting for the success and with a well-remembered sense of indebtedness I would like to pay tribute first to the volunteers in the Archives, particularly Joyce Henshaw and Nobby Clark who worked so hard during the early planning stages. They were joined by Kevin Kelly and Barry Williams who, with Les Davison of the Polytechnic Library, skilfully produced sound-recorded material for the Exhibition which served as a focal point of the whole conference. This exhibition of documents, photographs, artwork and artefacts from the 1914–18 Archives and working models of First World War aeroplanes from the Morpeth scale model flying club was accorded, thanks to the support of Norman Hunter, the Librarian, the excellent setting of half the main reception hall of the Polytechnic Library. The layout and display of the exhibition benefited from the professional flair of its designer, Rob Burton from the Faculty of Art. During the three-week intrusion of battle sound, aircraft engines, tape recorded interviews and crowds of visitors, all the Library staff were unstinting in giving every assistance despite the disturbance to their work, particularly by telephone calls. Reference must be made in particular to the two caretakers and to a special unit from Northumbria Police as their co-operation safeguarded material which was of course irreplaceable.

The Polytechnic Estates Division answered every call for help but the Exhibition was heavily dependent upon the outstanding generosity of Vaux Breweries P.L.C. of Sunderland through the understanding and enthusiasm of the Public Relations Officer, Mervyn Willers. The actual cost of mounting the displays was heavy and assistance in defraying this was given by Blandford Press of Poole in Dorset, Brassey's Defence Publishers of London, Michael Russell Publishing Wilton, Cornings Glass and Lloyds Bank both of Sunderland and there was also help in cash or kind from Edmonds Museum Cases of Birmingham, Joplings of Sunderland, Ward's Graphics of Dunston, Sunderland County Borough Museum, Scottish and Newcastle Brewery, The Polity Press Oxford, George Allen and Unwin Publishing of Hemel Hempstead, the *Sunderland Echo* and the *Newcastle Journal and Evening Chronicle*, the Esmée Fairbairn Charitable Trust, Mayday Printers of Gateshead and Stuart Stott of Hythe in Kent.

A special thanks in which I know every person who attended the Conference would want to be associated must go to Tony Gray and the catering and housekeeping staff. High quality food was plentifully provided and the service was always friendly, the Conference dinner being a triumph for all concerned in its management, a memorable evening made the more so by the rousing choruses of songs of the Great War in which we were led by the talents of John Hawkins and his accompanist Hugh Hedley.

Reid Wilford of the Polytechnic's Continuing Education Unit had in Norma Meeks someone who coped with graceful efficiency in all administration tasks, the technicians of the History and Geography Department copied the documents selected for display, Tom McKitterick of the Department of Civil Engineering copied the photographs, Kathleen Barnes and Gillian Mushens voluntarily undertook many tasks and then during the fortnight the Exhibition was open, Nick Henshaw, Douglas and Bill McIntyre and Bill Lawson were exemplary custodians while managing at the same time to run the popular bookstall provided by Hills of Waterloo Place, Sunderland, whose Directors had gone to endless trouble to show an extensive range of books on the Great War.

In these few words of appreciation, gratefully I acknowledge my good fortune in having the wholehearted support of my wife Louise for she frequently helped me to see in perspective, Conference difficulties which had seemed to loom alarmingly large but then diminished under the influence of a more detached but encouragingly positive approach.

One element which enhanced the proceedings of the whole Conference and something which will remain perhaps for longer than anything else as a happy memory, was the presence of First World War veterans as members of the Conference, in large numbers at a special reception and then again at the Conference dinner itself. By happy chance of fate the dinner was held on the precise anniversary date of great events in the lives of two of our guests at the Conference, Major Edward Cooper having his V.C. gazetted on 15 September 1917, and Bob Tate having driven a tank towards Flers Courcelette on 15 September 1916. In the September month of so-called mellow fruitfulness of the previous year, 1915, one guest Herbert Taylor, was languishing at Suvla Bay, Gallipoli while in the first September of the war, territorial Bill Allan another guest, was in full-time training preparatory to his service on the Western Front.

Our principal guest was Sir Thomas Harley and he made a welcome contribution in many ways. His First World War service on the Western Front and in Macedonia was recalled movingly but also with humour when he welcomed 1914–18 men to the reception and then when he spoke so eloquently at the Conference dinner. Old soldiers Cecil Slack and Tom Robson joined Sir Thomas on a number of occasions with pertinent anecdotal comment during the questions which followed the delivery of Conference papers, which leads me quite naturally to the papers here in their published form.

It is an honour to be the editor of such a collection and I do thank my fellow contributors for their support in making their work generally available. Unlike the chairman of a Party Political Conference, an editor of such a collection has no responsibility to produce a consensus viewpoint. This is just as well as at least two of the papers are in trenchant discord, those of John Grigg on Lloyd George and John Terraine on British Military Leadership. As editor I have done nothing to blur what are almost wholly opposed standpoints on a major issue and I judge it to be improper here to reflect an editorial inclination to one view or the other. All I need say is that the marshalling of facts, the cogency of argument and the force of expression will command the respect of the reader who will then have the enjoyable but equally subjective challenge of judging if anything were to have been omitted or anything overstressed.

The theme of "Home Fires" was introduced at the Conference by Dr. David Sweet of the University of Durham who paid particular attention to the role of Parliament in its essential link between national management and the shop floor of public opinion. The extent to which this link failed to hold working people to an acceptance that the exigencies of war were leading to sacrifices which were being borne equitably by all sections of the community was the theme of Dr. Bernard Waites of the Open University. Dr. Waites drew attention to the not by any means stilled voice of a sector of public opinion which receives little serious consideration outside of specialist publications and these publications themselves lose some impact by reason of their limited and perhaps ideologically committed readership.

Dr. Mike Pattison of Barry College of Further Education similarly puts the reader in his debt by an illuminating paper on a topic of fundamental importance but one concerning which there is too little readily available published work. Dr. Pattison's paper is on scientific development through Government established committees and agencies.

No single paper was exclusively devoted to opposition to the war. This was a pity but neither of the two men best qualified to give such a paper was free in September, Professor Arthur Marwick because of a long standing academic commitment in Poland. This disappointment is paralleled by the impossibility of printing in this volume Professor David Dilk's impressive research on the Department of National Service and its first Director-General as it was to be published later in 1984 in its larger context of the first volume of David Dilk's biography of Neville Chamberlain.

Major-General Tony Trythall's paper on Fuller and the Tanks, the editor's on the Gallipoli concept and its execution, the paper of Colin White (Royal Naval Museum, Portsmouth) on the War at Sea and that of Keith Simpson (Royal Military Academy, Sandhurst) on the British soldier on the Western Front contributed to the Conference on what might be called obvious or popular themes but Dr. Malcolm Smith of St. David's College, Lampeter offered his research on a topic which perhaps has not had the balanced treatment which so important a subject deserved, that of the application of air power over the Western Front.

Dr. Ian Beckett partnering Keith Simpson from the Royal Military Academy focused in sharp detail on the separate elements which together made up the 48th Territorial Division and from his research was able to make telling observations upon the "character" of Territorial Force units and of the performance of these units and their commanders in battle.

On a wider canvas Dr. Brian Porter from the University College of Wales at Aberystwyth examined both the diplomatic background and military campaigning against the Turks in Mesopotamia and Palestine, a theme which benefited from the demonstrated interrelationship between the two fronts. Dr. Porter's whole approach was one which educated those of us too frequently blinkered in our concentration upon some piece of research which we choose exclusively to "compartment".

For accepting the onerous burden of the preparation and delivery of two papers, Dr. Hugh Cecil of the University of Leeds well deserves the place of honour as rearguard at the conclusion of these introductory remarks. Having enlightened his audience at the Conference on the work of the British parent of the League of Nations (studiously steering clear of the performance of the offspring in question) he moved next to a magisterial survey of the substance and approach of the novels rooted in the experience of the First World War. Here, sheer literary labour was well-matched by scholarship. To Hugh and to all the contributors, to the volunteers and to the Polytechnic staff and by no means least to the members of the Conference who provided just the right atmosphere for intellectual stimulus in the delightfully informal circumstances which obtained throughout the Conference, the Editor expresses his warm appreciation.

Sunderland Polytechnic   PETER H. LIDDLE, F.R.Hist.S.
June 1985

The Foreign Fields

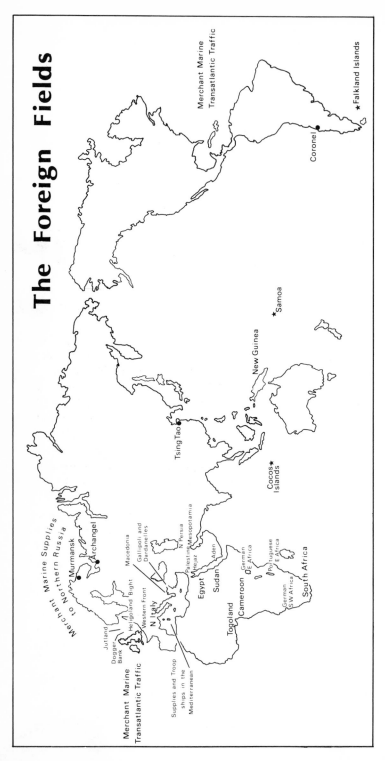

The Foreign Fields

An indication of the areas of active service for British and Commonwealth Forces in the First World War.

This map cannot do justice to the work of the Merchant Marine on trade and supply routes nor to the responsibilities and operations of the Royal Navy in for example the Baltic, the Aegean, the Eastern Mediterranean and the Sea of Marmora. Among the areas of service not indicated are the British bombing raids on enemy territory, the impact of enemy action from sea or air against the United Kingdom, the British Nursing Units in Serbia and the Royal Air Service Armoured Car Unit in Russia.

1

Lloyd George and Ministerial Leadership in the Great War

JOHN GRIGG

When the first great war of the twentieth century began in 1914 the British people did not at first receive, or expect to receive, effective war leadership from civilian ministers. As head of the Liberal government then in office, H.H. Asquith showed outstanding firmness, patience and skill in handling his Cabinet and party so that the policy of intervention was in the end accepted with only marginal dissent. But by temperament he was evidently not cut out to be a war leader in the style of Chatham or even Palmerston; at best he could only be looked upon as a potential Liverpool. Yet even that precedent did not really apply, because circumstances had so drastically changed during the century since the end of the war against Napoleon.

The most important change was that Britain had moved from a state of oligarchy to one of at least approximate democracy. The war of 1914–18 was the first in which the whole British people both felt involved and increasingly *was* involved. It was a war of peoples which, as Winston Churchill had shortly beforehand predicted, would prove more terrible than the wars of kings. The people had to be mobilized as never before, and for this inspiring leadership was needed. But who was to provide the inspiration?

At first the country turned, not to any civilian, but to a soldier whose prestige was already legendary: Lord Kitchener of Khartoum. In the summer of 1914 he was on leave in England from his post as agent and consul-general (in effect viceroy) in Egypt, but when the war broke out he was on the point of returning there. Immediately, however, there was overwhelming demand that he should remain and take over the running of the war. Asquith sent a message to Dover on 3 August to stop him crossing to France en route to Egypt, but did not at that stage intend to offer him the post of Secretary of State for War. This he (Asquith) had been holding himself since the Curragh incident earlier in the year, and his idea was that he should continue to hold it with Haldane as his deputy. But public opinion, as articulated by the Press, clamoured for Kitchener, and Asquith also perceived that appointing Kitchener as War minister was the price he would have to pay for Conservative support of his government in wartime.

1

In any case, Kitchener himself refused to serve in any other capacity. So on 5 August he was appointed.

Kitchener was an extraordinary man, with great qualities as well as great defects. As War minister he performed two invaluable services, both within his first weeks in office. At a time when almost everybody was anticipating a short war, he firmly stated that it would last at least 3 years, and brought a stunned Cabinet to accept his prognosis. The other vital achievement was to lay the foundations of a huge citizen army, such as the British had long been conditioned to regard as inadmissible. The famous poster with the pointing finger evoked a tremendous response.

As time went on, however, Kitchener's faults and limitations became painfully apparent to his colleagues, if not to the general public. Even as a soldier he was excessively aloof and self-sufficient, and he was therefore much more so when required to co-operate with a group of Parliamentary politicians. In fact, he did not co-operate at all; he did not even keep his colleagues informed of what was going on in the military sphere. Worse still, it soon became obvious that his autocratic and secretive methods were unlikely to win the war. Civilian power had virtually abdicated in favour of military power, but without the justification of probable military success.

The leadership that Kitchener exercised in the early weeks of the war was, in a strict sense, ministerial, since he had the status of a Cabinet minister. But of course he was a politician only in name and his character was totally unsuited to the task of leading a democratic nation at war. It was therefore necessary for somebody to emerge who both grasped the realities of the unprecedented ordeal that the country had to face, and possessed the political arts and talents appropriate for the task. Such a person existed in David Lloyd George, who had been Chancellor of the Exchequer since the formation of the Asquith government in 1908. Within a few months he had established himself as the civilian best qualified to give the country effective leadership, though unfortunately twenty-eight months had to go by before he became head of the government, with the full scope and initiative which only that office confers.

What did he achieve meanwhile? His first contribution was to steady the City of London and so help very largely to surmount the financial crisis which resulted from the international crisis of July–August 1914. But it took him several weeks to understand the nature of the war and the colossal dimensions of the challenge that had to be met. By mid-September he could see that the war would be long and desperately demanding, and a visit to France in mid-October convinced him that operations on the Western front had reached a condition of stalemate. From then onwards all his efforts were devoted to mobilizing the resources of the British Empire and its allies to match the resources of the Central Powers, and to trying to find an alternative strategy to that of attrition on the Western Front.

Realizing that public opinion was the key to all else, he set himself to give a clear exposition of the issues at stake in the war, and to ensure that the British people had no illusions about the sacrifices needed to win it. In a series of powerful speeches he combined instruction and inspiration in a manner far transcending the silent eloquence of Kitchener's recruiting poster. The most important of these speeches were delivered at the Queen's Hall in September, at the City Temple in November, and at Bangor on 28 February 1915. They were not only fully reported in the press and very widely read by a public then addicted to newspaper-reading, in addition, they were reprinted as pamphlets and translated into many languages. Later they appeared in book form. It is fair to say that, in the pre-radio age, their impact was entirely comparable with Churchill's broadcasts in the next great war.

At Bangor Lloyd George broached the theme of munitions, declaring that the war was "an engineers' war". "In the old days", he said, "when a nation's liberty was menaced by an aggressor, a man took from the chimney corner his bow and arrow or his spear, or a sword which had been left to him by an ancestry of warriors, went to the gathering ground of his tribe and the nation was fully equipped for war." But that was no longer the case. "Now you fight with complicated, highly finished weapons." He emphasized the need to use skilled manpower on the home front, where it could contribute most effectively to victory, and he also warned that industrial disputes and restrictive practices were out of place in wartime.

His concern about arms supply brought him into conflict with Kitchener, because the War Office had sole responsibility for ordering equipment and deciding what types were needed by the army. Even before the first coalition was formed in May 1915 he had already made some inroads on the War Office monopoly, and had negotiated a compact with labour under which a code of practice for War industry was agreed. But it was only when he became Minister of Munitions in the first coalition that he was able by degrees to gain control over the whole field, and to carry out what was little less than another industrial revolution. During his thirteen months in the job the State obtained powers in industry that it had never aspired to before, while government itself was transformed by the recruitment of businessmen for tasks which, on a conventional view, should have been confined to civil servants.

Lloyd George's preoccupation with the home front between the spring of 1915 and his appointment as War minister after Kitchener's death in June 1916 was partly due to his failure to influence war policy and strategy as he would have wished in early 1915. It seemed to him then that the generals' belief that the war could only be won by massive attacks on the Western front was a fallacy, quite apart from the tragic human cost of such attacks. In his view, the Central Powers were most vulnerable in the Balkans, where Serbia was still maintaining a dogged resistance, and where the hostility of Slavs, both inside and outside the Habsburg empire, was a source of weakness to the enemy that the Allies were well placed to exploit. He was opposed to the military landings at Gallipoli, mainly because he regarded Salonica and the Balkans as the more promising theatre. At the same time he was advocating the despatch of a high-powered mission, led by the foreign secretary or himself, to bribe, bludgeon or cajole the Balkan States into forming a united front against the Central Powers. But he did not get his way.

No doubt he underrated the difficulties that would have confronted him, but even when they are allowed for it seems that a great opportunity was missed. As a result Serbia was left to its fate, Bulgaria joined the enemy, Greece dithered, and Roumania eventually – in the autumn of 1916 – came in on the side of the Allies, but on its own and without the means to withstand attacks from several directions. It was Lloyd George's, and the Allies', misfortune that by the time he became prime minister in December 1916 all the most hopeful options in the Balkans had been closed.

His advent to the premiership was, however, decisive in many other ways, and probably (one is tempted to say certainly) if it had not happened the Allies would have lost the war in 1917. The situation was, indeed, critical when he took over from Asquith. Russia was exhausted and about to enter the revolutionary process which would impair what remained of her capacity to fight and in due course take her out of the war. America was still neutral, and making life very difficult for Britain through financial pressure. France had been through a terrible, if glorious, year with the struggle for Verdun claiming a further enormous toll of lives. In Britain there was a sense of growing disillusionment about the battle of the Somme, which had lasted from July to November with very little to show for it except interminable casualty lists. Worse still, German submarine warfare was during the year to threaten the country with early defeat and the Admiralty seemed to have no answer the threat.

Lloyd George began by drastically changing the machinery of government. Instead of the unwieldy peacetime Cabinet which Asquith had never been prepared to scrap, he created a small War Cabinet of five members including himself. To this was attached a secretariat under Maurice Hankey, formerly secretary of the Committee of Imperial Defence and of the successive Cabinet committees which Asquith had set up to discuss, though not to direct, the conduct of the war. Thus for the first time minutes were kept of Cabinet meetings. The new prime minister also established a secretariat of his own, which was housed in temporary huts in the garden of 10 Downing Street and so became known as the "Garden Suburb".

In his ministerial appointments outside the War Cabinet he made some striking innovations in structure or personnel, or in both. Five new departments were immediately brought into being: Labour, Pensions, National Service, Food Control and Shipping. The first two were entrusted to Labour men, as promised when Lloyd George was winning

Labour support for his government. But the most significant and unorthodox appointment was that of Sir Joseph Maclay as Shipping Controller.
Maclay was a self-made Glaswegian shipowner recommended by Bonar
Law, and then promptly appointed by Lloyd George. No member of the
government, apart from the prime minister himself, was to make a larger
contribution to victory. Lloyd George certainly shared the view that war
was too serious a matter to be left to soldiers – or sailors – and even in
peacetime he had shown that he regarded politics as too serious a matter to
be left to professional politicians. His government reflected both attitudes.

Without Maclay's masterly administration it is unlikely that the shipping
crisis would have been overcome. He was allowed to draft his own powers
and, after a fight with the Admiralty, obtained the responsibility for
allocating all the country's shipping resources. He was also an early
advocate of the convoy system and strongly influenced the argument that
led to its adoption. But his work to save the country from strangulation was
supplemented by the immense boost that Lloyd George gave to agricultural production, and by his measures to limit imports and to control food
consumption. By urgent action to tackle the problem in all its aspects the
most deadly threat to Britain's survival was, in the course of 1917, averted.

In other ways the year was not a happy one for Lloyd George, or for the
country. Though America became a co-belligerent in April, it was bound to
be some time before American participation in the war could be substantial, at any rate on land. Meanwhile Lloyd George would have liked a
defensive posture to be maintained on the Western front, but the High
Commands were already committed to further offensive action there. He
hoped, therefore, to make a virtue of necessity by achieving unity of
command under the newly appointed French commander-in-chief, Robert
Nivelle, by whom he was anyway much impressed. His manoeuvres to this
end somewhat miscarried, and compounded the ill-will that the British
commander-in-chief, Sir Douglas Haig, already felt towards him. Moreover the Nivelle offensive, when it took place, was a failure in relation to
the high hopes entertained for it, and the resulting disillusionment was
correspondingly great. The French army's morale came near to collapse
and there were serious mutinies, which were then used by Haig as a pretext
for launching his own favourite project of an offensive in Flanders. This
not only failed to realize the grandiose objectives that he had in mind, but
was also prolonged after the futility of further attacks, in appalling
conditions of weather and terrain, had become manifest. Haig showed
again in the third battle of Ypres the same blinkered obstinacy that had
caused him, the previous year, to continue fighting on the Somme long
after there had ceased to be any rational justification for doing so.

Lloyd George was against the whole campaign, and was particularly
appalled by the later stages of it, usually known as the battle of Passchendaele. Why, then, did he not get rid of Haig? The answer is that even a

strong and determined a prime minister as he was could not have removed a commander-in-chief who had powerful backing in the Press, and therefore in public opinion, and who also cultivated close links with Buckingham Palace and the Conservative Party. Lloyd George could not have carried the War Cabinet with him, let alone the Parliamentary majority (largely Conservative) upon which his government depended.

He had to be content with a first step towards Allied unity of command with the establishment, in November, of a Supreme War Council at Versailles, which was accomplished against stiff opposition from the C.I.G.S., Sir William Robertson, but accepted by Haig. Early the following year he managed to displace Robertson, and when in March the Germans launched their last big offensive, which at first carried all before it and posed an imminent threat to the Channel ports, an Allied supremo was at length appointed in the person of Ferdinand Foch.

Lloyd George's handling of the last great crisis of the war was admired by all who came in contact with him at the time. Churchill wrote of one evening when the outlook seemed particularly black: "I never remember in the whole course of the War a more anxious evening. One of the great qualities in Mr. Lloyd George was his power of obliterating the past and concentrating his whole being upon meeting the new situation. ... The resolution of the Prime Minister was unshaken under his truly awful responsibilities.[1] He took personal charge at the War Office, expedited the flow of reinforcements, and worked on the Americans to accelerate the build-up of their forces in France. Above all, he kept his own and other people's spirits up. As another witness recorded: "His work and anxieties are always with him, but he mingles them with bright and amusing conversation which lightens the burden."[2] And we should remember that the man who was showing this remarkable vitality and resilience had been in high office *without interruption* for eleven and a half years, including seven as Chancellor of the Exchequer and already eighteen months as prime minister.

Mention of Churchill naturally prompts the question: how does Lloyd George's war leadership compare with Churchill's in the ensuing war? The first point to be stressed is that Lloyd George's experience was without precedent. No minister before 1914 had had to lead the country in conditions remotely comparable with those of the first Great War. Lloyd George's efforts were those of a pioneer and Churchill in the next war was, as it were, standing on his shoulders.

Another point to bear in mind is that Churchill's position as prime minister was much stronger than Lloyd George's. He was the head of a grand coalition, with all the major parties wholly committed to it, whereas only about half of the Parliamentary Liberal Party adhered to Lloyd George's coalition. Moreover, after Neville Chamberlain's death in November 1940, Churchill became leader of the Conservative Party, which was the largest party in his government. In Lloyd George's government his party – or section of a party – was by no means the largest constituent; he had to rely upon a majority consisting largely of Conservatives.

Churchill also had the advantage of becoming leader in the age of radio, and in a country which had a system of public service broadcasting. Though he did not absolutely control the B.B.C. during the Second World War, it showed a natural and proper regard for the government's interests in wartime, and on balance he gained very substantially from its existence as the principal medium of mass communication. By contrast, Lloyd George had to deal with a miscellany of newspaper proprietors and editors, of whom the most formidable, Lord Northcliffe, acted virtually as a P.R.O. for Haig and the military.

In general there was, in the second War, much less of a psychological gulf between civilians and military than in the first, because in the second many civilian ministers had served on battlefronts in the earlier conflict and had been through experiences at least as unpleasant as any that the professional service chiefs could recall. It was, therefore, far less easy for the professionals to claim that civilian ministers did not know what they were talking about. In 1914 the only leading politician who had direct experience of warfare was, in fact, Churchill, but in 1939 many ex-servicemen were prominent in politics.

Finally, although Churchill became prime minister at a moment of extreme national danger, he had a relatively free hand and was starting from scratch, unhindered by allies and with no preceding strategic commitment to cramp his style. Lloyd George, as has been said, came to the premiership when many of the best options had been closed and when decisions had been taken by the Allied commanders which he did not approve but could not reverse. The danger from U-boats was scarcely, if at all, less great than the threat of invasion by Hitler, and public morale had none of the exaltation that it undoubtedly had in the summer of 1940.

Despite the comparative disadvantages, Lloyd George's leadership was not noticeably less successful than Churchill's. Indeed, one might argue that it was more successful. True, the second War was won at a much lower cost in British lives, but the difference there is to quite a large degree attributable to advances in medicine. In other respects the comparison surely favours Lloyd George. Whereas the second War lasted nearly 6 years in Europe, the first was won in 4 years and 3 months. Moreover, it really was won. Not only was the enemy defeated, but the country on whose behalf Britain had ostensibly gone to war was restored to freedom and independence. The same could not be said of Poland in 1945.

All in all, Lloyd George's leadership in 1914–18, both before and after he became prime minister, must surely rank among the most dynamic, resourceful and innovative in our own or any other country's history.

Notes

1. Winston Churchill, *The World Crisis*, vol. 11, p. 1291, Odhams, London 1938.
2. Lord Riddell, *Lord Riddell's War Diary*, entry for 24 March 1918, p. 321, Nicholson & Watson, London 1933.

2

The Domestic Scene: Parliament and People

DAVID SWEET

In his study of the British experience on the Western Front between 1914 and 1918, and the ways in which it has been subsequently "remembered, conventionalized and mythologized", the literary scholar Professor Paul Fussell observes that the prevailing mode of twentieth-century consciousness ever since the Great War has been the ironic: an observation entirely consistent with Sir Llewellyn Woodward's characterization of the generation of post-war British intellectuals as "scorched" by war. Professor Arthur Marwick, in his seminal account of British society in the Great War, has suggested that it was "in the nature of the war ... to foster scepticism, irony and irreverence".[1] No doubt the effect of the war on British society was rather less cataclysmic than was the case with those continental belligerents which suffered military defeat and consequential political dislocation: four great empires were dismantled as a direct consequence of military defeat, and their places were taken by successor states of a quite different character – republican, nationalist, and either totalitarian already or unstable and vulnerable to totalitarian pressures. To deny that it was the Great War which destroyed the traditional structures of nineteenth-century Europe and inaugurated the twentieth-century era of mass democracy, virulent nationalism, totalitarianism, and ideologically-validated violence, would be perverse; and recent attempts to do so have not been notably convincing.[2] Every European society that took part in the war was fundamentally changed by it, and we habitually regard the world of 1920 as being recognizably the contemporary world, whereas that which existed before 1914 looks remote and unfamiliar, having more in common with the Europe of (say) Metternich or even Bismarck than of Hitler and Stalin. In a less extreme form, this proposition appears to hold good even in the case of Great Britain. It is inconceivable that Britain should have gone through 4 years of total war without profound effects, without fundamental adaptations of attitudes and institutions, some of them perhaps impermanent, but others irrevocable and of great long-term significance. The salient features of the domestic scene during the war have been thoroughly mapped by generations of distinguished historians, and my debt to them will be obvious to any attentive reader. All that can be attempted in this brief paper, by way of introduction to some of the more specialized studies which follow, is to point to some of the more prominent features, and in particular to comment upon developments in that crucial three-way relationship between government, Parliament and people on which the successful prosecution of the war ultimately depended.

The Liberal administration of which Asquith was prime minister was able to secure general support for Britain's entry into the war, largely because it delayed going to war until the German violation of Belgian neutrality gave it the most impeccable arguments of international morality to present to Parliament and to the British people. But, initially at least, it conceived of its role in bringing the war to a successful conclusion in a very limited sense, largely because it failed to comprehend the nature of the struggle upon which it had embarked: Asquith and his colleagues shared the almost universal assumption that the war would be a short one, consisting of a few decisive engagements which would decide the issue in weeks or at most months. Only Kitchener, brought into the cabinet as Secretary of State for War in order to reassure public opinion at large (and the Conservative opposition in particular) about the government's competence as a war ministry, predicted that the war would last for years rather than months, and that it would require the mobilization of vastly greater resources of manpower than the small Expeditionary Force which was all that the War Office had at its disposal in August 1914. The role of the BEF in delaying the advance of the German First Army commanded by von Kluck, and in the Allied counter-offensive which halted the German offensive on the Marne in early September, was by no means negligible; but its decimation in the first battle of Ypres of October and November 1914, and the stabilization of the whole front from the Swiss frontier to the sea, the creation of entrenched positions which became on both sides increasingly invulnerable to attack as the war progressed, demonstrated decisively the accuracy of Kitchener's predictions. Thereafter the essential function of the British government, as conceived by Asquith and his colleagues, was to provide the military with the resources needed to achieve victory: to recruit, organize and supply the new mass armies which the nature of trench warfare on the Western Front dictated. The history of British government in the First World War is essentially the history of the progressive enlargement of state intervention, in order to maximize the mobilization of national resources for war. No doubt this process reached its culmination only after Lloyd George had succeeded Asquith as prime minister in December 1916, with the creation of new departments to manage labour, shipping, food, national service, and pensions; and perhaps with that ultimate expression of "war socialism", the introduction of food rationing early in 1918. It had however begun much earlier under Asquith's Liberal administration, with for example the assumption by the Board of Trade of the management of the railway system immediately after the outbreak of war, and the Treasury agreements of March 1915, by which Lloyd George secured the acquiescence of the trade unions in the dilution of labour in essential industries. Furthermore, the process was continued under Asquith's war coalition of May 1915, not only with Lloyd George's *dirigiste* management of the newly-created Ministry of Munitions, but also with the McKenna duties of September 1915, and of course most spectacularly with the introduction of conscription in two stages in the early months of 1916. In so far as the extension of state intervention required the assent of Parliament, it necessarily entailed fundamental adaptations in political attitudes (for which the Liberal party above all was ill-equipped), and it dictated changes in the previous relationship between government and Parliament.

In a characteristically trenchant lecture (delivered all of 25 years ago, yet as fresh and stimulating as ever), Mr. A.J.P. Taylor argued that Parliament was almost irrelevant to the essential business of managing the war effort.[3] There is undoubtedly a great deal of truth in this contention. Except for the handful of radical and socialist M.P.s who opposed the war and who could be disregarded, opposition was unpatriotic and therefore impossible. There were only very limited opportunities to debate the government's management of the war, and even constructive criticism required the most judicious language if it were not to breach the conventions of solidarity and security. Furthermore, the "unofficial coalition of silence" between the two front benches down to May 1915, and the formal coalition which operated thereafter, rendered the backbenchers more or less impotent to influence the policies of government. Instead of debating strategy, they found themselves more useful activities in the recruiting campaigns outside Parliament, and in contributing to the torrent of propagandist literature by which the war effort was justified and supported. There was consequently a remarkable absence of coherent resistance to the growth of state intervention, even to measures which in normal times would have provoked a Parliamentary storm, particularly from the Liberal benches. Only ten radicals voted against the McKenna duties, which abandoned the old Liberal cause of free trade. The introduction of conscription was, if anything, even more antipathetic to traditional Liberal principles, yet it provoked only one resignation from the Asquith coalition (that of Simon), and only 50 Liberals voted against the measure which imposed conscription on single men in January 1916. The introduction of universal conscription in April 1916 was made easy for the government by the patriotic surge of opinion which followed the Easter rising in Dublin and the British surrender to the Turks at Kut-al-Amara, and indeed Mr. Taylor goes so far as to maintain that this was the only occasion during the war when the House of Commons dictated policy to the government.[4] The formation of the Lloyd George coalition in December 1916 had the side-effect of creating also an official opposition, but one which did little to merit the name; and when it did divide the House against the government, at the end of the Maurice debate in May 1918, fewer than 100 Liberals voted against Lloyd George, and the unpopularity of Asquith ensured that there was no significant support from the other parties. In short, throughout the war Parliament was inhibited from exercising its constitutional function of controlling the activities of the executive.

None of this should be taken as implying that the political truce succeeded somehow in suppressing the normal political passions and animosities, but merely that they were driven into subterranean channels from which on occasion they erupted with devastating effect. In this way Parliament, responding to popular dissatisfaction, was able to end ministries even if it could not mend them, and to secure administrative reconstructions which at least held out the promise of a more effective management of the war effort. There were two such occasions – in May 1915 and in December 1916 – and on both it was backbench opinion which acted as the expression of public alarm and was of pivotal importance in dictating a change of government; and on both occasions it was Lloyd George who was the principal beneficiary. The resentment of Conservative backbenchers at the restraint imposed upon them by Bonar Law's support for the Asquith cabinet found expression in the Unionist Business Committee, which was formed to press for the introduction of tariffs. In the spring of 1915 it took up allegations in the press of an acute shortage of shells which was held to be the cause of the military failures in Flanders, and was stirred into open revolt against Bonar Law and his support for Asquith by a crisis in the Admiralty over the Dardanelles operation. In order to avert the threatened Parliamentary rebellion, Asquith was obliged to reconstruct the government as a coalition, bringing in Bonar Law and the other Conservative leaders, with Henderson as the representative of Labour. The question of shell shortages was settled with the creation of the Ministry of Munitions, with Lloyd George at its head, which assumed progressively wider powers over the control and organization of war production; and the Treasury agreements were given legislative force. The question of the Admiralty was solved to the satisfaction of the Conservatives with the substitution of Balfour for Churchill as First Lord, and the McKenna duties went some way towards satisfying the demand for tariffs. The last Liberal government was thus swept away by the rebellion of Conservative backbenchers, while Lloyd George secured the opportunity of demonstrating his energy and efficiency as a war minister. On the death of Kitchener in June 1916 he became Secretary of State for War.

The second occasion on which backbench opinion played a pivotal role in enforcing a change of government was in December 1916, when an elaborate sequence of political manoeuvre led to the appointment of Lloyd George as prime minister, and the formation of the War Cabinet. In spite of the higher level of state intervention which the Asquith coalition practised, and in spite of the introduction of conscription, there was increasing criticism in the press, and increasing dissatisfaction on the back benches, with Asquith's leadership and with Bonar Law for sustaining it. In November 1916 Carson led a rebellion of Conservative backbenchers which convinced Bonar Law that he could no longer rely on their acquiescence if he were to continue to support Asquith. Lloyd George, convinced by the catastrophic losses in the protracted battle of the Somme (July–November 1916) that Asquith's supine leadership and subservience to the policies of the generals would lose the war, set his loyal supporter Addison to sound out and organize backbench Liberal opinion. Addison was able to deliver the support of over 120 Liberals for Lloyd George as prime minister (but not for Bonar Law), while Bonar Law knew that the Conservative rebels would support Lloyd George and himself if they were to repudiate Asquith. Henderson for Labour was prepared to support whoever could offer the best prospect of winning the war. This piece of Parliamentary arithmetic falsified Asquith's expectation that only he would be able to form a new ministry, and on 7 December Lloyd George became prime minister at the head of the second war coalition, one whose structure and style of government were very different from those of its predecessor. (What we may legitimately call Lloyd George's revolution in government is discussed by John Grigg in his essay "Lloyd George and Ministerial Leadership".

In this manner, backbench opinion in the House of Commons, acting as the legitimate expression of widespread public alarm and dissatisfaction, played the decisive role in overthrowing a ministry regarded as unequal to its task of managing the national emergency, and in bringing to power the war leader best known for his impatience with the constraints of traditional methods of government. Lloyd George was the first people's prime minister of the twentieth century, his supporters the representatives of the anti-patrician tradition in politics, in business and in the press. The Addison Liberals, for example, were radical businessmen rather than the more traditional and patrician Liberals who went into opposition with Asquith. Men of business and industrialists were brought into government by Lloyd George to run the new departments, regardless of their lack of Parliamentary experience: thus belatedly fulfilling the demand for a government of "national efficiency" which had been canvassed at the time of the Boer war. In addressing the leaders of the Labour movement, Lloyd George appealed directly through them "from the ruling classes to the people".[5] Measures such as the control of prices and rents, food subsidies and rationing, the establishment of the Ministry of Reconstruction (under Addison), and the introduction of a democratic franchise, went a long way towards recognizing and appeasing popular demands for equality of sacrifice during the war, and greater social and political equality when it should be over. Although for almost eighteen months after the formation of the Lloyd George coalition the war against Germany went no better than it had done in 1916, the government's policies during the dark days of 1917 at least ensured that Britain avoided defeat, and was in a strong position to take advantage of the new military situation created by the entry of U.S.A. into the war, and the unsuccessful German offensive in the spring of 1918. When the tide of war at last turned and the Germans were forced to seek an armistice, Lloyd George was in a position of unassailable popularity as a successful war leader, and was able to make terms with the Conservatives (though not with Labour) for the continuation of the coalition after the war as a government of reconstruction.

One aspect of the activities of government during the war which has received less attention than it deserves, and which exemplifies the interaction between public opinion, Parliament and government, lies in the area of propaganda and recruiting.[6] At the beginning of the war, the general purpose of propaganda was to mobilize patriotic support for the war, and its specific and immediate purpose to encourage young men to volunteer in large numbers for the army. The task of recruitment in 1914 proved remarkably easy, so that the government did not find it necessary to set up an official organization to conduct propaganda: the war was popular, was greeted with widespread public enthusiasm, and was generally regarded as being just and necessary; and in this climate of opinion there was no difficulty about recruiting the mass volunteer army for which Kitchener called. The War Office, and the advertising agency which it employed for the purpose, stepped up its recruiting campaign with a series of flysheets posing pertinent questions to various social groups ("Have you a man digging your garden who should be digging trenches?"). The other main recruiting organization was the semi-official Parliamentary Recruiting Committee, an all-party body formed at the end of August 1914 to co-ordinate the activities of local constituency groups, and provide M.P.s with something useful to do which would divert their energies from attempts to question the government's policies or, still worse, to debate strategy. It was this Committee which issued the justly celebrated Kitchener poster (and the equally effective "Daddy, what did *you* do in the Great War?"). The main contribution of the government to the early stages of war propaganda took the form of a great campaign of public speaking undertaken by Asquith, Lloyd George and other leading politicians, who all emphasized the responsibility of Germany for launching the war, the violent character of the German offensive, and the duty of the British people to defend the values of European civilization. These relatively moderate statements of the main themes of British war propaganda were rapidly outstripped by the newspapers, particularly the Northcliffe press, which launched a campaign of hatred based on allegations of German atrocities: a campaign which was neither instigated nor endorsed by the government, but which was not disavowed either, for the sufficient reason that it was good for the business of recruiting. After the introduction of conscription the question of recruitment was unimportant, but the momentum of propaganda was maintained throughout the war by the press and by a plethora of unofficial organizations (such as the "Fight for Right Movement" which included many leading writers and intellectuals). The government itself was frequently the target of criticism for being insufficiently harsh in its condemnation of German methods, a charge which was only partially rebutted by the publication of the Bryce report in May 1915.

Until the formation of the Lloyd George coalition, the only government organization charged with responsibility for disseminating propaganda was the Secret War Propaganda Bureau, set up by Asquith under the Liberal politician Masterman to counteract German propaganda in neutral states, especially the U.S.A., and to enlist their sympathy for the Allied cause. In February 1917 its responsibilities were taken over by the Department of Information, with Carson as the responsible minister; and in February 1918 Lloyd George established the Ministry of Information under Beaverbrook, with Northcliffe as director of propaganda to enemy countries. This bureaucratic progression, from Bureau to Ministry, clearly reflects the increasing importance accorded by government to the business of propaganda as the war went on; and although their primary concern was with propaganda overseas, much of their best material (including a series of highly successful propaganda films) found its way on to the home front as well. In addition, in June 1917 an organization specifically directed at the home front was set up, the National War Aims Committee, which had an all-party executive and the two Chief Whips as joint chairmen. Its creation clearly reflects the anxiety of the government in 1917 that war-weariness was beginning to take hold of the British people, and that pacifist propaganda and calls for a negotiated peace were beginning to attract public support far beyond the narrow circle of pacifists and radicals to which they had previously been confined. It organized some 900 meetings in areas where left-wing influences were strong in the trade union movement and where industrial unrest was threatening the war effort. These meetings were addressed by politicians supporting the government's policy of the "knock-out blow" and were enlivened with patriotic songs performed by music-hall artists. This campaign provided the context within which Lloyd George outlined his programme of war aims to the trade union leaders on 5 January 1918, and with limited success appealed to the patriotism of rank-and-file trade unionists in his address to the Manpower Conference on 18 January:

> We could not turn Hindenburg out of Belgium with trade union resolutions, but we could with trade union guns and trade unionists behind them. . . . Democracy must mean that the people of all classes . . . must merge their privileges and their rights in the common stock.[7]

This official campaign against defeatism was, as usual, accompanied by strident utterances from the newspapers and from the unofficial patriotic organizations. As the war approached its end, they turned their fire upon any suggestion that Germany should be treated magnanimously in the peace settlement. The virulent tone of the general election campaign of December 1918 was set by the press, and candidates felt themselves obliged to compete with one another in the stridency of their demands for hanging the Kaiser, and making Germany pay. The overwhelming success of coalition candidates against those suspected of being soft on Germany provides a convincing demonstration that they had accurately gauged the public mood. How far that mood was the result of 4 years of propaganda, and how far a natural reaction to 4 years of war, privation and death, it is impossible to determine. But the result was that Lloyd George, when he went to the peace conference to attempt the reconstruction of post-war Europe, was saddled with a commitment to a Carthaginian peace which his own instincts told him was impolitic as well as unjust.

In the area of domestic reconstruction also, Lloyd George was not notably successful in fulfilling the optimistic expectations he had aroused, again largely because his freedom of action was drastically curtailed by the political situation in which he found himself after the general election. We may briefly observe how remarkably impermanent were those developments in the role of the state which had taken place between 1914 and 1918. Professor Marwick has identified three areas of government policy under the post-war coalition as "major examples of the burgeoning of collectivist social action" – namely education, housing, and unemployment insurance; but has observed that, for the rest, "reconstruction turned to retrenchment".[8] The new ministries of the war period were abolished or attenuated, the machinery of state intervention was dismantled, those industries which had been brought under government control were returned to private ownership. The reconstructive radicalism of the coalition Liberals was unable to defend itself within a governing majority dominated by over 350 Conservative M.P.s; Addison himself was sacrificed by Lloyd George to appease the Conservatives, and his housing programme was aborted. In the area of government action on social questions, the enduring results of the war were a good deal less impressive than the promises which had been held out to the people at its end. In the large and amorphous area of social attitudes, in which no precision is possible, historians have indulged freely in a wide range of speculative interpretations which vary according to taste, and which it would be unprofitable to pursue here. But there was one area of British life which was undeniably altered, permanently and fundamentally, by the war: those shifts in political attitudes and in popular political loyalties which enabled the Labour party to displace the Liberals as the alternative party of government.

Much of the recent discussion of this theme has turned upon the interpretation of the electoral effects of the Representation of the People Act of June 1918. This was a major item of the programme of reconstruction, carried through before the end of the war for the simple but sufficient reason that the political leadership was fully aware that, in the climate of expectation at home and with the example of revolution abroad, it would be politically unthinkable to hold a general election without enfranchising those voteless young men who had done the fighting, and by extension without recognizing the contribution made by women to the war effort. The introduction of universal suffrage for men, and of the occupancy franchise for women over 30, was the true inauguration of democratic politics in twentieth-century Britain; subsequent franchise reforms have done no more than carry to their natural conclusion the assumptions inherent in the 1918 Act. At the time its political consequences were quite unpredictable; it increased the electorate from less than eight million at the last pre-war election in 1910, to over twenty-one million in 1918, and there were no reliable predictions as to how these millions of new electors would vote. In the event, turnout in the election of December 1918 was under 60 per cent (compared with a turnout of over 80 per cent in the three previous elections), and we know that only about one in four of those in the armed forces managed to vote; so that the 1918 election, taken on its own, offers a most unreliable basis for the discussion of electoral behaviour. On the other hand, its results were nothing short of sensational. In terms of seats won, and more particularly of seats lost, it was unfavourable to all but the coalition parties (and of course Sinn Fein, but that is another story altogether); but it was most unfavourable to the Asquith Liberals, who were replaced as the largest opposition party by Labour, which before 1914 had been little more than a left-inclined adjunct to the Liberal party. The Liberals were never able to recover their position after 1918: even when the Asquith and Lloyd George factions were reunited for the 1923 election, they were unable to displace Labour as the major alternative to the Conservatives, and were indeed responsible for providing the 1924 Labour government with its brief tenure of office. Even more significantly, in every general election from 1918 to 1945 (with the single exception of the election of 1931, which was held in highly abnormal circumstances) the Labour party increased its share of the popular vote. It is tempting to suppose, and it has commonly been supposed, that the Representation of the People Act, by establishing a new and much enlarged electorate in which working-class voters enjoyed a much greater preponderance than formerly, provided the indispensable conditions for the rise of Labour to majority party status.[9] It has, however, more recently been argued (on the basis of a minute examination of the detailed operation of the pre-1914 franchise) that the old electorate was more working class, and the new electorate less preponderantly working class, than has previously been supposed.[10] Consequently, the rise of Labour must be explained not simply in terms of franchise reform, but of all the other political developments between 1914 and 1922 which combined to discredit Liberalism and elevate Labour as the party of reform: the abandonment of traditional Liberal principles in the face of wartime exigencies, and their evident irrelevance to post-war problems; the disastrous split of 1916, the feeble leadership of Asquith, and the popular repudiation of Lloyd George as the creature of post-war Conservatism; the credibility which Labour gained from its role in government during the war, and the revitalization of the party's organization and programme under Henderson and MacDonald after 1917. Set in this wider context, the franchise reform of 1918 takes its place as one of those interlocking consequences of the war which, taken together, brought about the major political realignment of twentieth-century Britain, the displacement of Liberalism by Labour. We may add one more (admittedly speculative) consideration: that old assumptions about the natural superiority of the governing classes, which had ensured for both major parties a large deferential vote before 1914, could not survive the painful revelation of their fallibility in the campaigns of the Great War.

Finally, it should be observed that a substantial number of those Liberals who deserted to Labour at the end of the war did so in the belief that only Labour offered a new start in foreign affairs, which would guarantee the open discussion and democratic control of foreign policy, and thus ensure that there would be no repetition of the secret diplomacy and power politics which they blamed for dragging Britain into the war. Several of them (Ponsonby, Buxton, Trevelyan for example) had been outspoken in their criticism of Grey's foreign policy before 1914; they opposed Britain's entry into the war; and throughout its course they isolated themselves from the great bulk of Parliamentary and public opinion by advocating a compromise peace. Many of them (though not Buxton) were associated with MacDonald, and with extra-Parliamentary radicals like Morel and Angell, in the Union of Democratic Control. When they divided the House of Commons on the peace issue, as they did three times during 1917, they were overwhelmingly defeated. Nor did peace candidates have any success at by-elections. The operation of the party truce for the duration of the war, by which the party leaders hoped to avoid political controversy, could not prevent the appearance of independent candidates who offered the electors a genuine choice. It is striking that the only independents who did well in by-elections were those who demanded a *more* vigorous prosecution of the war; two of them (Pemberton Billing and Tillett) were actually elected against official candidates, while Kennedy Jones was hastily found a Conservative seat after he had come close to winning a by-election as an independent. The peace-by-negotiation candidates, by contrast, did uniformly badly in by-elections; and of course in the general election of 1918 sitting members who had favoured a compromise peace, including MacDonald, Snowden, Henderson, Ponsonby, Buxton and Trevelyan, lost their seats. They were all however returned as Labour members in 1922, together with Morel. Thus the Labour party received an accretion of talent from former Liberals who now regarded Labour as their natural political home, largely because of foreign affairs: because of their shared experience with MacDonald in the Union of Democratic Control during the war, and because the Labour party had belatedly adopted the Union's programme as its official policy on foreign affairs in 1918. Not the least important of the reasons for the fusion of radicalism with Labour after 1918 was the determination that there should be no repetition of the Great War.

Notes

1. Paul Fussell, *The Great War and Modern Memory* Oxford University Press (London, 1975), pp. ix, 35, and *passim*; E.L. Woodward, *Short Journey* Faber and Faber (London, 1942), p. 122; Arthur Marwick, *The Deluge: British Society and the First World War* The Bodley Head (London, 1965), p. 297.

2. See for example Simon Schama in the *Times Literary Supplement*, 16 May 1980, reviewing Robert Wohl, *The Generation of 1914*, Weidenfeld & Nicholson (London, 1980).

3. A.J.P. Taylor, "Politics in the First World War", the Raleigh Lecture on History, 1959 (*Proceedings of the British Academy*, 1959), reprinted in *Politics in Wartime* Hamish Hamilton (London, 1964), pp. 11–44.

4. Taylor, *Politics in Wartime*, p. 27.

5. Taylor, *Politics in Wartime*, pp. 31–5; also Lord Beaverbrook, *Politicians and the War 1914–1916* Collins (London, 2 vols., 1928–32), vol. II, p. 309.

6. The best account of propaganda on the home front is Cate Haste, *Keep the Home Fires Burning: Propaganda in the First World War* Allen Lane (London, 1977).

7. David Lloyd George, War Memoirs, 6 vols., Nicholson & Watson (London, 1933–36), vol. 5, pp. 2660–2661.

8. Marwick, *The Deluge*, pp. 276, 284. For an even more pessimistic view, see Philip Abrams, "The Failure of Social Reform 1918–1920", *Past and Present*, 1963, pp. 43–64.

9. See for example H.C.G. Matthew, R.I. McKibbin and J.A. Kay, "The Franchise Factor in the Rise of the Labour Party", *English Historical Review*, 1976, pp. 723–752.

10. P.F. Clarke, "Liberals, Labour and the Franchise", *English Historical Review*, 1977, pp. 582–590; Duncan Tanner, "The Parliamentary Electoral System, the Fourth Reform Act and the Rise of Labour in England and Wales", *Bulletin of the Institute of Historical Research*, 1983, pp. 205–219.

3

The Territorial Force in the Great War

IAN BECKETT

The difficulties under which the Territorial Force laboured between its creation in 1908 and the outbreak of war in August 1914 are well known. So, too, are the problems which faced the Territorial Army after reconstitution in 1920. Strangely, however, beyond discussion of Kitchener's decision to raise his "New Armies" in preference to utilizing the existing machinery of Territorial County Associations as a means of expansion, modern studies of the Territorials have almost totally neglected the period between 1914 and 1918.[1] Yet, the war years are equally significant for any understanding of the continuing development of what may be termed the "amateur military tradition" in Britain. It is the purpose of this paper, therefore, to fill this gap rather in the way that the Territorials themselves were held to have "filled the gap" in the ranks of the B.E.F. in France and Flanders in 1914 and 1915. It will illustrate, firstly, how pre-war factors determined the employment of the Territorial Force during the war and, secondly, how the Territorials emerged from the experience of war with a deep felt sense of grievance. Some of the arguments here advanced have been developed at greater length elsewhere[2] but it is a subsidiary aim of the paper to indicate how surviving formation records may be utilized by the historian to yield rather more sophisticated information than has often appeared the case from regimental accounts and histories. In this latter respect, most examples utilized will relate to the 48th (South Midland) Division and its constituent units, notably the 145th Brigade and the 1/1st Buckinghamshire Battalion of that brigade.

The Territorial Force as it existed in August 1914 did not approximate to the original concept of its architect, R.B. Haldane, since crucial compromises had been accepted in the course of the evolution of the scheme. In particular, Haldane had conceived the Force as being both a means of supporting as well as expanding the Expeditionary Force with Territorial units being ready for overseas service after six months continuous training upon mobilization. However, through fear of political opposition, the Force was represented in 1908 purely as a means of domestic defence. As such it failed to attract any enduring popular support once an invasion scare in 1909 had subsided while being subject to increasing criticism. The latter derived both from the attitude of the military authorities, who saw little reason to expend limited resources on men not liable to overseas service, and also from those who advocated conscription as a more appropriate means of defence. Criticism of the military efficiency of the Territorials only generated more disillusionment and, from a peak of 270,041 officers and men in 1909, the Force declined to 245,779 officers and men, or some 66,000 short of establishment by September 1913. Some 80 per cent of the men had served for less than 4 years, many having failed to re-engage at the end of their first 4 years' term of enlistment in 1912. In addition, barely 7 per cent of officers and men had taken the so-called Imperial Service obligation committing themselves in advance to overseas service in the event of war.[3]

In some respects, therefore, Kitchener's decision to ignore the Territorial machinery in 1914 was understandable in view of the Force's pre-war failings although his specific reasons for doing so are still obscure. There were no plans for expansion through the County Associations and it would appear that it was thought they might be swamped by rapid expansion. Similarly, of course, the Territorials were not liable to overseas service unless they could be persuaded to take the Imperial Service obligation. Of course, it was equally true that the Adjutant-General's department of the War Office was also unsuited to the rapid expansion required while the ability of the Territorials to ready themselves for service was severely handicapped by the withdrawal of many Regular adjutants and instructors to staff the New Armies. Kitchener appears to have been reluctant to pressure married men into volunteering to go abroad and his pre-occupation with the possibility of invasion, against which the Territorials were the principal defence, must also be taken into account. Yet, the impression remains that the decision was an instinctive one for a Regular soldier who told Sir Charles Harris on the morning he entered the War Office that "he could take no account of anything but Regular soldiers".[4]

In numerical terms the Territorials' contribution to the war effort was far from insignificant, 318 Territorial battalions serving overseas compared to 404 New Army battalions, but it must also be acknowledged that Kitchener's intention in dispatching four Territorial divisions overseas in 1914 (the 42nd to Egypt and the 43rd, 44th and 45th to India) as well as a number of other Territorial units was specifically to release Regulars from Imperial garrisons for service in France and not to afford the Territorials greater opportunities. Partly, it was expected that Territorial units sent abroad might complete their training more quickly under service conditions, Major-General H.N.C. Heath of the 48th Division recommending this course for his formation in November 1914. But those divisions sent to India in particular were immensely dissatisfied with the conditions under which they served and continued to serve there until 1919 or even 1920 in apparent violation of Kitchener's promise to bring them back to France within a year. Moreover, Kitchener was only reluctantly persuaded to allow Territorials to "fill the gap" in the winter of 1914/15 before the New Armies were ready to take the field.[5]

There can be little doubt that there was unnecessary duplication of effort and competition in recruiting that damaged both the New Armies and the Territorials although there were certainly legislative difficulties, of which Kitchener was well aware, in employing Territorials abroad. The sad fact was that those difficulties were approached by the military authorities in such a way that the Territorials believed themselves to have been treated with insufficient consideration. A case in point is the problem of the Imperial Service obligation.

Before the war, only five complete Territorial units had volunteered for service overseas and an invitation was then extended to the remainder to undertake a similar commitment on 10 August 1914. Eleven days later units where 80 per cent of the men had volunteered for service (reduced to a more realistic 60 per cent on 31 August) were authorized to complete to war establishment while others not reaching the required rate of acceptance could combine to form service units. It is common to find units in which 80 or even 90 per cent volunteered immediately such as the 1/4th Gloucesters of what became 144th Brigade in 48th Division but this was not always the case and it must be recognized that many pre-war Territorials were older or had more family responsibilities than many new wartime recruits. Still others were too young since Territorials could enlist at the age of seventeen when the minimum age for overseas service was nineteen. Graham Greenwell, who served in 1/4th Oxford and Bucks Light Infantry in 145th Brigade, was originally kept back in England as under-age while a total of 402 other ranks, or approximately 42 per cent of the establishment, "being under 19, or for some other reason, were unable to proceed abroad at once" from the battalion. They were thus sent back to form the nucleus of the second line, a duplication of the Territorial Force being authorized as early as 15 August where units volunteered for service. Orders of 21 and 31 August, reiterated on 21 September 1914, authorized the unconditional duplication of the Force with a third line being established from November 1914 as first line units went abroad and for all that had not yet done so in March 1915.[6]

Similarly, the 1/1st Buckinghamshire Battalion of 145th Brigade returned approximately 30 per cent of its manpower to the second line but under slightly more unfortunate circumstances than those pertaining in Greenwell's battalion. When asked to volunteer on 11 August only 553 men did so although the number had risen to 600 by the following day. Some 240 men including many older NCOs and all 27 members of the band were separated from the battalion at Chelmsford, stripped of weapons and equipment and sent to dig trenches at Witham. Labelled "Never Dies" by the Commanding Officer they were, in the words of an officer of the 2/1st

Bucks Battalion, "not treated by either officers or men in the manner contemplated by the King's Regulations". There was lasting antipathy between the two battalions as a result which was not improved when the 2/1st subsequently refused to send any experienced NCOs to the first line battalion in March 1915 in return for men left behind when the latter proceeded overseas.[7]

Apart from those unwilling to serve overseas, there would also be those unfit to do so and evidence suggests that as many as 15 or even 20 per cent of the men in some units might be physically unfit for military service overseas. In the case of the 42nd (East Lancashire) Division, for example, medical inspection considerably reduced its strength upon mobilization and, in order to reach establishment, large numbers of men were drafted in from many different sources prior to embarkation for Egypt in September 1914. Upon arrival in Egypt there were further problems since many of those so hastily recruited or drafted were themselves totally unfit for service and the hospitals at both Cairo and Alexandria were all but swamped to the considerable annoyance of the GOC in Egypt, Sir John Maxwell.[8]

Related to the issue of the Imperial Service obligation was the ability of Territorials to continue to enlist for home service only until as late as March 1915. There were sufficient home service Territorials in Britain in April 1915 to form no less than 68 provisional battalions whilst still leaving over 80,000 home servicemen on Territorial returns. It was not until the introduction of conscription through the Military Service Acts of January and May 1916 that this not unattractive option was finally eradicated. The same legislation also eliminated the ability of pre-war Territorials to seek their discharge at the end of their 4 year engagement, a concession to which 159,388 Territorials would have been entitled between 1914/15 and 1916/17 although it was automatically extended by a year in wartime. There is little doubt that many did exercise that right of discharge prior to 1916 although others re-engaged for 4 years or the duration. It is impossible to state exactly how many opted for each course of action but, in the 1/1st Bucks Battalion, a total of 91 men, or almost 11 per cent of the establishment, went home time-expired between March 1915, when the battalion arrived in France, and the cessation of the concession in the following year. A further 33 men re-engaged during the same period while some 26 men were subsequently compulsorily retained in the service under the provisions of the Military Service legislation.[9]

But if the Imperial Service obligation, home service enlistment and the problem of the term of engagement posed problems for the military authorities in employing the Territorials, an even greater difficulty deriving from the Territorial and Reserve Forces Act was the integrity of Territorial units. In theory it was illegal to transfer Territorials between units, even within the Territorial Force, and equally illegal to amalgamate or disband

Territorial units. In view of the controversy raised by this issue during the war and its repercussions in the inter-war years, it is worth considering the ramifications at some length.

It was clearly stated on the standard form, E.624, which all Territorials signed in signifying their assent to overseas service, that an individual would remain with his own unit. However, the numbers of casualties suffered by the Regular army in 1914 soon exceeded pre-war expectations and, with the New Armies as yet untrained, only the Territorials were available as reinforcements once the relatively slim resources of the Army and Special Reserves had been exhausted. Some consideration was given in early 1915 to amending the Territorial and Reserve Forces Act and, briefly, between May and July 1915, the War Office unsuccessfully attempted to impose a new form, E.624A, by which those volunteering for service also agreed to possible transfer.[10] The second Military Service Act of May 1916 eventually enabled transfers to be made between Territorial and other units legally but, in the meantime, the problem of maintaining both Regular and Territorial units in the field had to be faced. As far as Territorial units were concerned, responsibility for reinforcing the first line had passed to the third line in March 1915 but the numbers of trained men required could not be found from the third line alone and there was periodic raiding of the second and even of other first line units. The results for the efficiency of those deprived of their own trained personnel could be disastrous as the performance of the 53rd (Welsh) and 54th (East Anglian) divisions at Suvla Bay in August 1915 testified.[11] Such expedients might have been acceptable had it not been for the fact that the entire drafting system in France and Flanders appeared to have broken down at an early stage. After December 1915, when direct enlistment into the Territorial Force was all but suspended, the drafting system became even more haphazard with what many Territorials regarded as harmful consequences as far as the Territorial "character" of the Force was concerned.

In 1914 many Territorial units enjoyed a unity born of close identification with a given locality but the process of change could begin almost at once. As already indicated, men would be lost through going home time-expired or through acceptance for officer training. Sickness would take its toll as would transfers. The biggest factor in change resulted, however, from battle casualties although much depended upon how soon a unit proceeded on active service and, once there, on the relative periods spent in quiet or active sectors or on actual operations. Charles Carrington, who served with 1/5th Royal Warwicks in 143 Brigade, recorded that in 1916 he spent only 65 days in the front line although 36 days were spent in close support and 120 in reserve. A further 73 days were spent "at rest" and 72 on leave, sick, travelling or attending schools of instruction. The 48th Division as a whole occupied a relatively quiet sector of the line around Hebuterne for twelve months between July 1915 and July 1916. Accounts of this period such as that by Frederick Grisewood, the well-known broadcaster of later years, who served with 1/4th Oxford and Bucks, indicate a degree of what has been termed "live and let live". The 1/1st Bucks Battalion even had a trench cow, one of only five mentioned in regimental accounts of the war.[12] But, from Hebuterne, the division moved to the Somme with the sudden commitment to active operations on a large scale making the resulting casualties probably all the harder to bear.

By the end of 1916 the 1/4th Royal Berks of 145th Brigade had ceased to resemble the original battalion. In the words of the distinguished historian, C.R.M.F. Cruttwell, who served with the battalion,

> As a result of these losses, and the impossibility of finding adequate local drafts, the Battalion during the latter half of the year gradually lost its exclusive Berkshire character which at the beginning of the war had been its unique possession.

Similarly, V.F. Eberle of the division's 475th Field Company calculated that the engineering company had lost the equivalent of 70 per cent of its establishment by November 1917. In the 1/4th Oxford and Bucks only 25 original members of the battalion served continuously through to the armistice, 16 of them in the signals or transport sections and 9 riflemen.[13]

Similar evidence is also available for the 1/1st Bucks Battalion which, in effect, suffered most if its wartime battle casualties in just two brief periods – attacks around Ovillers and Pozieres on the Somme between 21 and 24 July 1916, which cost 242 casualties, and an operation at St. Julien on 16 August 1917 during 3rd Ypres which cost 291 casualties. In the wake of the Somme operations, the battalion received its first draft of "strangers" from 1/1st Hunts Cyclists but further drafts were required in September while other original members were transferred to the newly-formed 145th Machine Gun Company and the 10th Lincolns. A draft of 239 men were received in July 1917 in preparation for renewed operations and, following the heavy losses at St. Julien, large drafts were received from the Army Service Corps (Motor Transport). A measure of the degree of territorial change can perhaps be gauged by a comparison of the places of residence and/or birth of men of the battalion who were either killed, died of wounds or died from other causes while on active service. In 1915 some 65 per cent of the battalion's dead had originated from Bucks parishes and 70 per cent did so among 1916 deaths. In 1917, however, the percentage from Bucks parishes declined to 34 per cent, rising marginally to 38 per cent among the dead of 1918. This cannot be a precise survey since losses may have fallen disproportionately within the battalion but it is at least persuasive in its implications and it should be said that similar results have been discovered in other battalions and formations.[14]

Naturally, the process of change also affected the officers of battalions. The 1/4th Royal Berks had lost a third of its original officers through various causes by the end of the first year abroad. Eberle was the only one of twelve officers in two engineering field companies of the division to remain serving in 1918. Of 30 officers who embarked with the 1/1st Bucks Battalion in March 1915, only two served with the battalion throughout the war. Of the remainder, four were killed, two died of wounds; twelve were wounded (of whom eight returned at various times to serve with the battalion), two were invalided home and eight moved to other duties. Indeed, throughout the entire period of active service a total of 142 officers passed through the battalion or approximately four times the original establishment. As in the case of the rank and file, replacements would rarely be Buckinghamshire men, the arrival of thirteen officers of the Essex Regiment in September 1916 being "it must be admitted, something of a shock". Greenwell's battalion received replacement officers from the Scottish Rifles at the same time and in some other Territorial battalions there are accounts of kilted officers or men arriving in English units.[15]

A number of consequences followed the arrival of drafts. The closeness of some Territorial units appears to have caused problems for newcomers and some accounts indicate a kind of caste system operating at least initially between "veterans" and newer arrivals. There was also rivalry on occasions between those drafted from a second line unit to its first line equivalent or vice versa which is understandable in that any large numbers of relatively experienced men arriving in a unit would have to be assimilated both socially and also in terms of seniority.[16] Fortuitously, some drafts later in the war might actually go some way towards restoring a unit's original character. In February 1917, for example, the 1/4th Oxford and Bucks received a draft of men from the Oxfordshire Yeomanry and the Royal Bucks Hussars which "thoroughly brought back the old spirit" while, at the end of the same year, the 1/5th Royal Warwicks received 100 men from the Warwickshire Yeomanry which similarly "rejuvenated" the Territorial spirit. Increasingly, however, men returning to a unit would find strangers – "Derbyites", middle-aged conscripts and, by 1918, eighteen-year-olds. To many Territorials the drafts were increasingly lacking in intelligence, physique and discipline. Thus Greenwell wrote in August 1917 of how, although the new men were generally good, "at times one yearns for the old crowd, they were so awfully different". Carrington, too, recorded new drafts in October 1917 as seeming "more vulnerable, coming and going, while a residue of tough old 'swaddies' among whom I could now number myself, seemed to go on for ever".[17]

In the case of the 1/1st Bucks Battalion, the arrival of the ASC personnel mentioned earlier coincided with a major increase in crime in the battalion. Newcomers after July 1917 accounted for 33.8 per cent of all crime throughout the entire war. The letter books of the Commanding Officer, Lieutenant Colonel L.L.C. Reynolds, also indicate that replacement officers were of declining quality as the war progressed. A few examples must suffice such as the 40-year-old platoon commander sent to the battalion in

March 1917 or the range accident in July 1917 caused because a newly arrived subaltern had had no revolver training. Two subalterns who arrived in March 1918 had had little command experience and one was eventually sent to Intelligence in September as he had shown no demonstrable powers of leadership. Eberle, too, had recorded in September 1916 that later replacements "had been given little opportunity for regular command or control of even a small body of men" while Greenwell's letters record another 40-year-old reaching the 1/4th Oxford and Bucks having previously been left behind by the 2/4th and one officer draft that included an epileptic. The diary of Edward Campion Vaughan, who joined the 1/8th Royal Warwicks of 143rd Brigade in January 1917, reveal another young subaltern regarded as "an inefficient young officer".[18]

At least the process of change would not usually materially affect the social composition of a Territorial unit. It is simply an error to assume that the Force as a whole corresponded to the London "class" corps drawn from the middle classes of the capital. Figures available for some London units do indeed indicate a preponderance of middle class personnel but the "class" corps were but a small percentage of the whole. There were a number of slum battalions in the Territorial Force and a number of predominantly working class divisions. The 48th Division showed that frequent mixture of town and country which was so common in Territorial divisions, brigades and even battalions. The 143rd Brigade consisted of four Warwickshire battalions of which three were characterized by Carrington as "townies", his own 1/5th Royal Warwicks having a BSA Company and a Mitchell and Butler's Company. Howard Green, who served with the 145th Machine Gun Company, has written that the 1/4th Oxford and Bucks considered itself "socially, to be a cut above the other battalions in the brigade". There was certainly a contingent in the battalion, as there was in the 2/4th Oxford and Bucks, from the teacher training college at Culham but Greenwell also records the employees of a Witney blanket manufacturers whose managing director was an NCO in the battalion. By the end of the war, too, a large number of miners had found themselves in the battalion. The 1/1st Bucks Battalion was also fairly representative. Of those constituting the battalion in April 1908, nine were professional men, 27 were tradesmen, 27 were clerks or in similar service employment, three had no known occupation, 147 were employees of the London and North Western Railway and 279 manual workers. Muster rolls for the Aylesbury Company and Chesham detachment attached to it show a continuing dependence upon manual workers down to 1914. Between 1909 and 1914 seven professional men joined the company together with 23 tradesmen, 36 clerks, one of no known occupation and 198 manual workers, the majority being printers. Over 100 Aylesbury printers went overseas with the battalion in March 1915.[19]

Another aspect of the problems of maintaining the territorial character of the Force was that the possibility of units being amalgamated or even disbanded steadily increased. There were some temporary amalgamations as early as 1915 and more permanent arrangements in the following year while many second line Territorial units were reduced during the manpower crisis in the spring of 1918. Of course, all these problems deriving from the transfer and reinforcement system did not affect the Territorials alone but, viewed from the perspective of the Territorials and their representatives in the House of Commons, it appeared that the military authorities intended the "gradual extinction" of the Force. London units naturally figured prominently in the criticism of the drafting system which reached a crescendo in the Commons in March and April 1916 but all Territorial Associations had reason to believe that their statutory powers, not least the ability to control the destiny of their own units, was being steadily eroded. There were attempts to fight battlefield amalgamations by associations. In the case of Bucks, for example, the Association urged that all Bucks men should be sent to Bucks units in March 1916 and, in the following month, complained at rumours of amalgamations at the front. In October 1916 it complained that the 3/1st Bucks was being made to wear OBLI badges and in March 1918 there was disquiet at the reduction of the 2/1st and the Association managed to extract a promise that no similar fate would befall the 1/1st Bucks.[20] Other associations, notably those in Scotland, attempted similar pressure but all remained powerless to control events. The role in recruiting was lost after 1915 and that in clothing even earlier. The Director-General of the Territorial Force lost powers to the Military Secretary in November 1916 and the Force's own Record Offices were closed in 1917. Only concerted pressure from a revived Council of County Territorial Associations saved Territorial depots from being closed down.[21]

The Territorials thus believed that they had good reason to feel aggrieved at the treatment accorded both associations and Territorial units, the ultimate betrayal of the latter appearing the reductions in 1918 when the 50th Division was reduced to cadre and reconstituted with only a single Territorial battalion and the 53rd and 60th Divisions in Palestine reorganized by despatching all but one battalion from each brigade to France and replacing them with Indian Army battalions. It is a measure of the Territorials' anger that the War Office felt compelled to issue a detailed defence of its actions over drafting in February 1919 in which it pointed out, not unreasonably, that military necessity had had to prevail over integrity of Territorial units. Nevertheless, the associations extracted the so-called "Pledge" upon reconstitution whereby integrity was guaranteed in return for an acceptance by Territorials of a general service liability for the future. The liability was, however, hedged with qualifications and continued to be a major source of friction throughout the inter-war years.[22]

Much of what has been described in this paper could and did happen to units of the New Armies and even the Regular Army but there was yet a further source of grievance among Territorials in that they also believed that Regulars adopted at best a patronizing attitude towards the Force if not one of outright hostility. This was not evident in the relationship at the level of other ranks although there does appear to have been friction between the Territorials and the New Armies at this level. Eberle, for example, felt that New Army men attached for trench familiarization resented being taught by the Territorials:

> They are supremely confident that the New Army will finish off this war, whereas we have been the stop-gap till they could come out. This attitude is rather different from that of the Regular Army units. They have helped and treated us as if we were younger brothers.

However, if there was friendly feeling at low level, this did not extend to commissioned ranks.[23]

When brigades had first been organized in the old Volunteer Force in 1888, Volunteers had often commanded them although fewer tended to be given the opportunity in later years. Haldane had also promised that Territorials would be given the opportunity of higher command but in 1914 only three Territorials commanded brigades, the first having only been appointed in 1911. It soon became clear that there would be relatively few others who would do so in war. In reply to increasing criticism from MPs, the Under Secretary of State for War, Ian Macpherson, announced in February 1917 that "no less" than eighteen Territorials had risen above the rank of Lieutenant-Colonel since August 1914 at the front and three at home. He also claimed that Territorial and New Army officers were filling an increasing proportion of the places on staff courses but this did not stem criticism and in January 1918 the Secretary of State, Derby, re-iterated the War Office case, arguing that four Territorials had now commanded divisions, that 52 had commanded brigades and 61 below the rank of Lieutenant in 1914 had risen to that of Lieutenant-Colonel. But many of the appointments were only temporary ones and Macpherson had to admit in the following month that only ten Territorials currently commanded brigades.[24]

In this regard the 48th Division affords a good example, During the war all five men who commanded it (two temporarily) were Regular officers and Regulars also filled the posts of GS01, A-A & Q-M-G, and B-G, RA. At the beginning of the war the divisional CRE was a Territorial but he was replaced by a Regular shortly after the division reached France and no Territorial occupied the post again until January 1918 and then only temporarily until another Territorial was appointed on a permanent basis in March 1918. Neither the 143rd or the 144th Brigades had any other than Regular commanding officers while the three Territorials who took temporary command of 145th Brigade at various times during the war managed only 42 days' command between them. Many of the junior staff posts in brigade and division were filled by Territorials but this hardly compensated for their failure to secure greater opportunities of command.

The attitudes displayed towards Territorials within 48th Division are also a microcosm of those elsewhere. When one elderly Regular took command of the 1/1st Bucks Battalion in January 1915 he apparently expressed surprise that his officers were "gentlemen" while Cruttwell's brother's memoirs record that although they liked their own Regular adjutant, the officers of the 1/4th Royal Berks had no great regard for Brigadier General W.K. McClintock of 145th Brigade. Neither did they like Brigadier General C.H.L. James of the 143rd Brigade who, on one occasion, was found in the Berkshires' trenches:

> I respectfully asked the Brigadier who he was (well knowing of course the old blighter by sight), and when he replied with some asperity, I said "Very likely you are Sir, but, etc, it is necessary for you to be identified as you are alone and you must, I fear, come along with me to my Company Commander's HQ." Spitting with fury, I escorted him to the Goat's HQ where he was detained, and entertained until, by field telephone, we persuaded his Brigade Major to come along and fetch him. He couldn't say a great deal but he looked more than he said!

By contrast, Greenwell recorded his impression of one new Regular commanding officer in June 1917 as "a very nice fellow indeed, like most regular soldiers".[25]

One problem in the relationship between Regular officers and their Territorial counterparts was the pre-war convention that Territorials ranked junior in their rank to Regulars which subsequently left many older and experienced Territorials junior to younger Regulars or New Army officers who came out to the front senior than those who had long preceded them. In some units and formations there is evidence of considerable friction and a number of accounts which indicate that some Territorials were moved to cut the "T"'s from their uniforms because they considered it a badge of inferiority. The irony, of course, was that the Territorial Force provided the Regular and New Armies with innumerable candidates for commission.[26] But, there are always exceptions to generality, and it must be acknowledged that many Regular officers were favourably disposed towards the Territorials. Sir John French, for example, who had been adjutant to a Yeomanry regiment at one time, was well satisfied with the performance of the Territorials in "filling the gap". Similarly, no reference to the 48th Division can be made without mention of Major General Sir Robert Fanshawe who commanded it from May 1915 until his dismissal in June 1918. "Fanny" was a Regular who clearly thoroughly understood how to motivate Territorial soldiers and virtually all accounts record the frequent visits of the "Chocolate Soldier" to the trenches, his pockets filled with chocolate bars to be distributed to officers and men alike.

There was considerable regret and anger when he was removed from his command by the Earl of Cavan in Italy after the division had been temporarily thrown back by the Austrian offensive on the Asiago plateau on 15 June 1918. Fanshawe had been one of the few divisional staff officers still on his feet after "mountain fever" had struck the 48th Division especially hard but it still recovered sufficiently quickly from the Austrian attack to inflict a major reverse on the attackers. Fanshawe's concept of "elastic defence" was not that of Cavan, who believed in a more rigid defence, while the chief British staff officer of XIV Corps, Brigadier-General the Hon. J.F. Gathorne-Hardy, may also have been involved in Fanshawe's removal.[27]

The reasons underlying the attitudes of Regulars towards the Territorial Force may well be connected to what a Director-General of the Territorial Force, Bethune, once called the "craft unionism" of the Regular army. Few officers appear to have expected much of amateur soldiers. Objective reports on the performance of Territorials in France and India dating from December 1914 and April 1915 respectively both concluded that Territorials showed little sense of interior economy while that from France found that Territorials were slow to move and lacking in instruction in both movement and entrenching. It was widely believed that Territorials had less recuperative powers than Regulars and that they would prove better in defence than in attack. It must also be borne in mind that the Territorials who first went overseas in 1914 were often poorly equipped, the celebrated attack of the 1/14th London (London Scottish) at Messines in November 1914 being undertaken with rifles incapable of rapid fire[28]. Indeed, the Territorials generally arrived in France even into 1915 with the obsolete Long Enfields, 15 pounders and 4.5" howitzers. Nevertheless, Territorials in India did remarkably well in the rigorous pre-war "Kitchener tests" and, although standards naturally varied, there was little to differentiate Territorial, Regular and New Army units by 1918. The most often criticized aspect of the Force was, of course, the alleged lax discipline in Territorial formations. This derived, however, from a basic misunderstanding of the ethos of the Territorials on the part of the Regulars. Major-General J.L. Keir, who commanded the 48th Division from July 1912 until July 1914, anticipated this well in the July 1914 issue of the *Army Review* in which he had written that problems would arise where Regulars and Territorials would be serving side by side "but practically judged by a different standard" in a war. The phrase that most commonly appears in Territorial accounts is "family" with a concept of self-discipline. Carrington has written of the "strong sense of unity" in his battalion, his brigade and his division and Eberle of the "family atmosphere" of his field company. It may well be that the reason for Vaughan's unpopularity in the 1/8th Royal Warwicks was that he had offended against the concept of family, a fellow officer telling him,

There is no room for personal dislikes; if our social relations are bad, we will never work together and the Battalion will lose the leading position that it has always had in the division.

Every other battalion in the 48th Division also appears to have believed that it was the best battalion and it is perhaps for that reason that it proved that "well commanded division but of no outstanding fame" of which Charles Carrington has written. It had a good solid reputation and, on occasions, had its moments, most spectacularly in the advance in Italy between 1 and 4 November 1918 in which it took over 22,000 prisoners and over 400 artillery pieces.[29]

The Territorial Force began to be disembodied in December 1918, the Army Council resolving that no special decoration would be issued to those who had taken the Imperial Service obligation in August 1914. There seemed little immediate role for the Force in the immediate post-war world with conscription now established as a precedent for large-scale conflict and the Territorials unlikely to consent readily to any wider service liability for smaller scale conflict without some guarantee of integrity. As already recounted, the Territorial Army got its guarantee in the "Pledge" but the post-war Territorials were still regarded as the most expendable part of the army at a time of financial retrenchment and were still denied command and staff appointments until the 1930s.[30] Prior to the cessation of voluntary direct enlistment into the Force in December 1915, some 725,842 men had enlisted in the Territorials, or approximately half the number who enlisted in the New Armies in the same period. It must be borne in mind, however, that the ability of the Territorials to recruit was restricted by official policy. Imperfect though it may have been as a means of expansion, the Territorial Force still made a major contribution to the war effort. Between 1914 and 1920 the Territorials had 577,016 casualties in all theatres and its officers and men won 71 Victoria Crosses. Among the most notable Territorial achievements during the war were the crossing of the St. Quentin Canal by the 46th (North Midland) Division in September 1918 and the surrender of Jerusalem to two NCO's of the 2/19th London on 8 September 1917 as well as that crucial role in "filling the gap". The Territorials' reward for such effort and sacrifice was little and it could not be said that the war materially improved its status within the army. That, as this paper has hopefully demonstrated, was both regrettable and unjust but only in keeping with the traditional fate of auxiliary military forces in Britain.

Acknowledgements

The author acknowledges the generosity of the following in enabling him to consult and quote from archives in their possession: the Trustees of the Imperial War Museum; the Duke of Edinburgh's Royal Regiment; the Council of Territorial Army and Volunteer Reserve Associations; the Ministry of Defence (Old War Office Library); Colonel John Christie-Miller; Major Elliott Viney; W. Ward-Jackson Esq; the County Record Offices of Buckinghamshire, Hampshire, Oxfordshire, Surrey and Worcestershire (Hereford and Worcester); the Guildhall Library; and those former officers and men of the 48th Division and/or 1/1st Bucks Battalion who have generously corresponded with the author or allowed him to interview them. Crown copyright material in the Public Record Office appears by permission of Her Majesty's Stationery Office. The short passage from *My Sapper Venture* by V.F. Eberle appears by permission of Pitman Publishing Ltd., London.

Notes

1. Edward M. Spiers, *Haldane: An Army Reformer*, Edinburgh University Press, 1980, pp. 92–115, 161–186; Peter Dennis, "The Reconstitution of the Territorial Force, 1918–20" in A. Preston and P. Dennis (eds), *Swords and Covenants*, Croom Helm, London, 1976, pp. 190–215; Peter Dennis, "The County Associations and the Territorial Army", *Army Quarterly and Defence Journal* **109**, 2, 1979, pp. 210–219.
2. See Ian F.W. Beckett, "The Territorial Force" in Ian F.W. Beckett and Keith Simpson, *A Nation in Arms: A Social Study of the British Army in The First World War*, Manchester University Press 1985.
3. Duke of York's Headquarters, Minutes of the C(ouncil) of C(ounty) T(erritorial) A(ssociations), 14 April 1913; Cd. 7254 (1914), *The Annual Return of the Territorial Force for the year 1913*.
4. Peter Simkins, "Kitchener and the Expansion of the Army" in Ian F.W. Beckett and John Gooch (eds), *Politicians and Defence: Studies in the Formulation of British Defence Policy, 1846–1970*, Manchester University Press, 1981, pp. 87–109; David French, *British Economic and Strategic Planning, 1905–1915*, Allen and Unwin, London, 1982, pp. 124–137; Sir Charles Harris, "Kitchener and the Territorials: First Hours at the War Office", *The Times* 28 August 1928, p. 13.
5. Major General N. Woodyatt, "The Territorials (Infantry) in India, 1914–20", *Journal of the Royal United Service Institution*, LXVII, 1922, pp.717–737 especially discussion after the lecture; PRO, Cab 42/2 (also Cab 22/1), Minutes of War Council, 19 March 1915; Surrey. RO., Minutes of CTA, 7 April 1919 and Minutes of General Purposes Committee, 19 April 1920; I(mperial) W(ar) M(useum), Henry Wilson Mss, Box 73/1/13, File 34A/18, Esher to Duncannon, 24 August 1918 (I owe this reference to Dr. Keith Jeffery).
6. Sir John Dunlop, "The Territorial Army in the Early Years", *Army Quarterly*, XCIV, 1967, pp. 53–55; MOD, W(ar) O(ffice) L(ibrary), *A Chronological Summary of the Principal Changes in the Organisation and Administration of the Territorial Force since Mobilisation*, 1918, pp. 1–5; IWM, V.G. Ricketts Mss (1/4th Gloucs), p. 9; Graham Greenwell, *An Infant in Arms*, 2nd edit., Allen Lane, London, 1972, p. 8; Oxon, RO., Minutes of CTA, 12 September 1914; WOL, *Chronological Summary*, pp. 1–5.
7. L.V. Crouch, *Duty and Service: Letters from the Front*, privately published, Aylesbury, 1917, pp. 24–25; Oscar Viney, "Reminiscences", typescript, 1960, pp. 70–74; IWM, 80/32/2, Christie-Miller Mss, pp. 28–29, 66–68, 79; Bucks. RO., D/X, 780/29, Diary of C.P. Phipps, 28 May 1915; Author interviews with Messrs. J. Stammers, A. Seymour and J. Tranter, 25 November 1980. Not all men of the 1/1st Bucks with family responsibilities opted for home service – see IWM, P329T, Gilbert Nash Mss.
8. E.V. Tempest, *The History of the 1/6th Battalion, The West Yorkshire Regiment*, Percy Lund Humphries, London and Bradford, 1921, P. 5; W.C. Oates, *The Sherwood Foresters in the Great War: The 2/8th Battalion*, J. and H. Bell, Nottingham, 1920, p. 23; Lord Silsoe, *Sixty Years a Welsh Territorial*, Gomer Press, Llandysul, 1976, pp. 27–28; PRO, WO 161/112, Winder to Williams, 17 October 1917; *Ibid*, Kitchener Papers, 30/57/45, 0047, Maxwell to Fitzgerald, 11 October 1914.
9. *Hansard* 5th ser., LXXIII, 2292, Tennant, 28 July 1915; F.W. Perry, "Manpower and Organisational Problems in the Expansion of the British and other Commonwealth Armies during the two World Wars", Unpub. Ph.D., London, 1982, p. 41; WOL,

Chronological Summary, pp. 12–13; *Ibid, Returns of the Territorial Force at Home*, 30 August 1915; IWM, V.G. Ricketss Mss, pp. 38–40; Bucks. RO., T/A 6/11–14, Casualty Books of 1/1st Bucks, 1915–18.

10. J.H. Lindsay, *The London Scottish in the Great War*, Regimental Headquarters, London, 1925, pp. 19–20; PRO, Cab 41/36/19, Asquith to the King, 29 April 1915; *Ibid*, WO 32/5452, Simon to Kitchener, 29 April 1915 and Derby to Sclater, 2 July 1915; Randolph S. Churchill, *Lord Derby: King of Lancashire*, Heinemann, London, 1959, pp. 185–186.

11. WOL, *Chronological Summary*, pp. 49–54; *Ibid, Circular Instructions affecting the Territorial Force*, HMSO, London, June and July 1915, passim; *Official History of the Great War* (hereafter *OFH*), *Gallipoli*, Heinemann, London, 1932, II, p. 314; C.H. Dudley-Ward, *History of the 53rd (Welsh) Division, 1914–18*, Western Mail, Cardiff, 1927, p.12.

12. Charles Edmonds (Carrington), *A Subaltern's War*, Peter Davies, London, 1929, p. 120; Frederick Grisewood, *The World Goes By*, Secker and Warburg, London, 1952, pp. 108–111; P.L. Wright, *The First Bucks Battalion*, Hazell Watson and Viney, Aylesbury and London, 1920, p. 17; T. Ashworth, *Trench Warfare: The Live and Let Live System*, Macmillan, London, 1980, p. 131.

13. C.R.M.F. Cruttwell, *The War Service of the 1/4th Royal Berks (TF)*, Blackwells, Oxford, 1922, p.99; V.F. Eberle, *My Sapper Venture*, Pitman, London, 1973, p. 135; Graham Greenwell to author, 19 March 1979; Author interview with Howard Green, 22 February 1980.

14. Wright, *First Bucks*, pp. 16–17, 36, 43, 83, 215–216; Bucks. RO., T/A 6/11–14; PRO, WO 95/2763, War Diary of 1/1st Bucks; *Soldiers Died in the Great War*, HMSO, London, 192, Pt. 47, pp. 53–63.

15. Cruttwell, *1/4th Royal Berks*, p. 47; Eberle, *Sapper Venture*, p. 197; Wright, *First Bucks*, pp. 179–196; A.F. Mockler-Ferryman (ed), *The Oxford and Bucks Light Infantry War Chronicle, 1917–18*, London, 1918, p. 243; Wright, *First Bucks*, p. 46; Greenwell, *Infant*, pp. 144–145; G. Harbottle, *Civilian Soldier*, privately published, Newcastle, 1983, p. 47; A.K. McGilchrist, *The Liverpool Scottish, 1900–1916*, Young and Sons, Liverpool, 1930, pp. 261–262; A. Rifleman (A.M. Bowes-Smith), *Four Years on the Western Front*, Odhams, London, 1922, p. 153; IWM, PP/MCR/86, A.G. Williams Mss, p. 316; J.Q. Henriques, *The War History of the 1st Battalion, Queen's Westminster Rifles*, Medici Society, London, 1923, pp. 108–109.

16. Arthur Behrend, *Make Me a Soldier*, Eyre and Spottiswoode, London, 1961, pp. 25–26; N. Gladden, *The Somme*, William Kimber, London, 1974, pp. 100–106; F.A.J. Taylor, *The Bottom of the Barrel*, Regency Press, London and New York, 1978, p. 47; W.V. Tilsley, *Other Ranks*, Cobden-Sanderson, London, 1931, p. 173.

17. Greenwell, *Infant*, pp. 139, 156; Charles Carrington, *Soldier From the Wars Returning*, Hutchinson, London, 1965, pp. 199, 229; W.L. Andrews, *Haunting Years*, Hutchinson, London, n.d., p. 213; Rifleman, *Four Years*, pp. 153, 332; W.H.A. Groom, *Poor Bloody Infantry*, William Kimber, London, 1976, p. 45; Greenwell, *Infant*, p. 190; Carrington, *Soldier*, p. 199.

18. Bucks, RO., T/A 6/11–14; IWM, 74/136/1, L.L.C. Reynolds Letter Books, entries for 11 April, 23 June, 15 July, 27 July, 20 September and 22 December 1917 and for 24 March, 30 March, 6 April, 7 May, 8 May and 9 September 1918; Eberle, *Sapper Venture*, p.101; Greenwell, *Infant*, pp. 143–145; E. Campion Vaughan, *Some Desperate Glory*, Frederick Warne, London, 1981, passim.

19. Carrington, *Soldier*, p. 101; Howard Green, "Retreat to the Hindenburg Line", *War Monthly* 7, 2, 1979, pp. 11–17; Grisewood, *World Goes By*, p. 110; Oxon. RO., Minutes of CTA, 31 October 1914; Author interview with A.H. Wootton, 9 June 1982; Greenwell, *Infant*, p.94; Bucks RO., T/A 6/1, Muster of 1st Bucks, 1908 and 6/2, Rolls of Aylesbury Coy, 1909-1914; Viney, "Reminiscences", p. 71.

20. Minutes of CCTA, 17 September 1917; *Hansard* 5th ser., LXXXI, 584–5, 924–5, 756, 1367–8, 1789, 1977–8, 2092–4, 2294; Bucks. RO., T/A 1/4, Minutes of General Purposes Committee, 6 April, 4 October, 5 October 1916, 4 October 1917, 2 January and 6 February 1919; *Ibid*, T/A 1/1, Minutes of CTA, 2 March 1916 and 7 March 1918.

21. PRO, WO 163/2, Minutes of Army Council, 30 October and 21 November 1916; *The Times* 27 January 1917, p. 7; Oxon. RO., Minutes of CTA, 27 January and 27 October

1917; Guildhall Library, Mss 12613,2, Minutes of London CTA, 20 February and 15 November 1917; PRO, WO 161/110, Order of 29 March 1917; Hants. RO., 37M69/3, Minutes of CTA, 16 March and 19 April 1917; Ibid, 37M69/4, Minutes of CTA, 21 December 1917 and 23 January 1918; Worcs. RO., 004.6, BA 5204/5, Minutes of General Committee, 20 October 1917; Minutes of CCTA, 17 September, 4 October and 7 November 1917 and 9 January 1918; WOL, *Chronological Summary*, pp. 6–11, 53–55, 59–62a.

22. Worcs. RO., 004.6, BA 5204/5, Minutes of General Purposes Committee, 1 March 1919 reprints statement by Army Council for 21 February 1919; Dennis, "County Associations", pp. 210–219.

23. IWM, V.G. Ricketts Mss, p. 16; *Ibid*, PP/MCR/86, A.G. Williams Mss, P. 86; E.H.G. Roberts, *The Story of the 1/9th King's in France*, Northern Publishing, Liverpool, 1922, p. 34; Behrend, *Make Me a Soldier*, p. 114; W.N. Nicholson, *Behind the Lines*, Cape, London, 1939, p. 207; E. Riddell and M.C. Clayton, *The Cambridgeshires, 1914–18*, Bowes and Bowes, Cambridge, 1934, p. 30; Eberle, *Sapper Venture*, p. 34.

24. *Hansard* 5th ser., XC, 1313, Blake and Macpherson, 21 February 1917; *The Times* 30 January 1918, p. 10; *Hansard* 5th ser., CIII, 936–7, Croft and Macpherson, February 1918; G.H. Barnett, *With the 48th Division in Italy*, William Blackwood, London and Edinburgh, 1923, p.x.

25. *OFH, Order of Battle of Divisions*, HMSO, London, 1936, Pt 2a, pp. 77–83; Viney, "Reminiscences", p. 84; Duke of Edinburgh's Royal Regiment, "Personal Recollections of G.H.W. Cruttwell", typescript, pp. 12, 14; Greenwell, *Infant*, p. 183.

26. IWM, 78/22/1, C.L.A. Ward-Jackson Mss, letter of 1 May 1915; C.M. Slack, *Grandfather's Adventures in the Great War, 1914–18*, A.H. Stockwell, Ilfracombe, 1977, pp. 74–75; *Statistics of the Military Effort of the British Empire, 1914–1920*, HMSO, London, 1922, pp. 234–235.

27. PRO, Kitchener Papers, 30/57/50, WA77, French to Kitchener, 7 March 1915; *The Times* 9 January 1917, p. 3; Richard Holmes, *The Little Field Marshal*, Cape, London, 1981, p. 256; Author interviews with Messrs Stammers, Seymour and Tranter, 25 November 1980; Author interview with A.H. Wootton, 9 June 1982; Author interview with Howard Green, 22 February 1980; Graham Greenwell to author, 19 March 1979; Charles Carrington to author, 20 January 1979; Mockler-Ferryman, *War Chronicle*, p.230; Vaughan, *Desperate Glory*, p. 78; Greenwell, *Infant*, pp. 183, 228; Eberle, *Sapper Venture*, p. 161; Carrington, *Soldier*, p. 226; Barnett, *With the 48th*, pp. 64, 95–96. There is considerable material relating to the Asiago battle and Fanshawe's role in PRO, Cab 45/84, being correspondence of Edmonds the official historian, with officers of the division. Sickness in the division was a crucial factor on 15 June 1918. Detailed sickness records are available from September 1917 but with the notable exception of that for June (see PRO, WO 95/2748 and 4245, War Diaries of ADMS). See also Charles Carrington, "Some Soldiers" in G.A. Panichas (ed), *Promise of Greatness*, Cassell, London, 1968, pp. 156–166.

28. Remark by General Sir E.C. Bethune at RUSI, 11 October 1922, *Journal of the Royal United Service Institution*, LXVII, 1922, p. 735; WOL, TF2, *Miscellaneous Letters During the War Period, July 1914 to June 1915*, no. 452, Report by DMT, 21 December 1914; *Ibid*, no. 516, Order by CinC., 11 January 1915; *Ibid*, no. 822, Donald to Wolfe Murray, 6 April 1915; Cd. 1734 (1922), Report of the War Office Committee of Enquiry into Shell Shock, pp. 45–6, evidence of J.G. Burnett; PRO, WO 32/3116, Report of the Committee on the Lessons of the Great War, October 1932, pp. 35–37; *OFH, France and Belgium, 1914*, II, p. 300, n. 71.

29. Major General J.L. Kier, "Some Aspects of a Territorial Division from Within", *Army Review* VII, 1, July 1914, pp. 128–141; Carrington, *Soldier*, p. 103; Eberle, *Sapper Venture*, p. 102; Vaughan, *Desperate Glory*, p. 153; Carrington, *Soldier*, p.123.

30. PRO, WO 163/23, Minutes of Army Council, 11 December 1918; *The Times* 28 December 1918, p. 3 and 30 December 1918, p. 5; *Statistics of the Military Effort*, pp. 238, 365–366; Brian Bond, "The Territorial Army in Peace and War," *History Today*, XVI, 3, 1966, pp. 157–166; Howard Green, *The British Army in the First World War*, privately published, London, 1968, pp. 36–45. For post-war developments, see Dennis,

"Reconstitution", pp. 190–215; Dennis, "County Associations", pp. 210–219; Peter Dennis, "The Territorial Army in Aid of the Civil Power in Britain, 1919–1926", *Journal of Contemporary History*, **16**, 1981, pp. 705–724.

31. The short passage from *Some Desperate Glory* is reprinted by permission of the publishers.

4

British Military Leadership in the First World War

JOHN TERRAINE

This is a subject that has been steeped in misunderstanding, prejudice and pure mythology for over 60 years and largely remains so to this day. The image of *"The Donkeys"* is firmly planted in many people's minds. That was the thoughtful title of a book by Mr. Alan Clark (now a junior Conservative minister) published in 1961 and consisting almost entirely of vitriolic condemnation of the two Commanders-in-Chief of the 1914–18 BEF – Field-Marshal Sir John French and Field-Marshal Sir Douglas Haig. The title was supposed to be taken from a conversation between General Ludendorff and General Max Hoffman, which according to Mr. Clark, went as follows:

Ludendorff: "The English soldiers fight like lions."
Hoffman: "True. But don't we know that they are lions led by donkeys?"

Curiously enough, when pressed, Mr. Clark failed to offer any source for this reported conversation. Even more curiously, the image of donkeys and lions does in fact have a variety of sources:

> thus, the London *Times* in 1870 used exactly that form of words for the French soldiers defeated by the Prussians: "lions led by donkeys"; in 1917 the Mayor of Poplar referred to the British as "a nation of lions governed by asses";
> and in April 1918 – significant timing – Princess Blucher, an English woman married to a Prussian aristocrat and living in Berlin, noted with great pleasure what she was told by members of the German General Staff: "the English generals are wanting in strategy. We should have no chance if they possessed as much science as their officers and men had of courage and bravery. They are lions led by donkeys."

It was in April 1918 that the lions led by their donkeys brought the most powerful offensive of the whole war to an absolute standstill without achieving any strategic objective whatever, and under the leadership of the same donkeys were soon to pass to a most triumphant offensive of their own, ending with a German delegation crossing the lines with a white flag! Not bad work for donkeys! As for Hoffman, I don't think we can rate his opinion as valuable, since he spent his whole war on the Eastern Front and never saw a British Soldier or a British General in action.

Yet the "donkey" image persists, and we find John Keegan, in *The New*

Statesmen in 1978, referring to "that hideously unattractive group, the British generals of the First World War"; the same enlightened publication, in 1979, accused me of "fantastic philistinism" for suggesting "that generals who presided over the demolition of a whole British generation were something more respectable than idiots". A letter in *The Spectator* in 1980 said that "with the honourable exceptions of Plumer and Allenby, it is difficult to find one great war general who answers to the adjective 'intelligent'". The magazine *War Monthly* (now called *Military History*) in April 1982, in an article by a Mr. Peter Chatt, fiercely attacking Lord Haig, quoted an unnamed reference saying:

> "It is hard for a connoisseur of a bad generalship, surveying the grey wastes of World War I, to single out any one commander as especially awful. There were dozens of them both sides"

which, as an example of pompous, arrogant rubbish takes some beating! Not to be outdone however, in July of the same year *The Army Quarterly* carried an article by a Mr. Keith Hammond entitled "Haig – A Suitable Case for Treatment?", seriously suggesting that the man who led the British Army in its most majestic series of victories was literally mad.

Prejudice and mythology die hard! Naturally what they thrive on is generalization, the broad sweep of the brush, the catchy phrase. Fair comparisons, statistical evidence, careful inspection of individuals, none of these are favoured; they spoil the myth. So let us now subject some members of John Keegan's "hideously unattractive group" to closer examination.

Who does he mean? – well, I think it is safe to say that he means above all the Commanders-in-Chief and the Army Commanders on the Western Front; the latter are less familiar than the former, so let us consider them. We have already heard mention of two: Plumer and Allenby; let us look at them a little more closely. General (later Field-Marshal) Sir Herbert Plumer commanded the second Army from 6 May 1915 until the end of the war, with a brief intermission in Italy from November 1917 to March 1918 (as Commander-in-Chief). Like many British senior officers of the period, he had had the enlightening experience of commanding Colonials in South Africa – very educative! *The Spectator* called him, in 1904, "emphatically a soldier's soldier", and so he remained, although Haig, in 1917, also called Plumer "this most reliable Army Commander". His affection for the troops under him and his care for them were well attested. He was often called "Daddy" Plumer, and he certainly did look like a sort of ideal granddad, with pink cheeks and fluffy white moustache and a little pot belly. But appearances are deceptive, as the Germans discovered. Plumer was a first-class Army Commander, a first-class practioner of battle, like Montgomery later, a master of the set piece as his victories as Messines (June 1917) Menin Road and Polygon Wood (September) and Broodseinde

(4 October) show – the last called by the Germans "the black day". In a war described as a "staff officer's war", in which the staff at times became exceedingly unpopular, it is interesting to note that Plumer and his own Chief of Staff, Sir Charles Harington, insisted that the staff of the Second Army must always be the servant of the fighting troops – a fact that was readily apparent and much appreciated by all. I have never heard a bad word about Plumer; how he or Harington can be called "hideously unattractive" passes my understanding.

What about Field-Marshal Sir Edmund Allenby? He is an interesting case. His fame rests on his achievement in Palestine in 1917 and 1918, and his overthrow of the Turks in a dramatic, swift moving campaign. This seems to be in marked contrast with the "static" and always bloody Western Front, and Allenby has been acclaimed accordingly. It is a view that fails to note certain important facts. First, in his final attack he enjoyed a numerical superiority of about 2 to 1, and an even greater advantage in material. Secondly, in Palestine he was fighting a secondary enemy: the Turks. They were tough soldiers, hard to beat – but nothing like so hard as the Germans, and they were exhausted by nearly 8 continuous years of war. On the Western Front, against the Germans, Allenby had not greatly distinguished himself. His one big battle – Arras – was a grim, costly business in which the only outstanding success was the brilliant storming of the Vimy Ridge by General Byng's Canadians – but they belonged to general Horne's First Army. Thirdly, open warfare in 1918 had returned to the Western Front also it was no longer "static". The great contrast is thus only achieved by false comparison. Fourthly, Allenby himself had no doubt that the Western Front was the place to seek a decision, whatever the difficulties. We need to take all this into account in assessing Allenby; the mere fact that he moved fast is not enough. What it finally amounts to is that Allenby's striking successes were won on a secondary front. In this they resemble those of the British generals of World War II, of whom only one – Lord Gort, for about three weeks in May 1940 – ever held high command on the main front against the main enemy. Allenby, like O'Connor in the next war, shows that dazzling success on a secondary front is not necessarily proof of the highest quality on the main front.

I mentioned Byng: General (later Field-Marshal) Sir Julian Byng was another British Officer who became well acquainted with Colonials in South Africa, and this stood him in good stead when he went to command the Canadian corps in 1916. Byng is the only one of the Army Commanders whose appearance might justify the phrase "hideously unattractive", because in all photographs he seems to be glaring with a menacing scowl into the camera. I say "might justify" – but only if you judge merely by appearances. As Jeffrey Williams points out in his excellent biography, *Byng of Vimy*, which came out in 1983, the thing about Byng was that he hated anything smacking of pomp, ceremony or publicity – and ne hated being photographed – hence the scowl. Byng was probably the most informal of our top generals, and this, of course, suited the Canadians well. They loved him, and when he became Governor-General of Canada later, the CEF veterans proved it by the warmth of their welcome to him wherever he went. So scowl or no scowl, Byng was a lovely man. When Allenby went to Palestine, Byng took over the Third Army. He pioneered the techniques of predicted shooting and massed tank attack at Cambrai in 1917. In 1918 his Army "stood off" the great German March offensive, and in August became the second prong of Haig's own final offensive.

In 1917, at Vimy, Byng came under General Sir Henry Horne, Commander of the First Army. Horne was another who shunned publicity; he was a quiet, retiring, competent Gunner. In World War II, I think one might match him with Sir Miles Dempsey, another able but retiring officer; such men never find the limelight, but Heaven help the Army that doesn't have them. Unfortunately, their shyness means that we don't know half as much about them as we should, and unless people like Jeffrey Williams come along, we never shall. Others are more fortunate – the limelight comes to them.

That was the case with Sir Henry Rawlinson, who commanded the Fourth Army. Rawlinson got off to a bad start on the Somme on 1 July 1916, that terrible day which I sometimes think is the only day in World War I that people know. But the war changed all the time, and most of the men in it were changing all the time. Rawlinson, whose set-piece daylight attack on July 1 was a disaster, tried a dawn attack on 14 July – and captured the German front positions with very small loss. And then came the everlasting ding-dong of attrition – the hard fight the German Army always made of it in this phase of the war. But Rawlinson was learning all the time, and in 1918 he put his lessons to good use. Beginning once again on the Somme, on 8 August 1918, his Fourth Army became the first prong of the final offensive, in the course of which it engaged 67 German divisions (2 of them 5 times) and took over 75,000 prisoners. I think comment is superfluous.

Two more Army Commanders must be mentioned. Sir William Birdwood was the English officer who had the hard task of commanding the Australian Corps. No one, I think, claims military genius for Birdwood – but he had genius of another kind. He made himself liked by the tough, proud individualists of the First Australian Imperial Force – they even paid him the rare compliment of calling him "Mr. Birdwood". He seemed to know every man in the five divisions of the Army Corps – and they certainly knew him. When he heard that he was to be promoted to Command the Fifth Army, he told the Australian Minister of Defence "I am prepared to be relieved of the command of my army rather than be cut off from my old comrades." He was persuaded to take the promotion when it was pointed out to him that otherwise he would be blocking promotion for an Australian officer. Was that "hideously unattractive", I wonder?

Then there was Sir Charles Monro, who left the Western Front in 1916 to become Commander-in-Chief, India. There it fell to him to create the Indian army with which Allenby in Palestine and General Marshall in Mesopotamia won their later victories. In fact Monro in 1916–18 did what Auchinleck did for Mountbatten and Slim between 1942–45. Monro has been called the best Commander-in-Chief of British India, even including Lord Roberts – which definitely suggests a touch of class!

I could go on: there were corps commanders, like Lord Cavan or Sir Claude Jacob or Sir Ivor Maxse or the two first-rate officers from the Dominions, Sir Arthur Currie and Sir John Monash. There were all the divisional commanders – not all excellent by any means; this was a weak area in the British Army – but including many very able men, like Tudor of the 9th Division, another Gunner, Babington of the 23rd, regarded by the other ranks as "a decent old bird" because of his pleasant, informal manner, but who nevertheless made his division one of the smartest and most efficient in the Army. And there was Boyd of the 46th, who failed the entrance examination for Woolwich, joined the Army in the ranks, fought in South Africa in the Devonshire Regiment, took a commission, and in September 1918 his division smashed through the Hindenburg Line, taking 4,000 prisoners and 70 guns for the loss of less than a thousand in one of the finest feats of the war. And these are just a few.

I am not going to talk about the Commanders-in-Chief. Sir John French's latest biographer agrees that he was not up to the job, and that is the general verdict of history. What I think of Sir Douglas Haig should be well enough known from my book *Douglas Haig: The Educated Soldier*. I look on him as one of only three British generals who have encountered the main body of a main European enemy (the others being the Dukes of Marlborough and Wellington) and the results speak for themselves. But one name I must add to this list: Field-Marshal Sir William Robertson, the only man to go from private to Field-Marshal in the Army's entire history. And this was no matter of mere honorary rank conferred as a kindness: Robertson rose to the Army's highest and most demanding position at the height of its most demanding war. I find it difficult to express the quality of character that enabled an ex-gardener's boy to do that in an Army some 75 per cent of whose officers in 1914 were from Public Schools. I will be the first to agree that Sir William Robertson was not in any degree "cuddly" – his best friends would admit that he was always light on charm. But clearly there was a rare fibre in him; I think if we are going to call that fibre "hideously unattractive" we must stop talking about soldiers altogether.

This misleading generalization is, however, only part of a larger one which has been expressed by a leading academic, Professor Sir Llewellyn

Woodward, who didn't think much of what he saw at first hand of the Army in the First World War. He was discussing with an Oxford colleague in 1919 why British leadership had been so bad, and the colleague soon found the answer: "the army was 'run by pass men'". (A "Pass" degree, of course, was the minimum educational standard required at Oxford and Cambridge to allow pursuit of really serious activities, like rowing, riding, rugby, ragging the swots and so forth). So here we have an extension of the "hideously unattractive" image: "all 'pass men'" – elsewhere called by Professor Woodward "a custom-bound clique". But then the Professor spoils it all: he lumps in the Allied generals also, and adds: "Fortunately for the Allies the enemy generals were equally obtuse." And there we have it in a nut-shell: all the generals, all over the World, in that generation were "pass men"! All I can say is, "if you can believe that, you can believe anything".

Let us consider what this means: this designation includes Germany, where the Officer Corps was still dominated by the aristocracy (despite industrialization and a great expansion of both the population and the Army). For example 52 per cent of officers of the rank of Colonel and above in 1913 were aristocrats, and in 1909 four fifths of the entry to the General Staff (considered the apex of military professionalism) were aristocrats. Not that statistics are all that important, because whatever the social origin, the imprint was aristocratic; in other words the whole German Army was dominated by the aristocracy and there was no possibility of the rise of a William Robertson. But apparently, the French were all "pass men" too, though in the French Army to be an aristocrat was positively a disadvantage. General Joffre, for example, a staunch republican, was openly praised for his broad mindedness in giving commands to aristocrats. In Imperial Russia contrary to many suppositions, the officer ranks were not a class privilege – in fact about 40 per cent of regimental officers up to the rank of colonel were sons of peasants. In America, of course, there were no aristocrats – but senior command was very much the preserve of the products of West Point and Annapolis, both of high educational reputation. Yet, all these people – to say nothing of the Austro-Hungarians, the Italians, the Serbs, the Turks – were all "pass men", all at once! I would submit that this is simply not a reasonable historical proposition; in fact I would say that it is merely silly.

How then should we approach British generalship, British military leadership in World War I? It is perhaps best to begin by putting the question, "what is the function of a general?" "What should we expect of him?" I think a perfectly clear and complete answer has been provided by one whose professional skill has never been disputed, and who was also, by common consent, humane, concerned, compassionate and much loved – Field-Marshal Lord Slim. Speaking of our early defeats in Burma in 1942 and 1943, Slim said:

"Defeat is bitter. Bitter to the common soldier, but trebly bitter to his general. The soldier may comfort himself with the thought that, whatever the result, he has done his duty faithfully and steadfastly, but the commander has failed in his duty if he has not won victory – for that is his duty. He has no other comparable to it."[1]

And that, surely, is true; that is what entitles a general to his badges of rank, the respect that is paid to him, and the salary he receives: that his professional competence should give his country victory – or at the very least, stave off the worst consequence of defeat. In this fundamental requirement, it is simple historical fact that the British generals of the First World War – unattractive or not, "pass men" or not, "donkeys" or not, did not fail in their duty.

It was not a British delegation that crossed the lines with a white flag in November 1918. No German army of occupation was stationed on the Thames or the Humber or the Tyne. No British Government was forced to sign a treaty like the one that Germany forced on Russia at Brest-Litovsk, or on Romania at Bucharest. The British generals had done their duty; their army and their country were on the winning side, not the losing. That is the only proper, only sensible starting-point for an examination of their quality.

I say "starting-point", because one has to ask whether the method by which they did their duty and gained the victory nevertheless nullified it and made it worthless – indeed, this had been said very often. Is it true? The only possible way of answering that question is by comparing their performance with that of their contemporaries. If it appears that, at the same time, in similar circumstances, other generals, other leaders displayed better methods, then the criticism would hold that, though the British generals had performed what was required of them, they had done it the wrong way. And how does one judge the right or wrong way? Obviously, one judges in relation to cost – above all to human cost, to casualties.

There are few more emotive subjects than the casualties of the First World War certainly here in Britain – few subjects more confused or calculated to confuse. Casualties mean death, often in horrible and painful forms, dreadful to see, sickening to read about; or wounds, also horrible, some permanent – blindness, paralysis, loss of limbs – wounds sometimes so bad one cannot help thinking death would have been better. They mean psychological injury, sometimes also permanent, madness, intermittent breakdown, intellectual incapacity due to shock – and all these on a terrible scale, measured by hundreds of thousands of human beings, even millions. And there straight away we come to the only language by which these dreadful matters can be understood: statistics – the cold, unfeeling arithmetical symbols which stand for the crushed, blasted bodies, screams of pain, the grief of bereaved families, the waste of promise. But statistics are what we have to use, they are all we have, if we want to understand. We just have to make the effort of imagination to try to convert the long rows of numerals and the percentage back to the flesh and blood they once were. When we do that, we find that there is nothing unique about the British experience in the First World War. Indeed, in a grim passage of the world's history, it may even be said that the British got off lightly.

Not only that, but we find that the 1914–18 war itself was not the uniquely destructive event that it is sometimes supposed. We shall never know exactly how many people were killed as a direct cause of the war; a consensus of opinion holds to a figure of about 13 or $13\frac{1}{2}$ million (which is, of course, unimaginable; no one can imagine even one million of anything). Yet that is our yardstick – that figure of 13 with six noughts after it; it is a dreadful figure, but not unique. Thus, the Thirty Years War, at the beginning of the seventeenth century, is believed to have killed some 8 million people in Germany alone (and populations then were far smaller than in the twentieth century; it was reliably said that the effects of that war could still be seen in Germany right up to this century). And in the Second World War it has been reliably stated that the military dead of the Soviet Union alone amounted to about 13 million, i.e. about the same as the total for all belligerents in the First World War. This, at any rate, is something that statistics can do – they can establish proportions and relations. It is important, when we feel our emotions rightly swelling over the losses of life of 1914–18, to remember that in 1939–45 the world loss was probably about four times as many. Immediately this is said, I think we begin to travel towards a proper perspective for the British experience – and therefore a proper criterion for British generals. One thing quickly becomes apparent: there is no point in comparing British generals in the two wars – the British role was entirely different, which is why the loss of life was so different: about 350,000 in 1939–45 and about 750,000 in 1914–18. I shall return to this contrast later on; what concerns us now is the 750,000 (that is the United Kingdom figure, the empire figure is about 1 million).

Does this figure of 750,000 represent a peculiar fate of the British Army due to incompetent handling by its generals? That is really what this whole subject boils down to, I think; and it is here that the confusion really lies, a confusion which unfortunately, as I said, can only be dispelled by statistics. The casualty statistics of the First World War, looked at carefully, tell us a great deal about that sad episode in history, but virtually nothing about the quality of British leadership, of British generals. The statistics show that the British experience was entirely normal, that British losses in great battles were generally about the same as anyone else's. They show exactly what any unprejudiced person would expect: that the British generals had their bad days and their good days, were sometimes lucky, sometimes not.

We all know – shall we ever be allowed to forget? – that 1 July 1916 was a bad day, in fact, one of the very worst in the Army's whole history. Our casualties on that day were 57,470, of whom nearly 20,000 were dead, and the gains were very small – it was indeed a black day. But surely the thing to remember is that it was unique – there was no other day like it – it was entirely abnormal.

July 1 1916 was, of course, the first day of the Battle of the Somme; there were 141 more days to go – a grim, grinding business, during which the British Army made its acquaintance with the war of attrition which the French Army had been experiencing all that year. By the end of the Battle of the Somme the British losses were 415,000 which means that the average daily rate of loss was 2,950. That was the norm – it compares with 4,070 a day in the 39 days of the Battle of Arras in 1917; 2,121 a day in the 105 days if the Battle of Passchendaele; 3,645 a day in the "hundred days" of the victorious final offensive of 1918. These averages show how extraordinary that First of July in 1916 really was – a combination of mistakes at all levels and sheer bad luck. But every army had its bad times. The British had the worst single day. But what about the worst week? There was a week in June 1916 when the Austro-Hungarian Army had 280,000 casualties – in just one week. If we want to look at a bad fortnight, we should pay attention to the last fortnight in August 1914, (actually 16 days) when the French Army lost 211,000 officers and men. There is nothing like that in the British Army's annals – we lost less than 100,000 in the whole of 1914.

Every army had its awful times: the Germans admit to 1,400,000 casualties in the year 1916; their worst time was the 6 weeks in March and April 1918 when they lost nearly 350,000, with a loss rate of over 8,500 a day. For a really horrible year, we have to look at Russia in 1915, when she suffered something like 2 million casualties – which takes us back again to the unimaginable stratosphere of numbers. The point I am trying to make is that casualties are not at all revealing about British performance or British generals – they only show that British soldiers and British generals belong to the human race and not to some species of mythical supermen. The famous French Marshal Turenne once said: "Speak to me of a general who has made no mistakes in war, and you speak of one who has seldom made war."

To me, the wonder is not that the British generals of the First World War made mistakes – that was inevitable in all armies – but that they did as well as they did.

We must remember that in 1914 Sir John French had never commanded anything larger than a cavalry division in war (about 6,000 men); his successor, Sir Douglas Haig, at that time had never commanded anything larger than a "column" (about 3,000 men) in war – yet when Haig took over from French in 1915 he inherited an army of over 1 million which rose to over 2 million (more than any population unit in the United Kingdom, except Greater London). Even in peacetime there were only three officers in the whole army who had held command of an Army Corps: Sir John French, Sir Horace Smith-Dorrien and Sir Douglas Haig. In any case, only one formed Army corps existed, by comparison with twenty French and thirty-five German. There was quite evidently a most serious lack of experience of handling large bodies of men (which is quite different from sand-table exercises, TEWTS or war games) which could only be compensated by intelligence, character, and finally by experience in the field. This is, in fact, the crux of the whole story. The British Army, from Commander-in-Chief to drummer-boy, had to be formed and trained *in the field*, in the face of a powerful, skilful, well-equipped and determined enemy – it is asking a lot.

The small size of the pre-1914 British Army, in fact, seriously affected the entire British war effort. As we have seen, it robbed British generals of their necessary training (though to some extent this could be remedied in India); the small size also robbed the New Armies and Territorials of the regimental officers and NCOs they needed for *their* training: it robbed the whole Army of munitions because the factories to supply a large army did not exist; and above all it robbed Britain of an independent strategy – which is why a great deal of criticism of British Generals is quite pointless.

This was a coalition war, and the senior partner of the coalition in the West was France; the main front of the war was where the main body of the main enemy was – in France. Until July 1916 the main body of the main enemy on the main front was engaged by the French, and the casualty figures reflect this: by December 1915, French casualties amounted to just under 2 million; British casualties (including Gallipoli and other sideshows) were by then just over half a million. The lengths of front held also reflect the weight of the effort: at the end of 1914 the BEF held 24 miles out of about 450; at the end of 1915 about 40 miles. I think these figures make it quite obvious who was going to be in control of strategy – clearly the French High Command (just as naval affairs were under the control of the British Admiralty, for the same reason).

Unfortunately, there were many who never understood the constraint that this imbalance placed upon the British commanders. In January 1915, for example, we find Lloyd George plaintively asking his friend Churchill: "Are we really bound to hand over the ordering of our troops to France as if we were her vassal?"[2] The proper answer, of course, should have been: "Yes – until we can match her effort." And this, whether they liked it or not, very quickly became apparent at the "sharp end" – to the generals concerned. So we find Haig, very shortly after taking over the Command-in-Chief, telling the Head of the French Mission at GHQ to say to General Joffre, the French Commander-in-Chief:

> "I am not under General Joffre's orders, but that would make no difference, as my intention is to carry out General Joffre's wishes on strategical matters as if they were orders."[3]

In view of the disparity of effort, this was the only possible policy, but to this day there are many who cannot grasp it. And as long as there was reasonable trust and cordiality on both sides, as there was between Haig and Joffre and later Haig and Foch, the policy worked out well enough. It broke down in 1917, when Nivelle replaced Joffre, and an atmosphere of trickery – much encouraged by Lloyd George – replaced the trust. It was restored when Pétain took over, but in 1918, when Pétain's nerve broke, Haig recognized that there would have to be a Supreme Commander of the Allies – but he also recognized that this would still have to be a Frenchman.

What makes this perception so remarkable is that by then the whole emphasis of the Western Front had changed. For what had happened in July 1916 was simply this: after twenty-three months of war, for the first time in its history, the British Army assumed the burden of fighting the main body of the main enemy in a European war. The Duke of Marlborough and the Duke of Wellington had held a supreme command of the coalition armies with which they fought, but the British component in their armies was always pretty small. Haig did not hold supreme command, but his army engaged the enemy's main body for the rest of the war, with only two brief intermissions. In the Battle of the Somme in 1916, the BEF engaged 95 1/2 identified German divisions out of 125 on the Western Front; in the Battles of Arras and Ypres in 1917, it engaged 131 German divisions out of 137 in the West, and in 1918, when the Germans attacked the British front, they threw 109 divisions against Haig's 60. Later when Haig launched his final offensive in August, he had 59 divisions, which met and defeated 99 German Divisions, some of whom were encountered twice, some three times, some even four or five. That year, with its great defensive victories in March and April, and the triumphant final offensive of August to November which brought about the Armistice, was in my opinion the "finest hour" beyond any comparison of the British Army. That was its achievement, and I cannot see how its commanders can be separated from it.

Of course, the cost was high – during that period from July 1916 to November 1918, the British Army in France had over 2 million casualties (just about the same number as the French in 1914 and 1915, when they were engaging the enemy's main body). In the next war, it was the turn of the Russians to do the same, between 1941–45, and, as I have said, it cost the Soviet Army about 13 million in dead alone. In both wars, the German Army proved to be very hard to beat. In World War II, the British did not see very much of it, which sufficiently accounts for their much lower casualties; but in World War I, for the only time in their history, they fought the German main body and beat it, and as I have said elsewhere, if that had not cost us appalling casualties as it had the French and would the Russians, it would have been a miracle requiring a supernatural explanation.

The disciplines of coalition war pressed hard on the British Army between 1914–18. They compelled it into actions for which it was not ready and not equipped in 1915. They forced it into the leading role in 1916, before it was really fit for that. And in 1917 they forced it into strategies which the British Command did not believe in, and which cost the Army dear. All this came as an unwelcome surprise, but, in truth, even that pales into insignificance beside the real burden of novelty which that unfortunate generation of generals had to bear. It is impossible in my opinion, to compare it usefully with any other, because no other generation faced such a catalogue of innovation as:

the impact of the *internal combustion engine*, introducing above all, *Air power*, and on land *mechanized transport, armoured cars, tanks*; the war thus became the *first mechanics' war*, requiring entirely new skills, new apparatus and equipment, and creating new strains (e.g. on line of communication); there was a revolution in *communication systems* creating vast complex telephone networks with deep buried cables, and introducing *wireless telegraphy* and *radio telephony*; this was the first war of *massed modern artillery*, the first to use *predicted shooting*, and the first to develop modern *fire control techniques*; it was the first war of *automatic weapons*, especially *machine guns* and the first to devise *counter machine gun tactics* (the British Army captured 29,000 of them in battle in 1918); is was the first war of *poison gas* (there were no fewer than 63 kinds in use by 1918); it was the first war of petroleum *flame-projectors* – what would later be known as napalm; and so on and so on.

For the British generals in particular this was also the first war of masses, with all that that means in the way of transportation, feeding, housing, medical services and welfare. In fact, no generation has ever faced such a simultaneous technological onslaught, such a surge of innovation and new techniques. Except in the obviously highly significant fields of nuclear physics, electronics and aircraft design, the Second World War cannot compare. Indeed much of World War II was spent relearning the lessons of World War I.

Technology between 1914 and 1918 made gigantic strides, but in two vital respects it just fell short of what was needed; a second generation would be required for fruition. These shortfalls were: first, mobility – conferred on armies from time immemorial by the horse (and the French, German and Russian armies were still largely horse-drawn in 1939–45). But the horse was no longer viable on a twentieth century battlefield, and horsepower really meant tanks, which between 1914–18 were always too few and feeble. This meant that generals had to make war in effect without a mobile arm, without an arm of exploitation – a most serious lack. The second shortfall was control: despite the immense progress in communication conferred by telephone and wireless, control in battle virtually lapsed. This was in fact the only war ever fought without voice control. Even platoon commanders had difficulty in giving orders, and generals were powerless just when they were wanted most. What they needed was the "walkie-talkie" – but what they had was a telephone line, probably broken in three places. Taking all these things into account, and taking into account also the undoubted conservative and traditionalist upbringing of most generals – certainly most British generals – it is to my mind staggering to observe how well they coped with it all. Behind the bristling moustaches and the granite jaws there was obviously a surprisingly high degree of broad-minded flexibility, an unexpected adaptability to change, a readiness to accept and use novelties which is absolutely contrary to the normally accepted image. It is perfectly clear that no "donkeys" could have absorbed this deluge of blinding science and directed it towards that succession of proficient victories which ended the war in 1918.

It was in that year that the real qualities of the British Army – which was, by then, as Lord Esher said, "the people in uniform" – were displayed from top to bottom. In that last "hundred days", Haig's armies captured 188,700 prisoners and 2,840 guns; all the other Allies, French, Americans and Belgians together, captured 196,700 prisoners and 3,775 guns. These, also, are statistics that cannot be argued with; they are statistics of absolute victory, the proof that the British military leadership was performing its highest duty.

Let me end on a somewhat different and, I think you will agree, somewhat surprising note. I will offer a view of British military leadership presented by a pretty junior officer, Captain Stair Gillon of the King's Own Scottish Borderers in the 29th Division, who wrote the history of the division in 1925;

> "The editor", he says, modestly referring to himself, "has never discovered that there exists any other point of view than that of the Higher Command. Broadly speaking, commanders and commanded have seen eye to eye."[4]

Notes

1. Field-Marshal Lord Slim, *Defeat into Victory*, p. 121, Cassell, 1956.
2. Martin Gilbert, *Winston S. Churchill*, vol. III Companion Part I, p. 472, Heinemann, 1972.
3. John Terraine, *Douglas Haig: The Educated Soldier*, p. 182, Hutchinson, 1963.
4. Captain Stair Gillon, *The Story of the 29th Division*, pp. xi–xii, Nelson, 1925.

5

The Tactical and Strategic Application of Air Power on the Western Front

MALCOLM SMITH

Any discussion of air power in the Great War, or any other war, involves issues of great theoretical and technical complexity. The Great War is particularly problematic in this respect because air power was so new. A quite basic issue in the British experience, however, was whether the future of air power lay in a development of the tactical role of aircraft, in close co-operation with and as an adjunct to land warfare, or whether it should develop an alternative strategy of its own. Between 1914 and 1918, the implication of the fact that modern war was fought not simply between armies and navies but between nations-in-arms was being thought through. Industrial production and the will to ward off the enemy nation proved to be the real basis of attritional potential. Since land and sea warfare had bogged down in stalemate, an argument emerged that air power might offer an alternative strategy to that of Field-Marshal Haig on the Western Front; if apparently vulnerable targets like the war economy and civilian morale could be attacked, the war would be won just as effectively as if the Army and Navy had been defeated. The argument had great appeal, and it still has to historians. Neville Jones, for example, has argued that the overriding influence of the Army, the constant and massive demands for tactical air power thrown up by the Western Front, prevented those with the clear foresight to see a larger and more independent role for air power from seizing the initiative. Unlike their successors 25 years later, Jones argued, the airmen of the Great War understood very well the limitations of the weaponry that they had available, and would therefore not have fallen into the trap of overstatement and underachievement that affected the Second World War offensive.[1]

The purpose of the present paper is not to discuss whether a Strategic Air Offensive would have been a success in the Great War, as such. To argue either way on this question would require a great deal more information than it seems to me that we have on the state of the German economy and transport system. Even if we had such information, there would still be a maze of problems – working back from recent discussion of

Harris' offensive, at least, relating to such matters as target selection, aircrew professionalism and, perhaps above all, the state of strategic air theory, particularly the role of counter-force operations (i.e. what to do about the German Air Force, which would certainly not – indeed did not – sit idly by while the RFC or the IAF attacked its targets). Rather than get involved in discussing yet another of the great "might have beens" of history, I would prefer to concentrate instead on the logic of the demand for a strategic air offensive as it evolved at that time, contrasting it with the arguments for tactical air power. I wish to examine how well practice mixed with theory, concentrating not simply on the question of military effectiveness but also on the military politics of the question, that complex of rivalries and feuds, relating to wide strategic issues, which so plagued the War as a whole and, in my opinion, played what in the last resort proved to be a quite crucial role in the development of the air war. I will be centring my discussion on four areas; first, the relationship between the development of the theory of air power and the technical development of the material to put it into effect; second, the relationship between the Military Wing and the Royal Naval Air Service in the structure of the Royal Flying Corps; third, the relationship between the Western Front and Home Defence in the strategic disposition of British air power; fourth, the significance for this question of the notorious "frocks vs. coats" dispute.

Air power developed extraordinarily rapidly during the Great War. When it started, flying was still very much in its infancy. It began to prove its worth, however, in the very first months of the war. It may well have been that the aircraft reconnaissance that spotted von Kluck's change of direction, as the Germans attempted to execute Schlieffen's Great Wheel, had a major bearing on the initial campaign; the air enthusiasts certainly believed so, at least. Within a year, the struggle for air superiority had proved to be a major element in the tactics of trench warfare, and the "Fokker scourge" had become a major element of debate both in military and in amateur circles. German Zeppelin raids brought the war to the home front, and in 1917 London endured its first blitz from aircraft. In 1918, the RAF came into existence and the Independent Air Force was pressured to concentrate on strategic bombing. If the war had continued into 1919, the RAF would have launched a heavy air attack deep into the heart of Germany, in an attempt to knock out the industrial supply and the will to war of the enemy country. By 1918, air power had tried everything it was ever to try, except the dropping of airborne troops. On the other hand, the real technical potential of aircraft still lay in the future, and if aircraft technology was developing rapidly, it was still outstripped by air theory. The Wright Brothers had first flown in 1903, and the years of development of the aircraft before 1914 had not made it clear that a great new weapons system, which would develop into a separate medium of war, was in the making. Much of pre-war experimentation was hare-brained and, quite frankly, simply dangerous. John Dunne, for example, before the invention of the elevator, used to gain height using the nerve-tingling expedient of warping his wings, literally bending the delicate frame and fabric, in the style but not with the grace of the great soaring birds.[2] Anecdotes designed to show that the military establishment was stupidly slow in realizing the potential of aircraft – for example, the officer who said that aircraft would never be any use to the Army because they flew too fast for anything to be seen – normally end up instead showing the extraordinary prescience of the pioneers. Certainly, when Bleriot flew the Channel in 1909, the military potential of aircraft should have been transformed. With that paranoid fear of anything which threatened to bridge the Channel, the British press responded as they had to the introduction of steam power in maritime warfare, but by 1911 the British still had only 10 serviceable military aircraft, compared with the French 220.[3] Training was clearly not taken all that seriously. Trenchard, for example, gave Tommy Sopwith seventy-five pounds to teach him to fly. Sopwith took him into the air for sixty-five minutes and pronounced him fit as a pilot. Three years later, the 40-year-old-major had become a 43-year-old major-general in command of the entire RFC in France. The formation of the RFC in 1912 at least provided the organizational stimulus to develop air power rapidly, quite apart from the unprecedented opportunities for promotion it provided.

Air theory had not moved a great deal forward since the time in the early nineteenth century when one man had worried about the possibility of man conquering the air, that "honour and virtue would be in continual danger if it were permitted to descend at all hours of the night into gardens and close to windows".[4] If this bizarre form of voyeurism had been the only problem mankind would suffer as a result of learning how to fly, then the world might have been a safer place. A small handful of writers wrote in the military journals, but since they had so little experience on which to build, none of them had all that much of interest to say.[5] It is on the level of the prophetic, rather than as strategic theory, that pre-1914 writing is of any interest. The ideas had been mooted that aircraft could not only contribute to traditional land and sea operations, they could also strike directly at the enemy homeland. To do so, they would require a separate administrative organization and their own specific share of the national resources. At the level of popular culture, however, in newspapers and in popular novels, air power had already merged with the fantastic, where it was to stay until air power finally acquired nuclear potential and made the fantastic real. H.G. Wells *The War in the Air*, published in 1908, accurately forecast the enormous amount of damage that an air fleet would be able to perform at some future date – in this case a German Zeppelin attack on the United States – damage made all the more grotesque by the inability of aircraft to hold air space.[6] This problem of the inability of aircraft to achieve full "command of the air" was indeed to be one of the central problems in the application of air power, making it impossible that it would ever become a self-sufficient medium of war. It was a problem that early air theorists soon latched upon, and it affected early air weaponry. The Military Wing of the RFC had not yet even worked out what it would require of its material in terms of weaponry, let alone whether it would be capable at some future date, of massive destruction. Aircraft design in the Military Wing was the monopoly of the Royal Aircraft Factory at Farnborough, which tended to concentrate on producing scientifically advanced aircraft which could fly both level and straight – no mean achievement in those days – and little attention had been given as yet to the question of armament.[7] The point really was that the Military Wing was not all that interested in provoking air fighting, if it could be avoided. All that was required was reconnaissance and spotting. This emerged from, and was reinforced by the view that a struggle for air superiority would be a wasteful and inefficient use of aircraft.

Among the most prominent of the early writers on air power in Britain was Frederick Sykes. At the time he delivered his first important lectures on air power, in 1913 and 1914, Sykes was Commandant of the Military Wing of the RFC at Central Flying School at Upavon; later he was Chief of Staff to Sir David Henderson when Henderson commanded the RFC in France; later still he was Chief of the Air Staff in the RAF, and chief instigator of the IAF. In these roles he played a major part in the definition of British air theory. Sykes believed that the difficulty in finding aircraft in the vast cubic air space available to them would mean that counter-force operations were unlikely to be worthwhile, unless both sides actually decided to make a fight of it. Sykes, however, saw this problem as a virtue, arguing that since they did not have to engage in a struggle for supremacy in the air, aircraft could get on with their role and ignore the enemy Air Force.[8] This was later to develop into the view that air power involved a complete break with the classical rules of warfare, that there was no need to defeat the enemy air force in being. Sir John French, belying the myth that he was not interested in military aviation, accepted Sykes' point but pointed out that aircraft should still fight when and if they did meet, because the result of that fight could well save the Army's eyes and blind the enemy.[9] Sir George Aston, writing in *Sea, Land and Air Strategy* in 1914, also accepted that, with the speed and range available to them, aircraft could indeed choose whether or not to get involved in a fight with other aircraft. Nevertheless, if aircraft began to have a substantial effect on the enemy, it was inevitable that the enemy would have to provoke a struggle for air superiority. It followed that the air strategist would have to decide on offensive and defensive priorities just like the traditional land or sea strategist.[10]

The significance of this apparently minor difference of opinion became clear once the war began, and became a critical point in the application of

British air power. Early on, the RFC found that its stable and airworthy machines – the BE series produced by Farnborough – were at the mercy of the increasingly specialized fighter aircraft that the Germans were putting into the air. Unwilling to commit itself to a policy of counter-force initially, and with the concomitant problem that the equipment policy that followed from the theory made it difficult to do so anyway, the RFC found itself in a constant technological race with the Germans. The RFC had to respond, both theoretically and technically. Practice indeed changed substantially when Trenchard took over the RFC in France and put full weight behind the offensive policy which had developed in response to German action, with standing patrols constantly threatening the German air force in being. The standing patrol policy was enormously expensive in men and material, but Trenchard found that there was no alternative to such a policy if the RFC were to perform its role of providing air defence for the Army, undertaking reconnaissance and spotting duties, and acting as a mobile artillery. Trenchard was quite clear that a struggle for air superiority was a primary intermediate objective for an Air Force; as he later put it, the conflict had to be initiated "by a struggle for air superiority, the achievement of which is of vital importance, in order that the full power of the nation may be wielded uninterruptedly through the air".[11] This struggle for air superiority could not be won in a one-off "big battle" moreover, but had to be constantly fought for as the enemy replaced men and material; up to 50 per cent of the force would have to be permanently engaged in maintaining air superiority by direct attack on the enemy air force. Trenchard was learning that attacks on the enemy targets would undoubtedly force the enemy to divert more resources to defence. Significant targets were, by definition, predictable and defenders would mass their fighters to defend them. To attack these targets with the weight and continuity necessary for success was, inevitably, to provoke a battle with the enemy armed forces in being; in no sense did the advent of air power mean a revolution in that basic rule of warfare.

This practical point had a major bearing on the whole argument for the development of an independent air offensive. All the leading airmen and air theorists were agreed that command of the air could not be achieved, that it was quite impossible to ensure that complete physical occupation of air space that was the only way to ensure that the enemy did not make good his losses. For Trenchard, this meant continued air fighting to maintain air superiority, but Sykes chose to subvert this basic problem and make it a positive attribute of air power. By 1918, Sykes was arguing that by deliberately avoiding the enemy air force, aircraft could overleap the military deadlock and destroy the total war effort of the German Empire behind the Western Front. In his *Review of the Air Situation* of June, 1918, Sykes laid down the operational concepts which he believed should guide the Independent Air Force; it would be a form of what he called "strategic interception". The Army would hold down the enemy forces in the field while air power, as a heavy and extra-long-range artillery, would destroy his lines of communication, bases of supply, and threaten the morale of the German people.[12] It should be noted here that not even Sykes was arguing for a wholly independent air strategy, rather for a strategic co-operation of two media of war, in which the long-range bomber force would create the opportunity for a decisive breakthrough on the ground; this is qualitatively different from the argument that, say, Harris was to deploy during the Second World War. In this sense, Neville Jones was right to argue that the argument for independent air action was much more realistically put in the Great War than it was to be in the Second, but the dent in the logic of the argument lay in how this could be achieved. Trenchard, as Commander of the IAF charged with putting through this strategy, found that well over a third of his force had to be devoted to counter-force operations, for example bombing enemy aerodromes, to prevent interference with his attack. Sykes complained that this was an unnecessary diversion of re-sources, but Sykes had limited experience of field command in comparison with Trenchard.[13] With the help of Sir William Weir as Director of Aircraft Production, a man who broadly agreed with Sykes' style of argument, specialized bombers were being produced by the latter stages of the war.[14] But to achieve the scale of damage that Sykes needed, bearing in mind the practical difficulties Trenchard faced and the limited bomb-carry of the Handley Page bombers, would have required a massive diversion of national resources. The Air Board had hoped that there would be 2,000 bombers available, each carrying approximately 1,000 lbs. In fact, Tren-chard rarely had more than 100 serviceable aircraft available at any one time during his command of the IAF.[15] As a result, the IAF only dropped 543 tons of bombs, and 220 of these were on enemy aerodromes. In other words, the theory had not developed in time, and the material had certainly not developed in time to make a strategic air offensive a viable proposition before the same end – destruction of German total war potential – had already been achieved indirectly by 4 years of trench warfare. Success would have depended, anyway, on developing another attritional cam-paign, a counter-force conflict in the air. Independent air power was an idea spawned by, and as a result of, the frustration resulting from the trench deadlock, rather than a fully fledged alternative strategy. It was an idea for the future rather than something that should obviously have been done at the time, and it had significant theoretical and practical flaws.

It could of course be argued that, if a fundamental commitment to expand strategic bombing had been made earlier, then the technical and produc-tion inadequacies would have been overcome in time for air power to have a real strategic effect. A similar argument could be raised about air power in the 1930s and 1940s; the counter-argument is the same, that an earlier commitment to provide the material would only have exposed the theoretical inadequacies earlier. But why were there such problems in providing an adequate supply of air material? Partly, no doubt, the reason is that Trenchard and the Western Front were using up aircraft and men at an extraordinary rate, but there was also a very wasteful system of dual control for most of the war. The RFC had been formed in 1912 to create a co-ordinating authority for naval and military aviation. There was no clear or homogenous war aim involved here, beyond a recognition of the importance of aviation for both services. It was reckoned that Army and naval requirements would be quite different and the two wings were therefore administered separately in effect. From the very beginning, the Admiralty adopted a highly parochial view of air power; in 1914, they virtually declared UDI by setting up the RNAS, even duplicating the flight training establishment. Certainly, there was some rationale for the Admiralty's attitude, in that naval needs were indeed quite different in the air. Even before the war, they had pioneered methods of deck take-off, and the long-range at which sea warfare was so often fought made it more likely that they would consider earlier than did the Military Wing the possibilities of penetration raids aimed at enemy naval shore establishments, port installations and even production facilities. Nevertheless, it was the close tactical support of the fleet that most in the Admiralty believed to be the chief import of naval air power.

The RNAS had enjoyed the vigorous support of Winston Churchill as First Lord of the Admiralty; engines and airframes more powerful than anything yet conceived at the Royal Aircraft Factory at Farnborough were ordered from civilian firms. The RNAS conducted long-range operations intermittently from the early stages of the war, bombing airship sheds and industrial targets in Alsace and in the Rhineland, for instance. But the activities of the RNAS No. 3 Wing soon came under intense scrutiny both from an RFC anxious to exert maximum pressure on the Germans in the air over the Western Front, and from an Admiralty equally anxious to know what these raids had to do with the naval war. It is too simplistic to argue that the Admiralty were being small-minded in this. Whatever the pros and cons of the argument for a unified air service with a separate war aim, such a service did not exist, and it is unreasonable to expect the Admiralty to have been self-abnegating enough to allow the RNAS to go its own way at a time when the function of air power within the Navy was, as yet, clearly only ancillary to the function of the battle fleet. But it was to save their own tactical air power, rather than to nip strategic air power in the bud, that the Admiralty jealously guarded what air resources they had, and repeatedly thwarted attempts to centralize aircraft procurement.[16]

The Admiralty was vying both with the airmen and the Army for the largest share of limited air resources. But even the most moderate airmen were arguing that the peculiar technological and training conditions in the air meant that it was essential to have a unified training and aircraft procurement establishment; specialist training and specialist aircraft could follow this minimum requirement. In this view, the arguments for unity were much stronger than those for continued separation. The Army, on the other hand, was really only interested in getting its hands on naval aircraft for use on the Western Front. These three points of view were clearly quite incompatible. The Joint War Air Committee was set up in 1916, under the Chairmanship of Lord Derby. This organization collapsed in a matter of weeks, however, Derby arguing that the problem of co-ordination could only be solved by the creation of an executive body. Derby also admitted that it was difficult to see how such a large administrative change could be accomplished in the middle of such a large-scale war. Curzon's Air Board was formed in May 1916, but lasted only seven months, during which time the differences of opinion between Curzon and the Admiralty became a matter of open comment in the press and in Parliament. Executive powers were given to the Air Board when the accession of Lloyd George to the premiership began to sweep away the previous "laissez-faire" style of war administration. Responsibility for the design and construction of aircraft passed from the services to the Air Board, which began a close liaison with the Ministry of Munitions; Sir William Weir, Director of Aircraft Production at Munitions, in fact did most of his work at the offices of the Air Board in the Hotel Cecil. There was, however, still no co-ordination of training or staff work between the two services, which continued to fight virtually separate wars.[17]

The Admiralty required that the RNAS should become more "naval" rather than more "aerial", and the leading light in naval aviation, Murray Sueter, found himself constantly supervised in his efforts to expand the role of the service. The appointment of Admiral Vaughan-Lee to supersede Sueter as Director of the Air Service was designed, in Geoffrey Till's words, "to integrate the Air Service within the Navy and to keep it in order".[18] Sueter's open dissent from the Admiralty view that there should be no unified air service secured him a posting to the Mediterranean, out of the Admiralty's way. When Jellicoe, one of the first naval officers to learn to fly, became 1st Sea Lord, the fortunes of the RNAS began to improve, and the service found a strong ally in Beatty. Reform of the RNAS did not save it from incorporation into the RAF, however, and Beatty's attitude towards the new service soon became hostile, not because he was opposed to a separate air service as such, but because he felt that the centralization of air resources around the notion of an independent air offensive denied the legitimate air needs of the Navy. The basic organizational problem, one which plagued air power from its inception in this and in other countries, was that independent air operations needed massive and centralized resources, which meant an independent air organization; but such an organization was extremely likely to concentrate on independent air operations at the expense of the tactical requirements of the other services, setting up frictions which were only to harden into outright hostility to the strategic aims of the rival organization. The theoretical argument for independent air action to break the strategic deadlock had latched on to the originally separate argument for co-ordinating training and supply in the name of tactical efficiency. The Admiralty did not believe that the tactical needs of the Army and the Navy were the same, and therefore argued against the co-ordination of supply. They could guess also that if a new organization was set up to co-ordinate aircraft procurement, it would very soon start to concentrate on independent air power, and the Navy would lose its tactical air support. This is precisely what happened, leading to internecine conflict between the Admiralty and Air Ministry until the Navy won back the Fleet Air Arm in 1936.

One of the reasons why Beatty may have been, initially at least, apparently willing to see the RNAS absorbed into a new organization, was the increasingly heavy responsibility for the air defence of Great Britain with which the Admiralty had been landed. Largely because the RFC was so hard-pressed in France, responsibility for the air defence of the home country often fell on the RNAS, though the RFC still officially retained control. It was not an enviable task for either of the air services, the Zeppelins proving so hard to catch, and even more difficult to shoot down if caught. It was also a real hot potato from the political point of view, since the press and public opinion reacted strongly to the apparent failure of the air service to protect the British population from its first real taste of total war. Sir David Henderson was forced to adopt the enormously wasteful policy of putting up standing air patrols along the routes of the Zeppelins, in order to try to allay public fears. But the Zeppelins could outclimb the BE2cs – it took British aircraft forty-five minutes to get up anywhere near them in the first place – and they could empty an entire magazine into the gas envelope with no visible effect. Even more problematic were the raids by heavier-than-air craft that began in May 1917, which was to introduce a third element into the rationale for superseding the tactical phase in the development of air power, namely the demand for reprisals. The first two raids on London were to be the most worrying, with 832 casualties among the civilian population, and some clear signs of panic that could be interpreted as a crisis of morale after a long and arduous war effort.[19] Even the Prime Minister himself was not immune from the consternation, though he issued libel writs against anyone who dared to print the rumours that he had packed and prepared to leave London.

Trenchard was recalled from France for consultations. His advice to the War cabinet was that the most effective antidote to the Gotha raids was the occupation of Belgium, which would rob them of their landing fields, together with immediate raids on the airfields behind the Western Front. Reprisals in kind Trenchard accepted as a possibility, but pointed out that they were likely to lead to an escalation of bombing on London.[20]

Trenchard believed, with the backing of Haig, that the only way of preventing the German attacks on London was to use the bulk of the RFC in France, forcing the Germans on to the defensive both in the air and on the ground. The Gotha offensive was having the effect of drawing a disproportionate element of RFC strength away from what Haig and Trenchard considered to be the decisive theatre of the war, the Western Front, for very little return in terms of shooting down enemy aircraft. In the 36 raids by aeroplanes from the beginning of 1917 until the end of the war, the Germans launched 397 sorties but lost only 27 aircraft. The number of hostile aircraft actually making landfall in any one raid never exceeded 33 and rarely exceeded 20, yet for this minimal outlay the Germans succeeded in tying down over 20,000 officers and men and nearly 300 British fighters during the crucial stages of the war on the Western Front.[21] The demand for reprisals, moreover, was intense, so much so that the kind of ideas that Sykes was putting forward, ideas which I have suggested were not that well thought through, were allowed to hold the ring. Trenchard complained that to operate the new IAF as a reprisal weapon, and independently of the winning campaign on land that Haig was able to develop after the failure of the German Spring Offensive series of 1918, was a serious misapplication of air power. In this argument he was unquestionably right; there was no way of stopping the German aircraft offensive against London, in the days before radar and the revolutionary fighter designs of the 1930s, short of a general advance of the Army on the Western Front. This would rob the Gothas of their bases, just as the advance of the Army in the Second World War was the only way of stopping the V1s and V2s. To use air power to any other end but backing the Army at that stage of the war was misguided.

What I have tried to argue in what I have said so far is that there was rather more to the development of air power in the Great War than a simple confrontation between proponents of tactical and proponents of strategic air power. Indeed Trenchard, who was to emerge from the war as the major architect of British air power, was to deny that the distinction between tactical and strategic air power was even a real or helpful one. I have tried to argue elsewhere that Trenchard was by no means the immoderate prophet of independent air power that RAF mythology would have us believe. His view was that the proper application of air power was in strict co-ordination with land and sea power, rather than in an independent war-winning strategy. The function of Trenchard's ideal Air Force was to prepare the way for a successful land offensive, in conjunction with the effort applied by sea power in blockade. In this task, it should be used either "strategically" or "tactically" as the circumstances demanded, though Trenchard believed that it was misleading to use these terms as distinctions given the role that he envisaged for air power.[22] Trenchard's disciple, John Slessor, put the Trenchardian case most succinctly when he wrote, in *Air Power and Armies*; "the men on the ground impose upon the enemy a situation in which an intensive flow of materials is vital, while the men in the air, by blocking that flow, create the opportunity for their comrades on the ground to progress to the point at which their action is decisive".[23] Superficially, this seems to be remarkably close to Sykes' thinking, but the differences between the two men were by no means trivial. The major differences consisted in the definition of the word "independent", in judging just where and when air power should be applied to the best overall advantage, and on the significance of counter-force operations. The final months of the war, the months of the short IAF campaign, were the nub. Differing judgements of that campaign, short though it was, became the basic talking points in the RAF during the 1920s. About the straightforwardly tactical work of the RFC and RNAS, no one seems to have bothered very much.

This in itself is revealing about the way the IAF campaign took thinking about air power in Britain on to a different plane. It was the point, I suggest, at which perspective and experience were downgraded in favour not of a new bright horizon but rather of a blinkered and dogmatic faith in the power of aircraft. The formation of the Air Ministry consolidated this trend organizationally by making the RAF co-equal (which was fair enough) but also administratively separate (strategically wrong) from the other services. Trenchard envisaged Army, Navy and Air Force working in close co-operation on what might be called the "Grand Tactical" level to produce a co-ordinated strategy. He was therefore very worried, and rightly so, about the continuing pressure to develop air power as a separate medium of war with its own administrative organization. The argument for a new ministry to control air affairs was an elision of the three separate trends in the development of air power in the Great War which I have outlined. First, there was the argument which Sykes had been developing over the years of trench warfare to use the increasing technological possibilities that aircraft seemed to imply, to leap over the problem of the trench deadlock and attack those vulnerable centres of supply behind the front line, without which the German field Army could not operate. Second, there was the clearly wasteful duplication of training and supply involved in having separate air wings for the Navy and Army, though this was complicated by the justifiable Admiralty argument that the air needs of the Navy were very different from those of the Army, and that separate training and supply organizations needed to be maintained. This Admiralty argument had been largely, though not wholly discounted in the decision to give control of aircraft design and supply to the Air Board. In turn, the large and rapid increase in aircraft production expected to follow the new arrangements reinforced the hopes of those who were arguing for a more independent use of aircraft in war. The fact that the really major increase in aircraft production which was expected did not really take place, did not discourage the air prophets. Third, there was the strong political pressure which followed in the wake of the first Gotha raids on London, pressure which took the form of a demand for reprisals centred round a long-range air offensive against Germany, which was not necessarily related to the immediate aerial needs of the battle raging on the Western Front.

These three separate trends converged in the famous Smuts Report of 17 August, 1917, a document with revolutionary implications which Smuts framed with the help and advice of Sir David Henderson and, almost certainly, with some real help from Sykes as well. The evidence for Sykes' influence is rather circumstantial – Sykes' not exactly self-demeaning autobiography – but there is enough of Sykes' ideas in the main flow of the Report to suggest that his may have been a decisive influence. This is especially true of the most famous section of the Report, which proclaimed that the time for the subjugation of the air service to the tactical needs of the Army and the Navy had come to an end: "As far as can at present be foreseen, there is absolutely no limit to its (aircraft's) independent war use. And the day may not be far off when aerial operations with their devastation of enemy lands and destruction of industrial and populous centres on a vast scale may become the principal operations of war, to which the older forms of military and naval operations may become secondary and subordinate."[24] The result was, of course, the setting up of the Air Ministry and the RAF in April 1918.

There is, however, yet another element in the equation which needs to be taken into account, and that is the way in which the rationale for strategic air action fitted into the wider argument, one of personality as much as strategic thought as such, commonly known as the "frocks vs. coats" dispute. Trenchard's distaste for the "frocks" was even more obvious than that of other senior commanders on the Western Front, and his infamously short stay at the Air Ministry as first Chief of the Air Staff was largely due to the fact that he refused point-blank to allow Lord Rothermere, Secretary of State, the kind of freedom of access to advice to which he was probably constitutionally entitled. Trenchard was no military radical, though his rumbustious personality was often to lead him into arguments which made him look like one. Field-Marshal Haig seems to have been the only military man he supported unswervingly; he only accepted the post of CAS in the first instance after consulting Haig, and only accepted the command of the IAF, fundamentally unsound though he believed the principle of the force to be, because he believed that he would at least have the confidence of the land commanders. Trenchard and Sykes, moreover, did not get on, a factor which undoubtedly hardened the theoretical differences between them. In turn, Sykes was close to Sir Henry Wilson, the epicentre of the alternative strategic wisdom in the War Office. Wilson, of course, was Lloyd George's great white hope for undermining the Robertson-Haig axis. There seems to me to be a great deal of justice to Andrew Boyle's judgement on the Smuts

Report: "What finally saved it from the waste-paper basket was not the logic of its demand for an independent air force, but the fears of the war cabinet about the general military outlook. It seemed, towards the end of August (1917), that the conflict would drag on indefinitely unless the strategic monopoly of Haig and Robertson could somehow be curbed."[25] It would be an oversimplification to describe the establishment of the Air Ministry, the RAF and the IAF as just another piece of Lloyd George skulduggery, but it is fair to say that the separate arguments for independent air action, for co-ordinating training and supply in the air services, and for reprisals against the Germans, were articulated together and given significance by the way in which they related to the friction between the political and the military leadership in the war. The establishment of the Air Ministry was, among other things, a vote of no confidence in Douglas Haig.

British air power moved very far and very fast in the Great War, but it was to be very easy to overestimate the significance of what had happened in the years which came after. The air weapon had established itself as a major element on the battlefield, with a crucial role to play in reconnaissance, in artillery spotting and in ground attack, either in close support of the surface forces or in a long-range role. To achieve significant success in any of these areas, however, it had also become clear that an Air Force would be as subject to the classical rules of warfare as any of the traditional media of war; there was to be no short-cut to victory by avoiding battle with the enemy armed forces in being. This was to be a lesson that the RAF was to forget in the ensuing years, one which it had to relearn during the Second World War. On the other hand, it could easily be argued, as it was in the interwar years, that air power had never been used properly in the Great War, that the separate air organization had developed too late to be able to show its true worth. Though Trenchard managed to moderate the claims of the more extreme air power proponents in the 1920s, on the basis of Great War experience, the heirs of Sykes were encouraged by expectations of technical development into ever more effervescent prophecies of the likely impact of aircraft on warfare. Independent air action had been only one of many lines of argument that had produced a separate Air Ministry, but it was one that threatened to dominate that Ministry from its very inception, to the exclusion of other possible roles. Trenchard had warned of the dangers, and continued to do so when he was interviewed by the historian H.A. Jones, when Jones was tracing out the ground that I have just re-covered: "It is not a question of the separate existence of an Air Ministry," Trenchard said, "but of a proper conception of the role of air power."[26]

What he meant and what he went on to argue for in the ensuing years, was the need for a Ministry of Defence to correlate the needs of all three services and to co-ordinate these needs with those of government. Trenchard was indeed a farsighted man, but not along the rather unrealistic line he is normally credited with. He was more of a pragmatist than a visionary and understood, more than most at least, that the air weapon would only develop as a useful medium of warfare if its limitations were seen as clearly as its advantages. It was unfortunate that the apocalyptic conception of air power, untried, theoretically flawed, and based on a wishful misreading of what had happened in the Great War, was allowed to drown the hard-won experience of 4 years of conflict. Haig's opponents had demanded a quick way of winning the war; the mobilization of huge resources by modern industrial nations dictated that there could be no quick way, apart of course from the most obvious solution, a negotiated peace. Air power had proved to be a major new dimension in warfare and, in the future, the surface forces would have to rethink radically their operational concepts in order to take air power fully into account. What air power had not proved, and could not prove, was that it could operate as a self-sufficient war-winner. To argue along these lines was to combine intuition and logic in a particularly appealing way, given the drawbacks of traditional warfare, but with very little basis in experience. In that it underpinned the argument that air power had radically transformed the conduct of war, the creation of a separate Air Ministry muddled the further development of air power in Britain.

Notes

1. N. Jones, *The Origins of Strategic Bombing*, William Kimber, London, 1973.
2. C.F. Snowden Gamble, *The Air Weapon*, Oxford University Press, London, 1931, Introduction.
3. For the pre-1914 development of military aviation in Britain, see Snowden Gamble; J.M. Spaight, *The Beginning of Organised Air Power*, Longmans, London, 1927; G. Norris, *The Royal Flying Corps: A History*, Muller, London, 1965.
4. For this and a host of anecdotes, see Snowden Gamble, Introduction.
5. See R.A. Mason, *Readings in Air Power*, RAF Staff College, Bracknell, 1980, Chapter 1.
6. H.G. Wells, *The War in the Air*, George Bell, London, 1908.
7. Spaight, Chapter 2.
8. F.H. Sykes, Military Aviation, *Aeronautical Journal*, July 1913 and April 1914.
9. Concluding comments on Lecture by Sykes, *Aeronautical Journal*, July 1913.
10. Sir G. Aston, *Sea, Land and Air Strategy*, John Murray, London, 1914, Chapter 10.
11. Address by Trenchard to the Staff College, April 1923, AIR 9/8.
12. *Review of the Air Situation by Sykes*, 27 June 1918, reprinted in F.H. Sykes, *From Many Angles*, Harrap, London, 1941, p. 546.
13. Sykes, Chapter 9.
14. See W.J. Reader, *Architect of Air Power: A Biography of Viscount Eastwood*, Collins, London, 1968.
15. A. Boyle, *Trenchard*, Collins, London, 1962, Chapter 11.
16. See G. Till, *Air Power and the Royal Navy*, Jane's, London, 1979.
17. Spaight, Chapters 6, 7.
18. Till, pp. 111–16.
19. See E.B. Ashmore, Anti-Aircraft Defence, *Journal of the Royal United Service Institute*, 1927; *Air Defence*, London, 1929.
20. Boyle, Chapter 9.

21. Ashmore, *Air Defence*, passim.
22. M. Smith, *British Air Strategy between the Wars*, Oxford University Press, London, 1984, Chapter 2.
23. J.C. Slessor, *Air Power and Armies*, Oxford University Press, London, 1936, p. 37.
24. J.C. Smuts, The Second Report of the Prime Minister's Committee on Air Organisation and Home Defence against Air Raids, 17 August, 1917, reprinted in E. Emme (ed.), *The Evolution of Air Power*, Princeton University Press, Princeton, 1959.
25. Boyle, p. 229.
26. Report of an Interview with Trenchard by H.A. JONES, 11 April, 1934, AIR 8/67.

6

Lord Robert Cecil and the League of Nations during the First World War

HUGH CECIL

When there is talk about the "peace movement" during the First World War this tends to refer to the rebels – the conscientious objectors or the foreign policy radicals who called for the end of the conflict and the abolition of secret diplomacy. In fact, members of British governments also took an interest in one important aspect of peace movement activity – schemes for the prevention of wars in the future. This was in part because such schemes had a recognized propaganda value – particularly in impressing a United States with our moral superiority to the Germans. Even before the U.S. entered the war on the Allied side, the high-minded ex-professor President Wilson was known to have a project for a future international league; once the U.S.A. had come into the war the British government continued to dabble in the idea of a league to reinforce the new alliance, as well as to pacify industrial unrest at home.

But some members of government circles themselves genuinely believed in the need for a League of Nations. "The army of the good" were not all outside the government. That being said, there was a wide political gulf between most of the "peace movement" in the country and even the sincerest government advocates of a league. Lord Robert Cecil – who forms the central figure of this paper – was to be the most devoted government exponent of the League from 1916; but he was particularly harsh in his denunciations of Philip Snowden and other foreign policy radicals in parliament who sought a compromise peace.[1] He invoked the Defence of the Realm Act to prosecute those who criticized the conduct of the war in their publications – notably E.D. Morel, the Secretary of the Union of Democratic Control (in 1918).[2] On their part, members of the UDC attacked the government interest in a League project as being a diversion from the central issue of disarmament. Some peace advocates suggested that it was simply a device to defend the old international and social order.[3]

Official thinking on the League followed two main lines. The first can be dismissed briefly as it bore no fruit though it did gain some support: this was the view put forward by the secretary of the War Cabinet, Maurice

Hankey – namely that the league should rest not on any abstract principle but on the organization and practices of the Interallied Supreme War Council which was set up in November 1917. Such a League, Hankey thought, should hold meetings to prepare suggestions for the decisions of individual governments. There would be no *obligation* to abstain from resorting to war and no machinery for enforcing decisions.[4] Hankey always felt that this was a more realistic proposal than the form of League ultimately set up – which tried to introduce an element of compulsion and some surrender of sovereignty. Hankey did not believe either in basing his system on the idea of the sanctity of international agreements – the rule of law – which he felt was an out-moded concept in foreign affairs.[5]

The other government line of approach to a League – which was more influential – rested very much on the idea of the rule of law and on a revival of the old nineteenth century Concert of the Powers system in a reinforced form. Sir Edward Grey, one of the first ministers to advocate a League, wanted to see a system whereby the Powers were automatically bound to go to the conference table in a time of crisis, all hostile action being suspended. Grey believed that the participation of the U.S.A. was crucial – as a disinterested peace-loving Anglo-Saxon power with international ideas similar to those of Great Britain. And Germany too must be included in such a League.

Grey discussed his ideas in 1915 and 1916 with a number of Americans in influential circles – notably with Colonel House, President Wilson's most intimate aide, who was over in Europe to sound out the possibilities of a mediated peace.[6] Wilson and House had already in 1914 discussed ideas for a future world order based on mutual guarantees of territorial integrity against aggression.[7] House, as was his fashion, responded enthusiastically to Grey's ideas, but could not offer a pledge of American adherence to Grey's League at this stage.[8] Grey's views strongly influenced Lord Robert Cecil who had been his parliamentary under-secretary from May 1915.

Cecil at this time was in charge of the Contraband Department at the Foreign Office; he had first-hand experience, therefore, of the power of the economic weapon in depriving the enemy of vital supplies; this gave him a useful lesson in coercion which he applied to his League project. He was the son of Lord Salisbury, the late Prime Minister and Foreign Secretary, and though a good deal more optimistic temperamentally than his father he shared with him hopes about future international peace which he strove in his lifetime to put into action. He was fond of quoting his father's Guildhall speech of November 1897:

"The one hope we have is that the Powers may be gradually brought together to act together in a friendly spirit on all questions of difference which may arise, until at last they shall be welded in some international constitution which shall give to the world as a result of their great strength a long spell of unfettered and prosperous trade and continued peace."[9]

Salisbury had been gloomy about the future but hoping against hope had wanted to see the old Concert of Powers system made more watertight. This Lord Robert Cecil set out to do.

Lord Robert was a lawyer by training and a politician by upbringing – though in the rather remote, albeit vigorous, atmosphere of Salisbury's house at Hatfield; he was a vehement, animated, long, thin, gangling man with a large nose. He dressed extremely shabbily like a cross between a poor clergyman and a navvy.[10] His political speeches before the war were almost entirely on old Tory causes – against Welsh Church Disestablishment and Irish Home Rule and in defence of the House of Lords. He was also opposed fundamentally to the application of a great Liberal principle that was to be one of the main planks of a later Allied Peace programme, the principle of nationality – that is, the reorganization of Europe on lines of nationality. In the end he himself came, grudgingly, to recognize that national self-determination could not be ignored but he was sceptical about it:

> "So far [he wrote to St Loe Strachey in 1917] its achievements do not seem to have been very encouraging: it produced a united Germany, unfortunately for us; it has kept Eastern Europe in a turmoil ... it is responsible for very wild and unreasonable aspirations in Italy, and it is a perfect curse to us in Ireland"[11]

As a strong free-trader, Robert Cecil also deplored the provocation that tariff reform ideas in England had given to Germany, the suspicion they created in the U.S.A. and the business-orientated nationalism that the Tariff Reform Scheme seemed to him to encapsulate.[12]

Cecil was passionately concerned about the maintenance of treaty agreements and this was one of the strongest reasons for his disapproval of the British foreign policy radicals during the war; their demands that Britain should repudiate the secret treaties she had made with Italy and Russia when they were revealed by the new Bolshevik government of Russia, called out a strong protest from him in February 1918:

> "When they ask us to repudiate treaties, it seems to me that these pacifists do not understand the elements of their creed. How are we ever to make any progress in international affairs unless we regard international obligations as sacred? It is the very essence of any reasonable system on International Relations."[13]

Hence he rejected any idea of a compromise peace which did not involve the restoration of Belgium. Here he was in agreement with all the British governments, even though it seems by no means certain that Lloyd George, for example, took such a strong line on the sanctity of treaty agreements in general. For example, when Lloyd George used a memorandum by Cecil as the basis of his speech to the Trades Unions in January 1918 on the future peace settlement he left out some of Cecil's most extreme paragraphs on the subject of treaty agreements, though he used the rest of the memorandum word for word.[14]

Cecil's views on the League were strongly bound up with his ideas as a fervent Anglican churchman: "I am, I hope, a pacifist in the sense that I regard war as the greatest blot on Christian civilization and would do anything in my power to diminish the chance of its recurrence," he wrote in July 1916.[15]

As Contraband chief, and from 1917 Minister of Blockade Cecil proved a successful and energetic leader who improved his political standing during the war in consequence. Lord Milner's comment on him in November 1917 sums up well the qualities needed in a War Minister. Milner suggested him at the time to Lloyd George for the job of First Lord of the Admiralty – a post he never in fact filled:

> "You want someone at the head, who is not easily satisfied, who is nimble-minded & critical & always ready to try new things. I don't say Cecil is ideal, but, as compared with the others, he has more brain-power, more drive, more restless eagerness to better things. He will keep his end up in Parliament . . . & he will be a more vital force in his office."[16]

Cecil's League ideas formed the core of a carefully considered set of peace aims which he felt to be vital and interconnected. First he wanted, through Allied victory, to re-establish the sanctity of treaties which had been undermined by the German violation of the Belgian treaty. Secondly, he wished for increased American participation in the maintenance of world peace. Thirdly, he wanted to see the militarist regime in Germany ousted and the Kaiser hanged if possible for his breach of the international law. Fourthly he wanted peace restored in post-revolutionary Russia through the establishment of strong government; he did not believe the Bolshevists could achieve this and considered them internationally unreliable; he therefore initially supported Allied intervention against them after the armistice; later the waste and inconclusiveness made him favour a truce rather than military victory.

Fifthly Cecil, in the end, did come to support the liberation of the subject nationalities of the Ottoman Empire, but only because it helped to undermine the enemy. He did not believe that the principle of nationality would ensure stability nor that it was intrinsically just. He made an exception for the Jews and Americans, however, because they were victims of religious persecution.

Finally, he was unsympathetic towards discussions about extending the British Empire in the Near East and in Africa; nor did he wish Britain to join an Allied economic boycott of Germany after the war. All in all, he believed his policy to be following directly in his father's tradition, aiming at peace and justice abroad.

Finally in this analysis of the leading member of the "peace movement" in government we should observe that he was responsible for one of the more disagreeable jobs in wartime – the starvation of Germany – which included depriving German children of milk; in a humane and sensitive man who was yet resolved to fight the war to the finish, this produced a strong reaction in favour of looking for a means of abolishing war in the future. In short, here was a man in government who was undeniably Tory in background but was quite as resolved as any of the idealists *outside* government to devise a scheme to achieve a lasting peace. Neither the Peace Movement outside government nor indeed Liberals or Radicals had a monopoly where such aspirations were concerned. But it must be added that Cecil *was* a political maverick – much more Tory and much more Radical than most of his contemporaries in the Coalition Government; in November 1918 he resigned from the Government over Welsh Church Disestablishment. In 1929 he worked with the Labour Government on the League of Nations, having left the Conservative Party. In short, his views cannot be regarded as typical of Conservative thinking.[17]

In August 1916, Asquith asked his War Council to prepare papers, individually or departmentally to help clarify war aims. Cecil, at the Foreign Office, wrote a memorandum on "Proposals for Diminishing the Occasion of Future Wars". In this appears his first suggestion for a League of Nations. Cecil's paper was the first in a line of documents from Government departments which was directly ancestral to an official British League plan.[18] At this stage, like Grey, he was thinking of an improved and enlarged concert of Powers and did not use the term "League of Nations". The powers that he wished to be involved in his scheme would be those which signed the peace treaty after the war. He considered the idea of arbitration but taking a leaf out of the diplomatic book of his father – who had favoured the extension of arbitration but saw its limitations – he pointed out that arbitration was insufficient to deal with questions where vital national interests were concerned; such vital national interests were the ones most likely to lead to war if endangered – and investigation of these issues and judging on them went beyond the establishment of fact or law. Cecil also included a suggestion that the post-war territorial settlement should have machinery for modifying it – by conference – at a later date. This was actually his most original contribution to the League idea, though it did not take the important place that he wished for it in the final League constitution, where it appeared as Article 19. His view was that the Conference of Powers should have a permanent international legislative function over and above making treaties. In fact he showed a characteristic over-optimism in believing that a conference would quite easily be able to revise the post-war peace treaty by peaceful discussion, boundaries always involve vital interests which make peaceful change without any element of threat almost impossible. He was thinking too much of the revision of international agreements in terms of English domestic legal practice, whereby a law *could* be revised or dropped if declared obsolete in the courts. But few countries in fact would ever peacefully cede territory on the grounds of a treaty's obsolescence. Over-legalism was in fact characteristic of British official League thinking altogether (Hankey apart), which aimed at producing a cut and dried legal document rather than something more flexible. Cecil's approach was also typically insular; too like many people with high international ideals in and out of government, he had little interest in foreigners or foreign practice. Though he had many friends in other countries, we can see from his Peace Conference diary of 1919 that he was frequently exasperated by national differences. When asked by his niece to identify one of the delegates at the conference, he replied, "I don't know, some ghastly foreigner!"

In the rest of Cecil's 1916 paper, he advocated a compulsory conference system bringing together at a time of crisis all the powers who would have signed the European Peace Treaty after the war. There would be a moratorium period while discussion took place and the public could hear the dispute aired. He expected the public to take a just-minded and unchauvinistic view of the situation – an element of pure faith in his thinking which contrasted with his scepticism on other matters – here again he showed a faith in public opinion which was typical of the "Peace Movement" in most of its forms.

In addition to the moral sanction of adverse opinion, he hoped to coerce a persistent aggressor by means of financial and economic sanctions using machinery similar to that employed for blockading Germany. This would be used not only to stop a breach of the moratorium period but to enforce a decision of the conference – a far stronger provision than anything that found its way into the final constitution of the League of Nations.

Finally in 1916 Cecil also advocated disarmament – subject to the setting up of the other machinery. Like the UDC policy programme of 1915, Cecil favoured the nationalization of armament industries. Nearly all of the ideas in his paper were general currency among League of Nations enthusiasts at the time.

The Cecil memorandum was examined by Sir Eyre Crowe, the formidable Permanent Under-Secretary of the Foreign Office. Crowe was sceptical but treated the project fairly. He never had an easy relationship with Cecil over the blockade during the war. Cecil regarded the punctilious Crowe (nicknamed by some irreverent colleagues "Herr Crowe") as a red tape fanatic. Crowe considered that Cecil received too much credit among outside observers for the running of the blockade. But like a good servant of HMG the capable and critical Crowe gave the paper his whole mind; he reinforced Cecil's caution about disarmament and encouraged him to think in terms of a wider more permanent organization, so that despite his scepticism Crowe made a constructive contribution to British official thought on the League which continued into the Peace Conference. "He is in a different street from all the rest", Cecil told his wife admiringly early in 1919.[23]

President Wilson's Peace Note of December 1916 to the belligerent powers was a signal to the British government to take an interest in the League project. Cecil wrote a Cabinet memorandum on a possible reply to the American president on 22 December;[24] in this he followed Grey in advising that we should press the U.S. government to declare how far they would be prepared to go in supporting a League. He shared Grey's view that America's adherence was essential and, like him, feared that the Monroe Doctrine and her isolationist traditions might prevent her from joining in the end. The official Allied reply sent to Wilson followed Cecil's line on the subject of the League.[25]

The British government became yet keener to discuss the League when America came into the war on their side in April 1917. It formed part of the agenda of the new Imperial War Cabinet which met for the first time in April 1917. It was clear however that the British official mind was fundamentally "agin" the whole concept. A sub-committee on the non-territorial problems of a future peace, chaired by Lord Milner, discussed the League; it examined Cecil's plan and reported unenthusiastically: anything as ambitious would only do harm – and certainly could only be contemplated in close co-operation with the other Allies.[26]

The Imperial War Cabinet discussed this committee report on 25 April. For the first time Lloyd George as Prime Minister contemplated the League project seriously. What did Lloyd George think of the League? At best his feelings were ambivalent. There was a strong residue of idealism in Lloyd George despite the effects of holding high office and war leadership. Apart from his sincere and long-standing feelings for the small nation oppressed by foreign tyranny, there was also his radical non-conformist background which made him naturally sympathetic towards disarmament policies – particularly if the choice had to be made between spending more on armaments or on reform at home. This was clear before the war; and at the Imperial War Cabinet discussion he expressed regret that the report had not mentioned disarmament. He felt there would be general disappointment after the war if there were no plans for limiting arms.[27] Electioneering considerations also played a part in these thoughts. As long as President Wilson's support and goodwill were needed, Lloyd George was content to use the League as a rallying cry – and even as a bargaining counter. But he never had much real use for it as a form of diplomatic machinery. His own diplomacy was a matter of lobby and alcove chat, breakfast persuasion, horse-trading and rousing speeches for the masses. Frank public discussion was not in his line and would have been a waste of some of his best talents.

According to Cecil, Lloyd George had no time for the idea at all: "Lloyd George always loathed the League," [28] he later wrote. But Lloyd George's attitude is perhaps most fairly summed up in the well-known entry in Frances Stevenson's diary for 10 March 1919, where she is writing about Queen Marie of Roumania:

"She gave a lengthy description of her purchases in Paris, which included a pink silk chemise. She spoke of meeting President Wilson on his arrival. 'What shall I talk to him about,' she asked, 'the League of Nations or my pink chemise?' 'Begin with the League of Nations,' said Mr Balfour, 'and finish up with the pink chemise. If you were talking to Mr Lloyd George, you could begin with the pink chemise!'"[29]

At the Imperial War Cabinet in April 1917 the members proceeded to discuss disarmament and showed, as Sir Eyre Crowe had, considerable reservations about it, particularly where British naval defence was concerned. The war had underscored Britain's need for naval superiority, and so future disarmament made no headway with her government during the war. The general response of the Imperial War Cabinet to the League idea at this stage was tentative and sceptical, but there were some who showed sympathy: Arthur Henderson, the Labour member of the War Cabinet, and Sir Robert Borden, the Canadian premier.[30] Discussion of the League occupied little of the Imperial War Cabinet's time – a part of two meetings in the spring – but it was the longest discussion of the question for over a year; and it was the most careful examination of it made by either War Cabinet until December 1918. With America's support assured, the British government took little further interest in the League idea, save as a slogan, for a long time to come.

During the summer of 1917, there were efforts by League supporters to induce the British government to take over the League question and study the schemes proposed to date.[31] The Foreign Office made no objection, provided it was clear that this was for the post-war period; moreover there would be no need to publish such findings unless Britain's allies wished it. A number of public men – including Cecil's brother Salisbury – signed a memorandum urging that the government should appoint a committee to look at League schemes. Lord Bryce sent this to Lloyd George. The Prime Minister did not reply;[32] nor did he raise the matter in the cabinet until October. Then, it was decided to adjourn the question until it could be discussed with Colonel House who was shortly expected in the country.[33]

Meanwhile Cecil himself continued to work towards getting the project off the ground. In corresponding with Colonel House, it came out that despite President Wilson's public speeches in favour of the League, the U.S. president was in fact anxious that there should be no general discussion of the subject in the U.S.A. and had put its leading advocates of the League to work on more immediate war duties to divert them from it.[34] Wilson was also against the European Allies conducting similar discussions among each other. His official reason was that it would distract men's minds from the conduct of the war. Subconsciously too, perhaps, he disliked the idea of others working on his own pet scheme while he, as American war leader, had no time to devote to it himself.

Despite this discouragement, Cecil went on pressing the Foreign Secretary, Arthur Balfour, to allow a committee of the Foreign Office to examine the League idea from an historical and juridical point of view, to test its practicability and to prevent "windy talk".[35] He was at the time (November 1917) in close touch with W.H. Dickinson of the new League of Nations Society and even had the support of Hankey for this plan.[36]

Balfour agreed lukewarmly and the well-known Phillimore Committee of law experts, Foreign Office officials and historians was set up.[37] The government also approved a speech delivered by Cecil in December 1917 explaining the role of the League in a future world settlement. He concluded this by telling the House of Commons that he would not remain a member of any government for a single hour which did not make the establishment of the League after the war one of its main objects. It was "the only thing worth struggling for in international affairs" – an illustration of *his* priorities on the settlement.[38]

Lloyd George was by this time intent on rallying organized labour for a renewed effort against Germany, and on beating off the challenge of the Union of Democratic Control and others whose calls for a compromise peace were beginning to have some support in war-exhausted Britain. He spoke publicly to the Trade Unions on 3 January 1918, telling them of the government's intention to support, among other things, a League of Nations after the war. The words he used on the subject were not his – he followed a memorandum of Cecil's, word for word on this topic.[39] After this, there was a general recognition from the "peace movement" in Britain that the government did seem to be taking the question seriously; bodies ranging from the London Ethical Society to the British Esperanto and Volapuk groups sent in their schemes for world organization to the Foreign Office and to Cecil personally.[40]

The Phillimore Committee produced a plan for a League which followed Cecil's ideas in many respects, though it gave less in the way of coercive powers .[41] However he was well content with this scheme for the moment, and wanted the Imperial War Cabinet and the House of Commons to discuss it. Subsequently, he hoped, the report's conclusions could be made generally known to the public. The War Cabinet, however, decided that the Commons and the Imperial War Cabinet should do no such thing.[42] Cecil was distressed and pressed Lloyd George further on the matter: "I think it could be regarded . . . as almost a scandal if . . . [the Imperial War Cabinet] should separate without having discussed a subject in which large numbers of people are deeply . . . interested." It was not a question, he argued, of the government becoming totally committed to the Phillimore plan, but of arriving at a future peace conference with a definite scheme backed at least in principle by public opinion.[43] He felt passionately that it was crucial, if the League was going to work, to have the public properly involved in the debate, while their hatred of war was at its height. The best way of achieving success was through public discussion preceded by an interallied conference on the subject. The Foreign Office duly circulated the Phillimore scheme to the other Allied powers;[44] but for the reasons already given, President Wilson put clamps on any public or interallied debates. He allowed the faithful House to send Cecil a possible American plan, a rather wishy-washy version of the Phillimore proposals.[45]

In Parliament, there were repeated demands for the League to be openly discussed, but as long as Wilson's veto operated, nothing further could be done. Cecil, replying, indirectly attacked the president's attitude and the passive acquiescence of the British government in this state of affairs.[46] The British War Cabinet finally gave the issue more detailed consideration in August 1918. Lloyd George now argued forcibly and with genuine conviction against the Phillimore scheme being published. He said he was afraid that the report could diminish the Allies' will to win at a very crucial and dangerous phase of the war. Germany was nowhere like accepting tolerable terms; if the German government said it would accept the British League scheme subject to certain conditions, it would have a disastrous effect on public opinion in the winter months.[47] Cecil did not take this point. He was disillusioned with his colleagues. Beyond expressing pious sentiments, the Cabinet had shown little enthusiasm and its main preoccupation had been with the future security and power of the Empire. He told his wife:

> "... I found the atmosphere very chilly – L.G. has never really cared about it and is almost against it now under the influence of Amery, Hankey and C [Curzon.] Not one of them except Barnes and possibly Smuts and AJB really approves ... Of the Colonials Hughes & Co. are definitely against – only Borden is with us wholeheartedly. I have always known that the Continental Bureaucracy is opposed to us and blood lust is obscuring the American vision – what ought I to do? Without the hope that this war was to establish a better international system I should be a pacifist."[48]

President Wilson's veto operated for the rest of the war. To be fair, his conception of the League was different from that of the British enthusiasts. He felt that it should begin as a series of principles and grow; he was in no hurry to work out a detailed constitution and did not feel so much the urgency of rallying public opinion at this stage. All the same, Cecil's agitation had the effect of making Wilson and House draw up a more definite scheme. There would have been no official American League draft at the beginning of the Peace Conference without it. Wilson also spoke publicly, laying down his principles for a League on 27 September 1918 in New York.[49]

The British Cabinet again discussed the question in October 1918 when George Barnes, the Labour member of the War Cabinet at this time, pressed for an Allied line on a League – otherwise, he warned, the Germans might forestall them with proposals of their own. The Cabinet were no more enthusiastic than before and remained content with President Wilson's view that no particular scheme should be publicized.[50] Questions by League supporters continued to be asked in the House of Commons and the questioners continued to be fobbed off with the answer that publication of the British and the new French schemes was inopportune and premature.[51]

After the Armistice, Lloyd George at last felt more ready to talk about the League in detail at meetings of the Imperial War Cabinet, but found that many of his colleagues, particularly Premier Hughes of Australia, were hostile to the idea.[52] It was not until 24 December that the Imperial War Cabinet did examine the various British ideas, including an independently conceived League Mandate scheme presented by General Smuts.[53] The upshot was that while Hughes and others had strong reservations about the value and desirability of the League scheme, Britain did go to the Peace Conference at Paris in 1919 with an official plan. As to publicity – the 1918 general election after the Armistice gave an opportunity to Cecil and others who were pressing for a League. However, the League, though on many candidates' lips, got no particular attention from most of them, nor from the public; demobilization and punishing Germany and post-war reconstruction were far more important to them. Lloyd George's statements on the subject were inadequate.[54] Many foreign policy radicals and Asquithian League supporters whose patriotic loyalty was questioned at the time lost their seats. Their belief in the need for an international organization for peace was certainly not enough to save them from their fate.

During the war, then, the burden of government work for a League fell almost entirely on the Foreign Office and on Cecil in particular. He had the strong support of a number of F.O. officials – notably Eric Drummond – and from members of the Foreign Office's new Political Intelligence Department. Crowe, despite misgivings, played a very significant part in the development of the idea. There were, however, many in the department who were actually hostile to it; its championship by Cecil, whom they regarded as too autocratic and arrogant in his capacity as Blockade Minister and Assistant Foreign Secretary, was no recommendation in their eyes.[55] Outside the F.O., Cecil did receive some other enthusiastic backing in official circles, from men in the interallied supply organizations like the energetic Arthur Salter who envisaged an international economic organization rising from the wartime network they had helped to create.[56] Even so, the government's support for a League was, overall, a lukewarm affair. Nobody in the Cabinet save Barnes, Henderson, Borden or Smuts gave it the same central and pre-eminent position as Cecil. This is not to say that the British government would have neglected the matter completely without Cecil's leadership. They would have been obliged to meet Wilson's wishes in some degree; Smuts, Barnes and Balfour would between them have authorized some scheme; but it is hard to imagine that the project would have been pursued with the same single-minded zest; nor is it easy to imagine a more effective head of the British delegation's League of Nations section at the Peace Conference. With the exception of Smuts, who as a

South African, came from outside British governing circles and Grey who retired at the end of 1916, nobody among the political leadership contributed, as Cecil did, any original ideas on a world organization for peace. Finally one should consider, in all this, the role of President Wilson. Certainly, without him, it is unlikely that the British War Cabinet would have bothered to look into the possibility of a League as much as they did. Without him, Cecil would have been hard put to it to achieve anything worthwhile. On the other hand it is striking during the war years how much the American president was also responsible for stifling discussion of the League of Nations idea in Britain as well as in the U.S.A.

Notes

1. See, for example, *Hansard*, 5th series, 1917, C.2091.
2. F.O. 371/3443. fII67II. I46603: minute by Cecil about U.D.C. pamphlets, (August?), 1918.
3. See A.J.P. Taylor, *The Trouble Makers. Dissent over Foreign Policy 1792–1939*, Panther edn., London 1969, p. 143: F. Jowett in the *Bradford Pioneer*, 21 Feb. 1919.
4. Stephen Roskill, *Hankey, Man of Secrets*, vol. i, Collins London 1970, 454, 462.
5. British Museum Addit. MSS. 49704 (Balfour Papers), f.4: memo by Hankey for Balfour, 25 May 1916.
6. See Viscount Cecil, *A Great Experiment, an Autobiography*, Jonathan Cape London 1941, p.47 and *The Intimate Papers of Colonel House* arranged as a narrative by Charles Seymour, vol.i., 1st edn Ernest Benn London 1926, p. 370, 428–9.
7. Alfred Zimmern: *The League of Nations and the Rule of Law*, 1918–35, 2nd edn., McMillan & Co. London 1939, p. 218.
8. *The Intimate Papers of Colonel House*, ed. Seymour, i, p. 370.
9. *The Times*, 10 Nov. 1897 – Report on Lord Salisbury's speech at the Lord Mayor's Banquet, 9 Nov. 1897.
10. See Kenneth Rose, *The Later Cecils*, Weidenfeld and Nicholson, London 1975, ch. 6.
11. F.O. 800/196, Strachey, St. Loe: Cecil to Strachey, letter, 13 Nov. 1917.
12. Viscount Cecil of Chelwood, *All the Way*, Hodder & Stoughton, London 1949, p. 87, p. 34.
13. *Hansard*, 5th series, 1918, CIII. 230.
14. *War Memoirs of David Lloyd George* (2 vol. edn.) Odhams Press London 1938, ii, 1491, 1513, and: CAB 24/37, GT 3181: War aims – draft statement by Lord R. Cecil, 3 Jan. 1918.
15. F.O. 800/242, p. 198: Cecil to Frederick Coudert, letter, 18 July, 1916.
16. Lloyd George papers, f/38/2/24: Lord Milner to Lloyd George, letter, 23 Nov. 1917.
17. See Cecil's authobiography, *All the Way* (note 12) passim.
18. CAB 29/1, p–18: *Memorandum on Proposals for Diminishing the occasion of Future Wars*, by Lord R. Cecil, (Autumn) 1916.
19. Information given to author by the late Dowager Lady Harlech.
20. Henry R. Winkler, *The League of Nations Movement in Great Britain, 1914–1919*, 1st edn., Rutgers University Press, New Brunswick, 1952, p. 13.
21. CAB 29/1, p–19: notes by Sir Eyre Crowe on Cecil's paper on the diminishing of future wars, 12 Oct. 1916.
22. Information given to author by the late 5th Marquis of Salisbury.
23. Cecil of Chelwood Papers, Hatfield House, CHE 6/7 Cecil to Lady R. Cecil, 8 Jan. 1919.
24. CAB 23/1, WC 16, Appendix I: memo by Cecil, 22 Dec. 1916.
25. L.W. Martin, *Peace Without Victory: Woodrow Wilson and the British Liberals*, Yale Hist. Publications, Misc. 70, Yale University Press New Haven 1958, p. 40 *et seq.*
26. CAB 29/1, p–15: Report of the Milner Committee on the terms of peace, 24 April, 1917.
27. CAB 23/40, IWC 12, item 19, 26 April 1917.

28. Cecil of Chelwood Papers, Hatfield, CHE 28/16 (undated) notes by Cecil on *Lord Riddell's Intimate Diary of the Peace Conference and After, 1918–1923.*

29. Frances Stevenson: *Lloyd George, A Diary*, (ed. A.J.P. Taylor), Hutchinson London 1971, p. 171 (10 March 1919).

30. CAB 23/40, IWC 13, items 3 & 4, 1 May 1917.

31. F.O. 371/3072, f.118460.118460: Marburg to Drummond, 18 May 1917.

32. F.O. 371/3439, f.13761.53848: Dickinson to Cecil, 16 Nov. 1917.

33. CAB 23/4, WC 253, item 17, 19 Oct. 1917.

34. F.O. 371/3439, f.13761.53848: Lord Bryce to Balfour, letter, 15 Nov. 1917.

35. F.O. 371/3439, f.13761.53848: minute by Cecil for Balfour, 20 Nov. 1917.

36. *Ibid.*, Hankey minute 22 Nov. 1917.

37. David Hunter Miller, *The Drafting of the Covenant*, Putnam's London 1928, vol. i.3, note 1.

38. *Hansard*, 5th series, 1917, c. 2096–2097.

39. See CAB 24/37/2, GT 3181: memo by Cecil, 3 Jan. 1918.

40. See F.O. 371/3439. f.13761.13761–50278.

41. CAB 29/1, p–26: interim report of committee on League of Nations, 20 March 1918.

42. CAB 23/6 WC 412, item 7, 15 May, 1918.

43. Lloyd George Papers, F/6/5/34: Cecil to Lloyd George, 26 June 1918.

44. F.O. 371/3439, f.13761.121790, Percy minute, 30 July 1918.

45. D.H. Miller, *The Drafting of the Covenant*, vol. ii, 7–11; and House Papers, Yale, House to Cecil, letter, 25 June 1918.

46. *Hansard*, 5th series, 1918, vol, CIX, 735–738.

47. CAB 23/7, WC 457, item 8, 13 Aug. 1918.

48. Hatfield, CHE 6/4. Cecil to Lady R. Cecil, 14 Aug. 1918.

49. See House Papers, Yale, Cecil to House, letter, 28 Sept. 1918.

50. CAB 23/8, WC 481, item 9, 2 Oct. 1918.

51. *Hansard*, 5th series, 1918, vol. CX 890–891.

52. CAB 23/42, IWC 38, item 10, 26 Nov. 1918.

53. See D.H. Miller, *The Drafting of the Covenant*, ii, 23–60 and CAB 27/24, p. 195 o.s., 9 Dec. 1918.

54. *The Times*, 6 Dec. 1918, p. 9, col. 1.

55. Hatfield CHE 93/148, Sir E. Grey-Cecil, letter, 24 Oct. 1916 on Cecil's relations with the F.O. The author is much indebted to the late Sir Owen O'Malley for an account of Cecil at the F.O. which was untinged by hagiography.

56. See Cecil's views on such ideas: *The Times*, 16 Aug. 1918, p. 8, col. 6.

7

Scientists, Government and Invention: the Experience of the Inventions Boards 1915–1918

MICHAEL PATTISON

The First World War highlighted the inadequacies of Britain's provisions for scientific and industrial research and, in so doing, marked the beginning of a new era in the relationship between science and government in Britain. Although, at the outbreak of hostilities, none of the protagonists was technically prepared for the type and scale of warfare that was to ensue,[1] in Britain the lack of preparedness carried a particular poignancy: it gave new credence to the arguments of those, like Lord Haldane, who accused the government of "the neglect of science".[2] More important, the war presented the government with a unique opportunity to correct those deficiencies, an opportunity that could not have existed in peace time. In particular, it created a climate in which limited State intervention became a pragmatic necessity, a climate which both allowed and encouraged the mobilization of scientists and the creation of new institutions for the promotion of civilian and military scientific research on an unprecedented scale.[3]

Of these new institutions, three were specifically created to organize inventive talent for military ends – initially by considering suggestions for weapons technology sent to them from the general public, and later by developing war-related research programmes of their own. Two such institutions emerged in the summer of 1915, viz: the Board of Invention and Research (BIR), established to study naval inventions, and the Munitions Inventions Department (MID), which examined ideas for land warfare. A third inventions board, the Air Inventions Committee (AIC), which was broadly responsible to the Air Board, became operational in May 1917. All three inventions boards employed scientists of the eminence of Sir J.J. Thomson, Sir Ernest Rutherford, Sir Oliver Lodge, H. (later Sir Horace) Darwin, and Dr. R.T. (later Sir Richard) Glazebrook.[4] A study of the inventions boards is therefore important in what it reveals about the deployment of some of Britain's foremost scientific brains during the Great War, and in what it discloses about the non-scientists' perception of military science at that time. This paper examines why and how the

HF–D

government set about creating these boards, and considers the often difficult early relationship between the scientists who worked for them and the military.

The Genesis of the Inventions Board

The encouragement of science in time of war is not a recent phenomenon. For centuries the open courtship of scientists and inventors by the military has been an important characteristic of warfare and its preparation. In the third century B.C., for example, Archimedes is said to have designed catapults for the defence of Syracuse against Roman invasion, and in the late fifteenth century Leonardo da Vinci furnished the Duke of Milan with designs for fortifications, military bridges, chariots, and mines. In Britain, the development of ordnance committees in the nineteenth century, and more particularly the creation of the Advisory Committee on Aeronautics in 1909,[5] the General War Committee of the Royal Society in 1914, and the Chemical Society's Consultative Committee in 1915, set a valuable precedent for the manner in which military scientific research was to be administered throughout the First World War.[6]

In August 1914, however, weapons research was not among the priorities of the War office. A prevailing belief that the war would be short-lived made such research seem hardly worthwhile, and the authorities were preoccupied with overcoming the desperate munitions shortage. Accordingly, the ordnance factories and armaments firms, on which, previously, the War Office had largely depended for technical innovation, were instructed to give priority to production over research. Moreover, throughout the first few months of war, despite the crucial importance of science-based industries such as explosives, dyestuffs, glass and pharmaceuticals, the authorities made no effort to prevent scientists enlisting for active service (although even in Germany, where the Imperial Government had long since recognized the strategic importance of a strong national science policy, scientists of the calibre of Hans Geiger were allowed to serve at the Front[7]). Pressurized by the "white feather" syndrome, or simply carried along on the wave of patriotic fervour that swept the country, some of Britain's brightest young scientists enlisted as soldiers. Many were killed, including thirty-five Fellows of the Royal Society and fifty-five members of the Royal Institute of Chemistry.[8] Among those who died, one of the most notable was Sir Ernest Rutherford's brilliant protege, H.G.J. Moseley, who was killed at the Dardanelles on 10 August 1915. "The loss of this young man on the battlefield," Rutherford wrote in *Nature*, "[is] a striking misuse of scientific talent." Indeed, even in Germany, Moseley's death was mourned.[9]

In 1917, Professor Andrew Grey, FRS, a physicist working for the MID, added his sentiments to Rutherford's bold indictment of the authorities' lack of foresight. In a memorandum prepared for the Ministry of Munitions, on the need to document the "special service record of men scientifically trained", he argued:

> "No effect of our unpreparedness for the present war has been more lamentable than the waste in ordinary trench and field fighting of highly trained young men, capable of doing excellent work in the scientific branches of the army, in the ships of the fleet, or in the researches required for the construction of new devices for warfare on sea or on land or in the air . . .
>
> ". . . It is in the highest degree discreditable to successive Governments of the country, that nothing was done to organize or even record the wealth of brain power, and of manipulative and technical skill, available in the nation to meet the attacks of a great power which for generations had made the study of war methods and war appliances, and the scientific efficiency of its army and navy, its chief aims and objects.
>
> "The arrangements made in this country on the outbreak of war for the recruiting of officers for the scientific branches of the services were inadequate and unjust."[10]

Initially, therefore, there was no serious attempt on the part of the authorities to encourage the application of science to warfare.

But by June 1915 change was in the air. Leading intellectuals and members of Britain's scientific community began publicly to argue, in the correspondence columns of *The Times*, that they were not being given sufficient opportunity to contribute their particular skills to the war effort. H.G. Wells informed its readers "Modern war is essentially a struggle of gear and invention," and warned:

> "Unless our politicians can add to the many debts we owe them, the crowning service of organising science in war more thoroughly than they have ever troubled to do it in peace, I do not see any very great hope of a really glorious and satisfactory triumph for us in this monstrous struggle."[11]

For almost a fortnight, *The Times* carried letters of support from such luminaries as Sir Philip Magnus, Member of Parliament for the University of London and a renowned champion of technical education, F.H. Royce and Claude Johnson, the Engineer-in-Chief and the Managing Director of Rolls Royce and J.A. Fleming, Professor of Electrical Engineering at University College, London. They urged the government that an inventions board should be created, "to organize the scientific intellect of the country", as a matter of priority.

Unknown to Wells and his fellow polemicists, there were already moves afoot, within the Admiralty, to establish an inventions board. Since the outbreak of war, suggestions for inventions had been arriving at the office of the First Lord, often at the rate of 100 per day. Most of these suggestions were quite useless, even eccentric, but all were forwarded to the Director of the Admiralty Technical Division, Admiral Dumas – much to his expressed annoyance. The admiral's diary provides a unique insight into why, among the many technical departments of the Services, there was a general feeling of contempt for aspiring inventors who turned their hands to munitions. "A proper bureau of inventions," he wrote on 18 June 1915,

"... would be worth anything if it saved me from futile and perpetual inventors," and, two days later, "all these would be assistants without any knowledge of the practical requirements are maddening."[12] Unfortunately, such contempt for inventors found further expression in a distrust, widely held among the military, of all civilian scientists and engineers.

But the political will and practical impetus for the navy's inventions board came from the First Lord, Lord Balfour, himself. Aware that it would "do much to satisfy a public demand", Balfour submitted a memorandum to the Cabinet in which he argued the case for "the institution of a Board of Inventions". One month later, in July 1915, the Board of Invention and Research was created. It was chaired by the controversial former First Sea Lord, Admiral Sir John Fisher, staffed by a consulting panel of sixteen distinguished scientists and industrialists, and charged with the following duties:

> "(1) To concentrate expert scientific enquiry on certain definite problems, the solution of which is of importance to the Naval Service;
> (2) To encourage research in directions in which it is probable that results of value to the Navy may be obtained by organized scientific effort, and to consider schemes and suggestions put forward by inventors and other members of the general public."[13]

A second inventions board, the Munitions Inventions Department, was established in August by the newly-appointed Minister of Munitions, Lloyd George. Since assuming office in June he, too, had been the recipient of a number of inventions suggestions: some of them – especially those from servicemen – showed great promise. As a result, in July Lloyd George approached Mr. E.W. (later Sir Ernest) Moir, a civil engineer who was already working with the Ministry of Munitions, to head his proposed inventions department. Moir agreed, and stayed in the post until December, when he took up a new appointment with the Ministry in the United States. He was replaced by Col. H.E.F. Goold Adams, a former officer of the Ordnance Board who had offered his services to the MID on a voluntary basis, and it was he who steered the MID through the difficult years that lay ahead.[14]

The responsibilities of the MID were similar to those of the BIR: "To receive particulars of ideas, inventions and suggestions likely to be of service in carrying on land warfare"; and "To carry out original research in connexion with mechanical, chemical and physical engineering subjects ...".[15] However, Lloyd George's department was larger than its naval counterpart: its consulting panel initially included twenty-five scientific and industrial experts, a number which had grown to forty-eight by the end of the war. Three of its scientists also served with the BIR (Sir J.J. Thomson, R. (later Sir Richard) Threlfall and R.J. Strutt, later Lord Rayleigh) and five later served with the AIC (H.L. Callender, R.T. Glazebrook, A.V. Hill, F.W. Lanchester and Sir Horace Darwin, who chaired the AIC). The demands made upon the scientists to attend meetings of the various sub-committees of the inventions boards were often great. F.W. Lanchester found his commitments so heavy that in 1917 he was forced to move from his Birmingham home to London in order to attend all the relevant meetings.

Before considering the nature of the work that the scientists undertook and the difficulties they encountered in seeking the necessary co-operation of the military, it is apposite to clarify the reasons for the creation of the inventions boards. There are three. Firstly, they were established to relieve the Admiralty Technical Division and the Ministry of Munitions from the burdensome task of sorting through the hundreds of letters which were arriving daily, suggesting often eccentric ideas for weapons technology. Secondly, their creation was undoubtedly useful to the government in stemming the tide of open criticism, from leading public figures, of its apparent unwillingness to involve scientific experts in the war effort. Finally, it was hoped that the creation of such committees would place the research and development of military technology on a sounder footing. From the very beginning, however, such hopes were tentative. When, on 28 July 1915, Lloyd George announced to the House of Commons his intention to establish a second inventions board, he concluded: "The new branch will have justified its existence if one project in a hundred, or even in one thousand, turns out to be of practical utility in the present emergency."[16] As events later proved, his caution was warranted.

Scientists and Inventions

In terms of the number of ideas they received, the inventions boards made a promising start. During the first six months of its life the BIR received five thousand suggestions, while, for the same period, the MID received almost twice as many. The quality of the ideas, however, was so poor that few were ever developed. It was the common experience of both boards that "The numbers [of suggestions] vary with the frequency of air raids, and the sinking of ships by submarine",[17] and many of the ideas they received were concerned with methods for dealing with hostile aircraft or U-boats. Among the schemes studied by the BIR, for example, was one to train cormorants, with explosives fastened to them, to swoop on surfaced submarines, and another to coat the ropes of barrage ballons with bird lime in the belief that Zeppelins would stick to them. Cormorants also featured in a suggestion put forward to the MID: it was proposed that flocks of them be trained to peck away the mortar of the chimneys at Krupp's factory in Essen, in the hope that the chimneys would then collapse on the munitions factory! One inventor, whose idea was given serious consideration by the BIR, claimed to have produced gold from quicksilver. Concerned that there might be questions in the House of Commons about the matter, Balfour consulted J.J. Thomson, but after conducting a series of experiments, Thomson was able to inform him that the inventor was wrong.[18]

The MID received its share of crackpot schemes, too. One man suggested that rubber tubes could be connected to soldiers socks so that they could warm their feet in the trenches by exhaling through the tubes, and that bullets with lateral grooves cut into them could be used by sharpshooters to tear down barbed wire fences. Another volunteered that, in order to facilitate gas attacks, given two hours notice he could summon a wind from any direction the War office required. In his autobiography, Admiral Sir Reginald Bacon, who replaced Goold Adams as Controller of Munitions Inventions in January 1918, recalls:

> "This last inventor was so angry at having his capabilities doubted, that he reported me as being obstructive to the conduct of the War to the Ministry of Munitions, the Secretary of State for War, the First Lord of the Admiralty, and the Prime Minister!"[19]

The possibility of harnessing electricity as a weapon also excited the fevered imagination of a number of aspiring inventors, and indeed was optimistically considered sufficiently realistic for its investigation to be listed among the terms of reference of the MID's Instruments Committee.[20] Those who envisaged such a possibility were to be disappointed, although for a while a scheme submitted by Russell Clarke, a radio ham employed by Naval Intelligence, was considered by Professor Bertram Hopkinson and Sir Oliver Lodge to stand "a good chance of success". The idea, which Clarke professed to have been developing since 1911, was to generate a deadly heat ray using electricity as the energy source. The principle was described thus:

> "If a generator could be discovered for producing electrical oscillations of very short wave length, and of sufficient power, these very short waves could be reflected by a carefully laminated reflector composed, say, of a number of wires arranged on a parabolic surface like the ribs of an umbrella. The oscillations could then be concentrated in a beam, and when impinging on an unlaminated metallic body, would generate intense eddy currents in it, and if the effect could be made powerful enough, the body would be melted."[21]

Clarke claimed he had discovered such a generator, but preliminary MID investigations determined that ". . . there are many likely causes of failure", and warned "Complete failure seems much more probable than the most limited degree of success."[22] In view of the likely expense that experiments would have entailed, James Swinburne, a member of the Instruments Committee and a pioneer of electrical engineering, was asked to produce a detailed report. His enquiries lasted only a few days, and his conclusion was:

> "The Russell Clarke scheme is quite hopeless. (1) The generator is impractical. (2) The radiator is not designed. (3) Accurate reflection of such waves is impossible. (4) A fallacy underlies all schemes of projecting waves on a target."[23]

Swinburne's objections were accepted, and the project was duly closed.

Evidently, one of the key probems which inventors faced was the need for precise information on the requirements of the armed forces. For their publicity the inventions boards were principally dependent upon the Press (although the MID also produced its own publication, *The Ministry of Munitions Journal*, which was circulated among firms controlled by, or associated with, the Ministry). Such publicity, however, was of limited value, for there were severe restrictions, both official and practical, on the kind of information that could be imparted. For example, an article by the MID, published in *The Times* on 7 September 1915, urged inventors to give careful consideration to the practicability of their schemes before submitting them to the department.[24] This was met with demands, in *The New Statesmen*, that the inventions boards should publish more stringent details of what was required by the Services, in order that inventors should have some definite problems to tackle and in the hope that inventions would therefore be more relevant and fruitful.[25] An article in *The New Statesmen*, in October, supported this view:

> "The organization of invention is not merely a question of advertising for brilliant ideas. Something, undoubtedly, may be done in that way, and it ought not to be neglected. But by itself it belongs essentially to the order of "muddling through" methods . . . The truth is that the great mass of inventive work is done not by men who have brilliant ideas 'out of the blue', but by men who have deliberately set themselves, or have been set, to devise a machine or method to achieve a certain definite object."[26]

Yet, what many inventors apparently failed to realize was that in publishing details of suitable projects which they might undertake, the inventions boards would also have provided the Germans with valuable and accurate information about the deficiencies of the British forces. Secrecy was of the utmost. Moreover, in 1917, an article in *The Ministry of Munitions Journal* countered continued demands for such details with the claim that publication would not guarantee more realistic suggestions, nor was it always possible to predict what the future requirements of the forces would be. "It would be easier," the article concluded, "to make a list of things not wanted . . ."[27]

Secrecy was essential in inventions work not only to prevent new ideas from falling into enemy hands, but also to protect the patent rights of those inventors whose ideas the inventions boards were developing. In practice, however, such rights could not always be guaranteed. There were two principal categories of patent operated by the inventions boards: "secret" and "ordinary", the difference being that while secret patents were *never* published, in peace-time ordinary patents were usually published after inspection by the Patent Office. During the war, however, the publication of *any* specification likely to be of service to the enemy was prohibited;[28] which, in theory, ensured the absolute secrecy of most inventions with which the boards were concerned. In fact, the need to co-operate with the allies, particularly in avoiding unnecessary duplication of research, prompted the government to introduce a certain amount of flexibility into the patent laws. After much consideration, a meeting of inventions boards was convened in April 1918 to discuss problems presented by the patent laws, and it was decreed that ". . . Inventions likely to be of use to the Allies should be communicated to them at the Department concerned and that before communication takes place the inventor should be given an opportunity to patent the invention in the Allied country."[29] The United States was particularly co-operative in this regard: it offered to compensate British inventors for any of their devices which it adopted, and made the offer legally binding.[30] Not even secret patents were exempt from this ruling, for it was added that ". . . the free interchange should take place [between the allies] of all secret patents that may be material to the conduct of the war even though it is almost certain to be the case, each interchange would compromise secrecy after the war." The important military requirements of secrecy was therefore eventually compromised to the scientists' demand for open discussion.

Another problem which confronted the inventions boards was that of time. The urgency of war had a telescoping effect on scientific activity, and scientists and inventors often worked under great pressure in their efforts to produce new war-winning technology.[31] Projects which in peace-time would have taken years of patient calculation, planning and experimentation, in war had to be perfected within a much shorter time-span, sometimes only a matter of months, for lives were often at stake.[32] Consequently, research which it was thought could produce quick results assumed special importance, particularly during the early stages of scientific involvement in the war.[33] It was not until 1916 that the possible long-term benefits of many of the projects of the inventions boards became a significant consideration.[34]

Despite this urgency, delays inevitably occurred – especially during experiments and trials. In December 1917, the matter aroused sufficient concern to take precedence over all other business at the third general meeting of the Air Inventions Committee.[35] At that meeting, the cause of these delays was identified as the customary caution of the experimental scientist, and the members resolved that, in some cases, the risks involved in hurrying tests on inventions were worth taking, in view of the possible benefits that an early introduction to the battlefield could bring. A.V. Hill expressed cynical concern that scientists were becoming as cautious as government officials, and F.W. Lanchester remarked that ". . . as a rule scientific men are disinclined to come to a decision on insufficient data and in dealing with inventions for War purposes the attitude should be modified."

In April 1918, Horace Darwin summarized his considered opinion on the matter in a three-page memorandum to the Ministry of Munitions:

"It is most difficult to decide how much time should be taken in the trial of new inventions before they are adopted. In perhaps a few cases proceeding somewhat more slowly would have led (sic) ultimately to a quicker supply, but in most cases it would seem that the new appliance would have been sooner in use if less time had been spent on experiments. . . . The risk of failure is increased or the invention when adopted may not be so efficient; in war time this risk should be run."[36]

Thus, the principle of systematic scientific investigation was tempered by the exigencies of war, although these observations were made too late for subsequent action to have any noticeable effect on wartime inventions work.

As Darwin's comments suggest, the inventions boards were able to develop a number of inventions in time for them to be utilized by the Services. By the end of the war the MID had received nearly 50,000 ideas, of which 226 had reached extended field trials or had been adopted into full military service. Among the more successful of these were designs for bomb throwers, gunsights, devices relating to machine-guns and signalling, height- and range-finders, and the Stokes mortar.[37] The BIR also had some successes in the development of inventions, particularly with regard to aerial photography (both in camera design and photographic interpretation), in the production of smoke bombs and non-corrosive metals, and in the manufacture of a compound internal combustion engine, designed by H.R. (later Sir Henry) Ricardo.[38] However, the discrepancy between the number of ideas received by the BIR and those which proved actionable was greater than for the MID. Although he may have been exaggerating that discrepancy, J.J. Thomson recalled: "I should think that before [the war] ended the number [of suggestions] had increased to well over 100,000; of these not more than 30 proved to be of any value."[39]

It is hardly surprising, therefore, that the initial enthusiasm of some of the scientists began to wane. The most striking example was Rutherford, who eventually became so frustrated with the burden of committee work and the commuting from Manchester which it entailed, that he began to seek sanctuary in his own research interests. On missing a panel meeting at the BIR he gave the following celebrated excuse: "I have been engaged in experiments which suggest that the atom can be artificially disintegrated. If it is true, it is of far greater importance than a war."[40]

Within six months of their creation, it was clear to anyone who cared to study the work of the inventions board that unsolicited schemes submitted by the general public were, on the whole, of limited value. Consequently, a gradual shift occurred in the emphasis of the work which the boards undertook. The task of evaluating inventions, for which they had been established, soon became secondary to the ultimately more rewarding function of initiating and sponsoring a wide variety of war-related research. The response of the military was mixed. Occasionally serving officers who were approached by the scientists, either to request that they be allowed to observe military exercises, or to ask for the loan of equipment for trials and experiments, proved quite co-operative. More often, however, the scientists were regarded with suspicion and their requests met with obstruction. Two examples best illustrate the difficulties which the scientists encountered in dealing with the military: the BIR's anti-submarine research and the MID's anti-aircraft research.

In November 1915 a group of BIR-sponsored scientists were attached to the Royal Naval Experimental Station at Hawkcraig. They were led by the physicist, Professor W.H. Bragg, from University College, London, and included A.B. Wood, a Research Assistant in physics from Liverpool University, F.W. Pye, a mechanic, also from Liverpool, and Harold Gerrard, a lecturer in electrical engineering from Manchester. Their task was to assist the station commander, C.P. Ryan, in the study of underwater acoustics and the development of hydrophones for the detection of submarines; an undertaking that assumed particular importance in view of German attempts, since February, to impose a U-boat blockade on the British Isles.

Despite initial progress in their research,[41] the relationship between the BIR scientists and their naval counterparts deteriorated rapidly. Bragg's biographer, G.M. Caroe, notes: "Personally, the scientific staff were on cordial relations with Commander Ryan and his dog (which persistently stole the scientists' dinner from the canteen table, until they attached a high voltage battery to a steak one day); but over the work, relations were uneasy from the start, and became increasingly difficult."[42] As Roy MacLeod and Kay Andrews have identified: "To the serving officers the scientists appeared unaware of naval customs and procedures, while to the scientists the officers appeared peremptory and unsympathetic."[43] By March 1916 the scientists were becoming exasperated at the Navy's apparent unwillingness fully to co-operate. In a letter to Ernest Rutherford, on 22 March, Albert Wood complained:

> "The usual difficulties in obtaining a second ship or submarine still exist. Commander Ryan informs that we have no right to demand two ships and we are only allowed to have them when he considers it convenient. ... With regard to submarine B.3 ... he said that it was to be used by both of us [the Navy and BIR]. He could not tell us, however, when we could have it for our own use; indicating that it would be possible for us to have it only on those occasions when he did not require it himself – which occasions from our previous experience will probably be rare."[44]

There were other incidents. A telephone link between two BIR huts was removed by the Navy without explanation, and a sailor, completing a manoeuvre for Professor Bragg, was confined to barracks by Commander Ryan.[45] It is, perhaps, not so difficult to understand why the Navy should be reluctant to release vital ships and submarines to scientists on civilian attachment, but these minor incidents of obstruction are far less easy to excuse.

The scientists' complaints soon reached the BIR in Whitehall. They were brought to the attention of Lord Balfour, who was told that the situation had deteriorated so badly that the BIR was considering discontinuing its anti-submarine research. This prompted the Admiralty to institute a number of minor reforms, including a doubling of the BIR's annual budget to £20,000 and a promise of greater co-operation from Admiralty technical departments. Although these reforms enabled further progress in directional hydrophone research, their effect upon the relationship between the BIR scientists and the Navy was minimal. Complaints at the lack of naval co-operation continued to filter through to Whitehall, and a report on the anti-submarine work of the BIR, drafted in March 1917, reflected:

"From the commencement of their researches the Board of Invention and Research have supplied the Admiralty with reports of all their results.

"They have received *no reports* in return as to experiments carried out by other Departments or Establishments, such as the "Vernon" Torpedo School, which are also investigating the same or allied problems.

"At Hawkcraig the Board of Invention and Research were officially requested to carry out experimental work on submarine detection in conjunction with Commander (now Captain) Ryan, R.N. His work was carried out independently and reported monthly to the Director of Naval Ordnance.

"From April to August 1916 no reports of Captain Ryan's work were furnished by the Director of Naval Ordnance to the Board of Invention and Research, nor were they informed of the orders as to experimental work given to Captain Ryan by the Director of Naval Ordnance."[46]

By the time the report was drafted, however, several important changes had been implemented. In December 1916 the Admiralty's Intelligence Division and the Anti-Submarine Committee were merged into a single new department, the Anti-Submarine Division. With these reforms came an opportunity to tackle the thorny problem of the BIR. In the face of continued criticism from the scientists, Bragg's team were moved to new quarters at the Admiralty Experimental Station at Parkestone Quay, Harwich. Here experimental facilities were vastly superior to those at Hawkcraig, and the scientists found the naval staff far more co-operative. A.B. Wood recalls: "Some of [the] senior officers were very helpful in discussions of problems relating to submarine detection. . . . In addition to advice, they frequently provided us, on request and at short notice, with submarines for experimental purposes."[47]

The reforms appear to have worked. By the summer of 1917 important advances had been made in the development of underwater detection methods,[48] and at Harwich the groundwork was laid for the development of ASDICS, or Sonar (although this was never used in action during the Great War). The improvements were such that Albert Wood went on to pursue a distinguished career as a naval scientist, continuing to work with the navy, for a while, after the war. Once the civilian scientists had been given the opportunity to demonstrate their skills, in some practical way, to the Admiralty technical departments, the Navy was more willing to accept that such people might be of value to them.

A clear and interesting comparison can be drawn between the problems encountered by Bragg's group and those encountered by the MID's Anti-Aircraft Experimental Section, which was also heavily dependent on the co-operation and involvement of the military. The Section was formed in the Autumn of 1915 under the charge of A.V. Hill, a young physiology graduate from Cambridge who was noted for his inventiveness. Its work included the development of height- and range-finders, research into the location of aircraft by sound, the study of wind and barometric effects on ballistics, and, later, the investigation of German anti-aircraft devices. In order to set about these tasks, Hill gathered a team of Cambridge academics, chiefly mathematicians, and enlisted the help of the staff of the National Physical Laboratory, whose director, Sir Richard Glazebrook, took a keen interest in the Section's investigations.

By March 1916, the team was ready to conduct initial tests on early height- and range-finders, and began to look for a suitable airfield from which they might be allowed to work. Clearly, in order to test the devices effectively, the group required access to an aeroplane, pilot, and gun. Hill was soon to discover that such access would not be granted readily. Although the Section had been offered accommodation at the airfield at Northolt, no further *active* co-operation was forthcoming from the staff on the base. Hill later complained:

> "There was a certain amount of indifference and apathy from the start on the part of the people at the aerodrome, the majority of whom regarded us as a set of rather uninteresting cranks who wanted to make a science out of a thing which they intended by nature to remain a sport: and although they did to some extent attempt to help us in our work there was obviously no real desire to take any interest in it. One or two of the younger pilots were, as a matter of fact quite interested in seeing the records of flights which they themselves had carried out, and one man in particular was very anxious to get attached to us in order to enable us to make records of his flights and the "stunts" which he practised; the attitude, however, of the authorities there was chilling."[49]

Again, the lack of co-operation from the authorities undoubtedly arose from their concern for the proper use of valuable aircraft and the safety of carefully trained pilots, but it reflects, too, their failure to comprehend the value of Hill's work. Indeed, prompted by the indifference of the authorities and the need for improved experimental facilities, after only two months Hill began to search for an alternative base.

One possible site, which Hill considered, was the Experimental Ground at Shoeburyness. Here the Section had previously organized a number of trials, and the station's Chief Instructor in Anti-Aircraft Gunnery, Major D.H. Gill, was anxious that Hill should move the Section there permanently. Although Gill had "no great scientific knowledge himself", Hill recognized in him "very strong scientific interests and instincts". The same could not be said, however, of Gill's commanding officer, General Sclater-Booth, who blocked the move. Apparently he regarded Hill as "a wild fellow" and told Gill: "We have a Superintendent of Experiments here and if there are any experiments to be done he ought to do them." Hill believed there were other reasons for his objection: "Probably, of course, there was some obstruction in the War Office too."[50]

On hearing about the difficulties which Hill and his team were experiencing, Glazebook invited them to establish their base at the National Physical Laboratory, at Teddington. Once there, the Section made appreciable progress in improving height- and range-finders,[51] and, in an attempt to convince the military of the value of their research, they arranged a number of trials to which officers were invited. The trials were effective in two ways. Firstly, they encouraged active liaison with the military and gave the Section opportunities to prove the practical worth of their investigations, eventually leading to the arrangement of field trials in France. Secondly, after witnessing trials at Gorleston, the officer commanding the Naval Gunnery School at H.M.S. *Excellent* on Whale Island invited the Section to establish a permanent headquarters there. Thus, in September 1916, the team moved again. This time the facilities they were given were ideal, particularly as they now had ready access to anti-aircraft guns, and the Section was able to expand its work on ballistics and, later, to begin investigations into the location of aircraft by sound.

As was the case with Bragg's BIR team, the contribution of Hill's group to the development of war-winning technology was limited. Although height- and range-finders devised by the group were used in France from the summer of 1917, the crude tactics of anti-aircraft gunnery remained largely unchanged throughout the war and sound locators were developed too late to be put to any great effect. The greatest contribution of both groups, therefore, lay not in the technology that they produced; rather, it lay in the impact that they had on the introduction of scientific techniques to the solution of military problems, and in awakening the military to the value of scientific advice. This was achieved either by persistent complaints from the scientists about the lack of military co-operation, in the hope that Whitehall would eventually listen and enforce the necessary reforms, or by organizing trials which were specifically designed to interest the military in the scientists' research. It therefore remains to consider what, in retrospect, the scientists felt about their experiences with the inventions boards, and what it was that made the idea of co-operation more palatable to the military.

The First World War has been the only war in which the British government established as many as three inventions boards specifically to investigate scientific and technological ideas received from the general public and to provide experimental facilities for aspiring inventors.[52] The boards had been created to organize, though not to direct, individual scientific initiative of the kind, historically, armies had employed whenever the need arose. What the experience of the First World War proved, however, was that because of the increasing scientific sophistication of military technology, without proper direction, such individual initiative was no longer likely to produce important results. *The New Statesman* was sufficiently alert to identify this fact as early as October 1915:

> "... there is no doubt that a great deal can be done by inviting all and sundry to send in their ideas to the [inventions] departments, but still more, probably, can be done by a deliberate effort to stimulate the inventive faculties of selected individuals. It is not enough that the department should have one or more military representatives at the front. It is of great importance that men of wide and varying knowledge should be given the fullest facilities for studying military problems on the spot. ... The [Munitions] Inventions Department ought, therefore, to be always sending relays of technical men to the front where their minds may be quickened by seeing concrete things in active operation."[53]

In fact, as we have seen, not a great deal was achieved by inviting "all and sundry to send in their ideas". The most promising technical contributions of the inventions boards (ASDICS and anti-aircraft defence research) were not tackled by individual inventors, but by teams of scientists and engineers, directed towards particular goals.

This led J.J. Thomson to conclude that inventions boards were initially established more for their political effect than for the value they might have in encouraging technical innovation. Writing of the BIR (although his argument applies equally well to the other inventions boards) he observed:

> "Though very little that was important for the prosecution of the war came out of this cloud of inventions, its political effect was very considerable. Every invention sent in was examined by experts: no one could say that he had sent in an important invention of which no notice was taken. If there had not been the BIR, many would have written to the newspapers, and created the impression that the government were too casual about the war."[54]

Indeed, Balfour's Cabinet memorandum which first outlines definite proposals for an inventions board identified public concern as a reason for creating such a body (although he claimed to attach "no great value to public sentiment on such a subject").[55] Thomson's assertions are undoubtedly correct: in dispelling public concern about the need to organize science and to counter German war technology, the inventions boards were effective.

Yet a fundamental conceptual flaw underlay the thinking behind such public demands: viz: the Victorian assumption that science and invention are one and the same, and that academic scientists are therefore capable of producing war-winning technology from public inventions suggestions. Science is systematic and formulated knowledge which depends upon abstract, theoretical constructs; invention, on the other hand, is often a matter of chance.[56] The failure of all concerned to recognize this distinction led to the early frustration, and in some cases disillusionment, of the scientists with their work on the inventions boards. The simple screening task which these eminent scientists were performing was not, in most cases, beyond the ability of any competent engineer. It achieved very little, and only served to reinforce the initial belief, commonly held among the Services, that these people had little to offer.

More promising were the research projects eventually devised by the scientists themselves, which required them to approach the Services in order to learn about the nature of particular military problems to which scientific solutions might be found. Although, at first, the military showed little interest in such projects, by the Summer of 1916 they could no longer afford to be dismissive. In that year, contemporary technology began to have an increasing impact on the conduct of the war. It was the year in which the tank was first used, in which the more accurate gas shells replaced cylinders, and in which aircraft designed to fulfil more specific roles were being produced. Moreover, scientists were at last able to demonstrate the practical fruits of their early labour (e.g. anti-aircraft and anti-submarine trials) and were increasingly being called upon to provide sophisticated countermeasures against new enemy weaponry.[57] Although few of these projects were developed in time to affect the conduct of the Great War, a number of scientists who worked for the inventions boards and survived to witness the next war believed that they had laid the foundations for the way in which science was to be used in the Second World War.[58] Thus, ironically, the key contribution of the inventions boards was not in the production of war-winning gadgets, but in fostering a closer collaboration between scientists and the military, which paved the way for the continuing involvement of civilian scientists in the administration of military science.

Acknowledgements

I would like to thank Professor R.M. MacLeod and Dr. S.B. Sinclair for their support throughout my research; Dr. L.F. Haber for giving so generously of his time and ideas; Professor D.K. Hill for allowing me to use the A.V. Hill Papers and the Master, Fellows and Scholars of Churchill College, Cambridge, for permission to use their archives. My warmest thanks are extended to Peter Liddle, without whom this paper would never have been written.

Notes

1. There is no shortage of accounts both of the general lack of unpreparedness for war among the belligerents, nor the acute deficiencies of Britain. For the general context see, e.g., R.J.Q. Adams, *Arms and the Wizard* (Cassell, London 1978), 2; B.H. Liddell Hart, *History of the First World War* (Faber & Faber, London 1930), *passim*; and L.F. Haber, *The Chemical Industry 1900–1930*, (Clarendon Press, Oxford 1971), chapts. 7 & 8. For a discussion of the more specific problems faced by Britain see, e.g., David Lloyd George, *War Memoirs*, (Odhams Press, London 1933), Vol. 2, chapt. 19; A. Marwick, *The Deluge: British Society and the First World War*, (Macmillan, London 1965), chapt. 7; H.

& S. Rose, *Science & Society*, (Penguin Harmondsworth, 1969), chapts. 2 & 3; R. & K. MacLeod, "War and Economic Development: Government and the Optical Industry in Britain, 1914–18", in J.M. Winter (ed.), *War and Economic Development*, (Cambridge University Press, Cambridge 1975), 165–203; and I. Varcoe, "Scientists, Government and Organised Research in Great Britain 1914–16: The Early History of the D.S.I.R.", *Minerva*, (1970), Vol. 8, 192–216.

2. See E. Ashby and M. Anderson, *Portrait of Haldane at Work on Education*, (Macmillan, London 1974); D. Sommer, *Haldane of Cloan, His Life and Times*, (George Allen & Unwin, London 1960); H. & S. Rose, *op. cit.*; and D.S.L. Cardwell, *The Organisation of Science in England*, (Heinemann, London 1957), Revised ed., 1972, 223–5.

3. Throughout this paper a distinction is made between "civilian science" and "military science". For the purpose of this study it is assumed that science *per se* is a particular objective body of systematic and formulated knowledge. "Military science" is the application of pure science to military ends; "civilian science" the application of "pure" science to civilian ends. Thus, e.g., the physics of sound transmission in water ("pure" science) becomes military science when applied to anti-submarine detection (i.e. when producing military technology), and becomes civilian science when used to devise means for detecting shoals of fish. (For a note on "invention" see n. 56.)

4. *J.J. Thomson* (1856–1940), educated Owens College and Trinity College, Cambridge; second wrangler and Smith's prizeman in the mathematical tripos, 1880; succeeded Lord Rayleigh as Professor of Experimental Physics at the Cavendish Laboratory, 1884; FRS, 1884; PRS, 1915–20.

    Sir Ernest Rutherford (1871–1937), educated Canterbury College, N.Z., and Cavendish Laboratory, Cambridge; MacDonald Professor of Physics, McGill University, Montreal, 1898; FRS, 1903; Professor of Mathematical Physics, Manchester University, 1907; announced nuclear theory of the atom, 1911; succeeded in splitting the atom for the first time, 1918.

    Sir Oliver Lodge (1851–1940), educated University College, London; Professor of Physics, University College, Liverpool, 1881; FRS, 1887; first Principal of Birmingham University, 1900–1919; President of the Society for Psychical Research, 1901–04, President of the British Association, 1913.

    H. Darwin (1851–1928), civil engineer; 5th son of Charles Darwin; educated Trinity College, Cambridge; established Cambridge Scientific Instrument Company, 1885; FRS, 1903; adviser on all questions relating to instruments for Advisory Committee on Aeronautics, formed 1909.

    R.T. Glazebrook (1854–1935), educated Dulwich College, and Trinity College, Cambridge; FRS, 1882; assistant director of Cavendish Laboratory, 1891; Senior Bursar, Trinity College, 1895; first Director of National Physical Laboratory, 1899; member of Advisory Committee on Aeronautics, 1909.

5. The Advisory Committee on Aeronautics was created to supervise the aeronautical investigations of the National Physical Laboratory, and to provide general advice on scientific problems arising in connection with the work of the Admiralty and the War Office in aerial construction and navigation. It comprised mainly civilian scientific advisers and was the brainchild of Lord Haldane, then Secretary of State for War.

6. Both the Royal Society and the Chemical Society established independent advisory committees of civilian scientists to "organize assistance to the Government in conducting or suggesting scientific investigation in relation to the war". See D. Lloyd George, *op. cit.*, (n.1), Vol. 2, 617.

7. See R.W. Reid, *Tongues of Conscience*, (Constable, London 1969), chapt. 4.

8. A.D. Cruickshank, *Government, Industry, and Scientific Research: Twenty Years of the Department of Scientific and Industrial Research – 1915–35*, B. Litt. thesis, Wadham College, Oxford, 1979, 19.

9. J.L. Heilbron, *H.G.J. Moseley: The Life and Letters of an English Physicist 1887–1915*, (University of California Press, Berkley 1974), 124–5; and R.W. Reid, *op cit.*, (n.7), 38–9.

10. PRO MUN 7/326, *Memorandum on the formation of a record of a special service record of men scientifically trained* (sic), by Prof. A. Gray, 1917.

11. *The Times*, correspondence columns, 11 June 1915.

12. *The Naval Diaries of Admiral Philip Dumas*, Peter H. Liddle's "1914–18 Archives", housed at Sunderland Polytechnic.

13. PRO ADM 116/1430, Secretary, Admiralty, to Lord Fisher, 14 September 1915. See also R.M. MacLeod and E.K. Andrews, "Scientific Advice in the War at Sea 1915–1917: the Board of Inventions and Research", *Journal of Contemporary History*, Vol. 6, no. 2 (1971), 7.

14. For a detailed history of the MID see M. Pattison, *The Munitions Inventions Department: A Case Study in the State Management of Military Science, 1915–1919*, unpublished Ph.D. thesis, Teesside Polytechnic, 1981.

15. PRO MUN 5/357/700/1, *Formation and Organisation of the Munitions Inventions Department.*

16. *Daily Telegraph*, July 29 1915. A cutting is included in PRO MUN 5/43/263/8/7. A slightly abridged version of the speech is published in D. Lloyd George, *op. cit.*, (n.1) Vol. 2, 621.

17. PRO ADM 116/1601 *Southern Holland Report. 1917.*

18. PRO ADM 116/1601, *BIR Papers (Misc.)*

19. Admiral Sir R.H.S. Bacon, *From 1900 Onward*, (Hodder & Stoughton, 1929), 300.

20. PRO MUN 5/357/700/1, Annexure 6, *Munitions Inventions Department: Committees of the Advisory panel.*

21. PRO MUN 7/305, *Russell Clarke's Heat Ray.*

22. *Ibid.*, Memorandum by Goold Adams, 8 December 1917.

23. *Ibid.*, letter from Swinburne to Goold Adams, 10 January 1918.

24. *The Times*, 7 September 1915, "War Inventions", 5.

25. *The New Statesman*, correspondence, 11 September 1915, 359.

26. *Ibid.*, 9 October 1915, "Inventions and the War", 8.

27. *The Ministry of Munitions Journal*, February 1917, "Notes on the Investigation of Inventions", 68.

28. PRO MUN 7/332, *Official Secrecy re. Inventors*, letter from Ministry of Munitions to Major Anson (MI5), 9 December 1918.

29. PRO AVIA 8/9, *Report of the Conference called to consider various questions in connection with Patents*, April 1918.

30. PRO MUN 5/118/700/19, *Memorandum re. the Transmission of Inventions by British Inventors to the U.S. Government without loss of Patent Rights in the United States*, 1918.

31. See, e.g., W. de C. Prideaux, "Seven Years Effort", lecture to the Wessex Branch of the British Dental Association, 1st July 1922, (privately printed), temporary deposit, National Science Museum.

32. This was particularly true of anti-gas research; e.g., J.B.S. Haldane, working with a small team at the Central Laboratory, G.H.Q. France, devised a respirator for protection against chlorine gas attacks within a fortnight of the first such attack. See R. Clark, *J.B.S., The Life and Work of J.B.S. Haldane*, (Quality Book Club, London 1968), 39–40; and interview between L.F. Haber and Lieut.-Col. L.J. Barley, March 1972, Imperial War Museum.

33. Among these were tests with a high pressure water cannon which, it was hoped, would destroy the German trenches. See Lloyd George Papers, D/10/3/3, D/10/3/18, D/10/3/21, and D/10/3/22, House of Lords Record Office.

34. This was particularly true of the work of the MID's Nitrogen Products Committee. See, e.g., W.J. Reader, *Imperial Chemical Industries, A History*, (Oxford University Press, Oxford 1970), Vol. 1, 347–59; V.E. Parke, *Billingham, The First Ten Years*, (ICI, 1957), chaps. 1 & 2; and L.F. Haber, *op. cit* (n.1), 207–8 & 225.

35. PRO AIR 1/2423/305/18/38, Minutes of the third general meeting of the Air Inventions Committee, 19 December 1917.

36. *Ibid.*, "A plea for more rapid adoption of New Inventions during the War", memorandum by H. Darwin, 16 April 1918.

37. Out of a total of 19,000 trench howitzers produced during the war, 11,500 were Stokes mortars, and throughout 1917 and 1918 the Stokes mortar was the only form of light trench howitzer to be manufactured. See PRO MUN 5/1610/5, *Outline History of the Stokes Gun and Shell*, and D. Lloyd George, *op.cit.* (n.1), Vol. 2, 620.

38. R.M. MacLeod & E.K. Andrews, *op.cit.* (n.13), 15–18.

39. J.J. Thomson, *Recollections and Reflections*, (Bell & Sons, London 1936), 213.

40. G. Hartcup, *The Challenge of War*, (David & Charles, Newton Abbot 1970), 21.

41. By 1916 work had begun on a single diaphragm directional hydrophone by which, under

ideal conditions, it was possible to detect a submarine at a range of four miles. Later that year work also began on a Portable Directional Hydrophone, by which it was possible to determine not only the range, but also the direction of sound under water. See R.M. MacLeod & E.K. Andrews, *op. cit.* (n.13), 20–21.

42. G.M. Caroe, *William Henry Bragg: 1862–1942, Man and Scientist*, (Cambridge University Press, Cambridge 1978), 86.

43. R.M. MacLeod & E.K. Andrews, *op. cit.* (n.13), 21.

44. *Ibid.*

45. *Ibid.*, 21–22.

46. PRO CAB 21/7, *The BIR and the Submarine Menace*, 29 March 1917.

47. ADM 218/4, *From BIR to RNSS*, A.B. Wood.

48. These included the development of the Fish Hydrophone, which could be towed astern of vessels, and the application of sound-ranging techniques to the detection of underwater minefields from onshore hydrophone stations.

49. A.V. Hill Papers, AVHL 1/37, Churchill College Archives, Cambridge.

50. *Ibid.*

51. In particular the group developed electrical transmission for height- and range-finders, and improved a height-finder devised by W. Hartree, a Cambridge mathematics graduate working with the Section, which was later produced by Pye in Cambridge and used in France from the Summer of 1917.

52. For the early development of inventions committees see O.F.G. Hogg, *The Royal Arsenal, its background, origin and subsequent history*, (Oxford University Press, London 1963), Vol. 2, 1432–39. During the Second World War only one inventions committee was established, the Advisory Committee on Scientific and Technical Development, which formed part of the Ministry of Supply and was concerned primarily with engineering and purely technological research. Much of the inventions work of this committee was, in fact, left to only one man: Prof. E.N. da Costa Andrade; see R.W. Clark, *The Rise of the Boffins*, (Phoenix House, London 1962), 80–85.

53. *The New Statesman*, 9 October 1915, "Inventions and the War", 8.

54. J.J. Thomson, *op. cit.* (n.39).

55. PRO CAB 37/130/322, Cabinet memorandum by Balfour, June 1915.

56. A useful distinction between science, technology, and invention is supplied by J.K. Gusewelle in his account of the BIR: "Science and the Admiralty During World War 1: The Case of the BIR", in *Naval Warfare in the Twentieth Century*, G. Jordan (ed.) (Croom Helm, London 1977), 105–17. "The scientist is concerned with abstract relationships, theoretical constructs, mathematical frames of reference, generality. This is not to say that he is indifferent to utility, but only to suggest that his orientation is not toward immediate application of principles to devices. . . . The technologist, on the other hand, uses insights, principles, theories, relationships, developed by science for the specific purpose of direct and immediate use. He may well be ignorant of the theory behind the application. Invention, by contrast, is frequently a matter of pure chance and mechanical gadgets may be developed by skilful tinkerers who gave little or no knowledge of either science or applied technology."

57. This was true not only of anti-submarine and anti-aircraft research, but also particularly true of gas warfare in which it was important for each side to establish a technical lead. See L.F. Haber, *The Poisonous Cloud*, (forthcoming, Oxford University Press).

58. See J.G. Crowther, *Fifty Years with Science*, (Barrie & Jenkins, London 1970); R.W. Clark, *op. cit.* (n.52), 32; and A.V. Hill's comments to C.P. Snow (author's interview with C.P. Snow, 10/11/1978).

8

The Dardanelles Gallipoli Campaign: Concept and Execution

PETER LIDDLE

In essence this campaign became a Combined Operation designed to capture the Gallipoli Peninsula in 1915 in order to facilitate the forcing of the Dardanelles and the passage of an Anglo-French naval force into the Sea of Marmora and so to Constantinople and the Bosphorus. The presence of the naval squadron at the Golden Horn, it was hoped, would stimulate revolutionary forces in Turkey, the Government would fall, the Ottoman Empire would be withdrawn from the War and then, so some leading spirits in the British War Council judged, a succession of significant military, strategic and political consequences would ensue.

Lord Kitchener, Secretary of State for War is reported in the War Council of 8 January 1915 to have averred:

> "It would re-establish communication with Russia, settle the Near Eastern Question, draw in Greece and perhaps Bulgaria and release wheat and shipping now locked up in the Black Sea."[1]

Lieutenant Colonel Hankey, Secretary to the War Council recorded his own view:"It would give us the Danube as a line of communication for an army penetrating into the heart of Austria and bring our seapower to bear in the middle of Europe."[2]

There was more to this splendid vision: a new security would reduce concern and defence cost commitment for India, Suez, and British oil interests in the Persian Gulf, influence would be exerted upon Italy to join the Entente and the Germans would be forced to drain their men and material from the Western Front to help their Austrian ally, confronted by her newly sustained enemy Russia, as well as by British naval power. An Anglo-French breakthrough on the Western Front would now be possible using the troops, artillery and ammunition no longer needed in the Near and Middle East, indeed nothing less was being forecast than the real prospect of a quicker end to the war.

Now with this in mind, anyone who continues to examine the record of War Council deliberations may well ask how it was that three weeks after the landing of the first troops on the Gallipoli Peninsula on 25 April, Lloyd George, the Chancellor of the Exchequer, was expressing not merely his own but shared War Council misgivings stating that:

> "There was no doubt that we had underestimated the resisting power of the enemy at the Dardanelles – personally he felt very doubtful whether the army could force the position."[3]

At the same meeting of 14 May Lord Haldane was noted as accepting that withdrawal was unthinkable, rapid advance impossible and therefore he counselled something far removed from the glorious January prospect: "To adopt a policy similar to but rather better than a state of siege – as it would result in holding the Turks there, and a British attack had already relieved the pressure on the Russians at the Caucasus."[4]

As further evidence of disillusionment before failure was openly acknowledged, we actually have a book published during the campaign: *What of the Dardanelles?* The author, Granville Fortescue, lambasted the "lack of foresight shown by the mind that conceived the plan of smashing a channel through to the Black Sea."[5]

What was wrong or what had gone wrong? There were some who even in the recent aftermath of defeat continued to defend the idea. H.W. Nevinson, who after all had been there in 1915, expressed his view in the 1918 publication *The Dardanelles Campaign* that it was: "a strategic conception surpassing others in promise".[6] With far more time for reflection, Major-General J.F.C. Fuller in his *Decisive Battles* though qualifying his point, still considered that as a "problem of pure strategy it was brilliant."[7] Much more recently still, the distinguished American historian, A.J. Marder, addressing himself more to the practical problem of carrying out the venture, considered that the navy might well have achieved success by perseverence in April with mine-sweeping by newly available Beagle class destroyers. The stakes, considered Marder, would have justified the effort and losses involved.[8]

It may be judged rash to question the assessment of men whose work is quite properly honoured but it still seems to the author of this article that too readily some ignore or diminish the significance of a point stressed in the published report of the Dardanelles Commission of Enquiry. The signatories of the report considered that fundamental in all consideration should have been an indissoluble link between the concept and the practical means of its fulfilment.[9]

Does it make sense for the historians to evaluate a wartime idea of grand strategy without consideration of whether the means existed to bring it to fruition? Troops, ships, ammunition, time, intelligence, suitability of location, communications, logistics, political factors are, in their degree of adequacy, going to be either the proper foundations of the whole edifice or the deficient plans and building materials which will ruin all at some stage.

It may be proper for the philosopher to consider ideas completely at a remove from their application but there is a particular reason why the Gallipoli historian should not be tempted into such speculation and that is because he has no fixed concept for evaluation. There is no pinned butterfly awaiting dissection, the nature of the so-called Gallipoli concept was never static but constantly and bewilderingly in a state of change during those vital months of January, February and March 1915. The record of this state of change can be examined in Colonel Hankey's notes of the War Council meetings and Hankey's own Boxing Day Memorandum, but before reference is made to this record, let us keep in mind the inexorable, undeniable logic of the war as it was and yes perhaps as it had to be, with a grim primacy of the Western Front: of Neuve Chapelle in March, of the German offensive of 2nd Ypres in April and May and of allied offensives in May, to say nothing of the September Battle of Loos. Both World Wars seem to provide lessons of the need to focus on soundly assessed priorities but perhaps it is an ironic tendency of the engine of war to set up eccentric motion which achieves an independence of its own so that the planning and conduct of war on geographically separate fronts becomes cocooned in airtight or idea-tight isolation, cared for by men with no shared realistic vision, no agreed understanding of strategic priorities.

It was on 25 November 1914 that the War Council first discussed the possibilities of the Dardanelles. Churchill, First Lord of the Admiralty, distanced by 3 years from his Cabinet Memorandum declaring the impossibility of forcing the Dardanelles, suggested that the ideal method of defending Egypt was by an attack on the Gallipoli Peninsula. If successful this would give the allies control of the Dardanelles and terms could then be dictated at Constantinople. "This however was a very difficult operation requiring a large force."[10] The "large force" was not defined but by the previous wording and the geographically extended area it can be justifiably presumed that ships and soldiers would be involved.

A month later and with the Western Front becoming trench and breastwork deadlocked, Hankey, man of influence as well as of secrets, committed to paper his thoughts on the alternatives to a war of attrition.

"Germany can perhaps be struck most effectively and with the most lasting results on the peace of the World through her allies and particularly through Turkey. . . . If Bulgaria guaranteed by the active participation of the three Great Powers could be induced to cooperate, there ought to be no insuperable obstacle to the occupation of Constantinople, the Dardanelles and the Bosphorus. . . . It is presumed that in a few months time we could without endangering the position in France, devote three Army Corps to a campaign in Turkey, though sea transport might prove a difficulty. This force in conjunction with Greece and Bulgaria ought to be sufficient to capture Constantinople."[11]

Hankey's thoughts, it may be noted, presume the involvement of Russia,

Greece and Bulgaria as well as France, approximately 150,000 British troops, unspecified sea transport and supplementary naval support.

A few days later on 2 January there came to the Government the famous Russian request for help in launching some diversionary attack to relieve them of Turkish pressure in the Caucasus. Churchill seized the opportunity to put forward a "practicable" proposal which in using exclusively naval resources appeared attractively economical. His signal to the Admiral in Command of the Eastern Mediterranean Squadron and Sir Sackville Carden's response are well known. A naval operation of the sort Churchill had in mind was judged to be feasible but would take time and would incur losses.

Kitchener was cautiously optimistic at the 8 January War Council. "150,000 would be sufficient for the capture of the Dardanelles but he reserved his final opinion until a closer study had been made."[12]

Churchill's enthusiasm and power of persuasion seemed to preclude the need and indeed the time for such an assessment. On 13 January he confidently reported the Admiralty as studying the question and believed that a plan could be made for systematically reducing all the forts within a few weeks. Once the forts were reduced the minefields would be cleared and the fleet would proceed up to Constantinople and destroy the Goeben."[13] Somewhat unfortunately he went on to affirm that they would have nothing to fear from field guns or rifles which would be merely an inconvenience.

The conclusions reached at that meeting of 13 January were momentous: "The Admiralty should prepare for a naval expedition in February to bombard and take the Gallipoli Peninsula with Constantinople as its objective."[14] This was of course a complete reversal of what had previously been considered necessary for success. The combined ingredients of collective depression over the Western Front, the economy of means deemed necessary to achieve success, the exotic fruits to be anticipated from that success, all presented by the 1st Lord's personal magnetism, produced a simple unsophisticated Anglo Saxon recipe for success somewhat surprisingly accepted by French political chefs.

From the earliest days thereafter, Churchill sought to expand the plan but other members of the Council expressed their qualifications. Kitchener curiously commented that a merit of the plan was that if satisfactory progress were not made, the attack could be broken off. At the same 28 January War Council, Hankey recorded Fisher's response to Churchill's search for a general declaration of commitment to the Dardanelles as a major priority that: "he had understood that this question would not be raised today. The P.M. was well aware of his views in regard to it." These views were not stated officially and whether or not the Admiralty cleaning ladies were to have known them, the official silent sulkiness of Sir John

Fisher's disapproval was as damaging to the need for full evaluation as it must have been embarrassing to the 1st Lord.

On 9 February, Kitchener promised the assistance of the Army at a later stage if it were required and anyone subsequently examining the evolution of the campaign is in a position to observe a further stage in the development of an idea, the economy of which is being shed even while in its original form it is being put into practice for, on 19 February, the naval bombardment began. Three days earlier the War Council had decided to approve the sending of the 29th Division, a Regular Army Division, to Lemnos, an island the main harbour of which was just over sixty miles west of the entrance to the Dardanelles. The War Council also approved that the Admiralty should build: "Special transports and lighters for the conveyance and landing of a force of 50,000 men at any point where they may be required."[15]

On the very day of the bombardment, the War Council was informed that with the failure of the Turkish attack on the Suez Canal, the 39,000 Australian and New Zealand troops in Egypt were to be substituted for the 29th Division as they were already on the spot and available to support a naval attack on the Dardanelles. The 29th Division would be held in readiness to be sent later if required. Furthermore the Royal Naval Division was being sent out.

Despite this clear evidence of a general realization that troops would be needed, the naval shelling was not held up for such troops to be assembled and the necessary plans made for a combined operation yet it was Churchill who warned his colleagues that: "We should never forgive ourselves if this promising operation failed owing to insufficient military support at the critical moment."[16] It was as if the small print clauses were now being read out aloud.

On 24 February Kitchener asked Churchill directly if he were now contemplating a land attack. Churchill replied that this was not the case: "but it was quite conceivable that the naval attack might be temporarily held up by mines and some local military operation required."[17] When challenged by Kitchener as to what he was going to do with the large military forces assembling in the Eastern Mediterranean, Churchill's range of possibilities, five in all, drew sarcasm from Lloyd George and a further searching enquiry from Kitchener. The First Lord took refuge in a statement that: "That troops would be required to support our diplomacy."[18]

The debate was renewed at a Council on 26 February. Churchill now claimed that: "if a disaster occurred in Turkey owing to insufficiency of troops he must disclaim all responsibility".[19] His efforts to enlarge the original January proposal were not over. On 3 March he advocated the use of a Russian Army Corps: "With three divisions from Greece, a French

Division and our own troops from Egypt we should dispose of 120,000 to 140,000 men."[20]

In this discussion of expanding the means towards achieving the original end, a touch of unintended humour rewards those who examine the record. Kitchener considered that it would be a good plan to use aeroplanes to drop leaflets in the area announcing that: "we were coming as the ancient friend of the Turk".[21] As we know of the RNAS Commander Samson's aversion to dropping leaflets and that it led to his compromise of dropping bombs on the gatherers of the paper harvest, we may legitimately doubt the effectiveness of both the theory and the practice of this form of persuasion.

On 18 March, without Russian, Bulgarian, Greek, French or even British troop support, the Anglo French naval force entered the Narrows for a close range bombardment of the inner forts. It was of course designed to allow unharassed mine-sweeping by the mainly North Sea trawlers which, under heavy shell fire, had been slowly butting their way against the swift outward-flowing current. The day's action resulted in the loss to mines of two old British battleships, one French and severe damage to others.

On 19 March the War Council was informed of these losses and the fact that the newly appointed Commander of the Mediterranean Expeditionary Force, Sir Ian Hamilton, had reported after his reconnaissance that: "all the arrangements for defence (of the Peninsula) seem to have been made with German thoroughness".[22]

The conclusion reached by that War Council Meeting was that the naval Commander, Vice-Admiral J.M. de Robeck, could: "continue the operations against the Dardanelles if he thought fit."[23] It was further stated by Lord Kitchener that the War Office had insufficient information to form a detailed scheme of disembarkation. Clearly the Council was now anticipating a navy-supported army landing the responsibility for which would fall upon the two force commanders on the spot.

March 18 with its losses had been followed by weather conditions considered unsuitable for resumption of the naval operations and on 22 March, the Commanders, in conference aboard the new battleship *Queen Elizabeth*, had come to a conclusion which formulated more precisely that which seemed implied by the War Council deliberations. Staffwork now began the race against time swiftly to prepare detailed, effective plans. The Turks, warned by damaging demonstration shelling as early as November 1914, rewarned in February 1915 and now incontestably in March, were to use well in defensive preparations their remaining five weeks of grace.

Taking a final look at the War Council record of deliberations before the Gallipoli landings were actually attempted, there is revealed a further grim irony in Churchill's 6 April retort to Hankey's anxiety about getting the troops ashore against opposition: he (that is Churchill) "anticipated no difficulty in effecting a landing".[24]

Such is the pedigree of the Gallipoli concept and as such surely it is powerful evidence against those who would separate this particular concept from its plans of execution. It is difficult to listen in sympathetic accord to those who would put all the blame for the Dardanelles Gallipoli failure on the Commanders charged with carrying out operations the background to which had changed like a tidal shoreline during a day at the beach. Perhaps the simile is insufficiently strong as irreversible changes had taken place with the tide, notably the gift of time to the Turks and the surrender of all hope of preserving the assailant's most precious commodity, surprise.

The pursuit of hypotheses not infrequently involves historians in lengthy fruitless verbal safaris with no real likelihood of an acceptable game bag at the end. To the reasonable enquiry as to whether more perseverance by the Navy in March and April might have led to success after all, it is as reasonable to respond that some of the factors required to sustain such a thesis were also unknown at the time, weather conditions, the exhaustion of Turkish ammunition supplies and the degree of revolutionary sentiment in Constantinople. It is furthermore not easy to dispose, even theoretically, with the danger of the mines, the potential menace of the Sea of Marmora and the Goeben and Breslau. How does one judge the certainty of holding a necessary sufficiency of British ammunition, oil, coal, fresh water and food supplies in the event of prolonged naval hostilities. It might be added that these factors still obtain when considering a delay until the end of the second week in April, when faster mine-sweeping destroyers were available. As for a combined operation planned as such from the start and with no warning preparatory bombardment, when could it have been launched with adequate military intelligence, planning, troops, artillery, ammunition, landing-craft, medical arrangements, supply and support facilities and what would have been adequacy in any of these factors? Again we are in the realm of conjecture.

Mindful of the foregoing, it is still proper to examine Sir Ian Hamilton's conduct of the military operations. To do so it is necessary first to have an idea of what he attempted, what was achieved and what was done with the frustrated effort to steer it clear of overwhelming disaster.

On 25 April 1915 Hamilton landed his regular troops, the 29th Division, at five separate beaches around the variable cliff-backed beaches at Cape Helles, the tip of the Peninsula. Across the Narrows on the Asiatic shore, a diversionary assault at Kum Kale by French troops was designed to prevent the sending of Turkish reinforcements to the defence of the Peninsula. It may be added here that the French mounted a feint landing operation at Besika Bay a little more than ten miles south of Kum Kale.

The Australian and New Zealand Army Corps was to be landed about nine miles further north along the coast from the most northerly of the Cape Helles landings. Coming ashore just north of the prominent Gaba Tepe headland, they would strike across the Peninsula to command the high ground inland and then the Dardanelles-shore village of Maidos. This would cut the Turks at Cape Helles from their land communications with the head of the Peninsula and Constantinople.

North again at a spot which seemed to invite attack by reason of the narrowness of the Peninsula, but which had significant disadvantages from an attacker's point of view, men from the Royal Naval Division were to give the appearance of being about to effect a landing – again with a view to drawing Turkish forces to this area.

The beachheads were in all cases secured by regimental officer and NCO leadership, the valour of all concerned and of course with the support of the Navy. "Y" beach at Helles was evacuated and has left a special legend of what might have ensued if swift reinforcement and a determined push inland were to have been made to take the village of Krithia and the crown of Achi Baba, the single dominant hill in the area.

Firmly resisting the temptation to describe landings in detail worthy of their imperishable niche in human endeavour, two exceptions in the form of personal testimony will be made, each chosen because the evidence has a wider significance than in describing merely one man's experience.

First for the Anzac landing: the troops were landed by naval error a mile further north than had been intended and were in consequence against a lunar landscape of dry gullies, washaways, ridges and precipices. It was hopeless terrain for co-ordinated, speedy progress towards any clearly-defined visible objective but it provided country which befriended neither attacker nor defender to the other's disadvantage if they were both to chose to stay put.

The vital objective was to reach and secure the heights of the third ridge inland as it commanded both sides of the Peninsula and gave a vision of the Dardanelles in their shimmering majesty and strategic significance. A Turkish Colonel wrote to his father twelve days after the landings: "For three or four days what anxieties were endured God alone knows. All actions developed upon myself . . . above Ari Burnu there is a fairly high hill called Koja Chemen Dagh that completely overlooks the Straits. The enemy's intention was to seize this hill suddenly, but on my timely insistence, the force held in this neighbourhood arrived in time to occupy the hill before the enemy and to force the latter into a steep very rough and rather narrow ravine between the hill and the sea. Although three attacks were made to throw the enemy into the sea, they were foiled again by naval and machine-gun fire and by the ruggedness of the land and the enemy's defences. We suffered great losses but those of the enemy were even greater and he had not achieved his purpose. That he has a few troops on land is of no importance. He can land troops wherever he likes but his main purpose is to seize the Straits and for that great self sacrifice is required. Of this there is however no sign for the morale of his troops has sunk so low as to be beyond description as we can see for ourselves and learn from prisoners.

These fellows will eventually have to embark their troops at Ari Burnu and remove them one of these nights. They cannot advance one step further but it will be a bit harder to chase them from Seddul Bahr."

It is scarcely surprising that a Colonel with such prescience was sure-footedly on the rungs of a military promotion ladder which would lead him to the very top of his profession.[25]

For Seddul Bahr or Cape Helles the exception is that of the letter of a young naval officer writing a fortnight after the landing: "The Turks and Huns having had plenty of time to prepare, have taken full advantage of all the natural advantage of their hilly country and have fairly dug themselves in: also they seem to have an enormous number of guns in concealed gullies so its going to be some job to shift them. I can assure you that all of us here are pretty fed up with the breezy manner in which a lot of newspaper rags have been spouting about getting to Constantinople etc., as if it were a mere walk-over."[26]

The Turkish Colonel and the Royal Naval Officer were on the same mark: what had been won was only dubiously worth the effort. At Anzac and Cape Helles the Turks held commanding positions overlooking the invaders. In both sectors dissimilar though they were in terrain, the men dug in. Frontal attacks proved ruinously costly without discrimination as attack was followed by counter-attack.

Allied reinforcements were never on a scale-tipping size but in August a new plan was worked out by Hamilton and it offered some prospect of success. Diversionary attacks at Helles and on the right at Anzac were to coincide with an ambitious three column night march up unreconnoitred gullies on a left flank approach to Anzac's vital third ridge, the Sari Bair ridge. There was also to be a new landing by Kitchener Army divisions just north of Anzac at Suvla Bay.

From the night of 6 August the geographically separated but concep-tually linked assaults were launched. There followed three critical days of grimly heroic sacrifice in the diversionary attacks, particularly at Lone Pine and the Nek at Anzac, of over-demanding physical strain, intense stress of prolonged battle and confusion for those attempting the Sari Bair heights and most bewilderingly of all a lack of vigorous leadership worsened by a shortage of water for those troops landed at Suvla. Here they saw an open scorched plain before them towards the amphitheatre of the surrounding ridge of hills, hills which each day seemed to serve more effectively as natural overlooking emplacements for more Turkish artillery and troops. The British troops were urged forward into determined assault too late.

The rest is anticlimax with the trappings of tragedy. Trench warfare, dysentery and in late November, floods, snow and frostbite were stoically endured before the allies wrought some unlikely success out of so consider-able a failure. A brilliantly planned evacuation was carried out in two stages, skilfully at every level and by 9 January all the troops were off the Peninsula none having been lost in the final hazardous exercise of stealing away under the very eyes of the Turk.

It has been claimed that the Turkish army had been critically weakened by its stubborn defence of the Peninsula. This and other long-term benefits difficult to accept have been put forward too as consequences of the allied endeavour but no recitation of the nonfulfilment of the January 1915 high level hopes is needed to drive home the British humiliation – and the cost, with a total of about 45 thousand allied dead.

Churchill, the political father of the campaign, had resigned in May 1915, Hamilton, the military midwife, was sacked in October. From the very first Hamilton had too little time, too few troops, too little artillery and ammunition. His stores had been incompetently stowed so that material essentially linked was carried in different ships and resources needed first were in the deepest recesses of the holds. His troops were scattered and there was no suitable base. He had insufficient engineers and signallers, no armoured landing craft and no help from the man who should have been in loyal support despite his own responsibilities, Sir John Maxwell, Commander in Chief in Egypt.

If these were not handicaps enough he had one outdated, inaccurate map and about as little chance of launching a surprise attack as could be imagined. Hamilton's predilection for security was indeed a drawback in some respects as lower level commanders were given too little awareness of the larger scheme in which their task was an integral part, but one must have sympathy with a man whose force was so openly designated for Constantinople. With surprise virtually gone, he had to make plans for a classical *coup de main* the success of which was plainly dependent not least on keeping the Turks guessing about the location of his main thrust.

Hamilton has been accused on both general and specific charges. On the broad canvas it is argued that he lacked those qualities, difficult to define but essential to the inspiration of his force at all levels – "the magic touch" it might be termed. He certainly had the experience and the professionalism on which such an attribute had necessarily to be based but somehow the regimental officers, the NCO's and men of the Mediterranean Expeditionary Force didn't see enough of him, didn't feel his presence sufficiently for it to be a potent factor in their personal and collective endeavour.

It is perhaps reasonable to point out in extenuation that the conditions under which the war had to be conducted scarcely made this easy but the constricted geographical location and time scale perhaps make a special case. Allenby, no conspicuous success in France, fortunately found in Palestine a theatre where he could exercise the "magic touch" as did Maude in Mesopotamia. Monash, with little in the Gallipoli August offensive to commend him, did show exceptional qualities in France in

1918 and there is of course the man well described by John Terraine as "the most consistently reliable and successful British Army Commander of the First World War",[27] "Daddy" Plumer, who achieved deserved fame in that singularly unpromising campaign area of Flanders.

On more specific charges Hamilton made no decisive intervention at moments of crisis in the first days of the landing. In August too his personal intervention was delayed and by then ill-judged. These must be points of significance in assessing his execution of the task of high command. It should be remembered that he supported Admiral Thursby's sturdy unwillingness to re-embark the Anzac force on the night of their April landing when their two Divisional Commanders and the Brigade Commanders in depressed anxiety requested this. There was resolution in Hamilton's stern admonition: "dig, dig, dig until you are safe",[28] but his philosophy of Command which involved the independence of Brigade, Divisional and Corps Commanders once an operation was launched, not only denied him the opportunity of exercising potentially decisive influence but threw a great weight of responsibility on men who might not have the capacity to fulfil imaginatively a responsibility widened into virtual independence. Sadly there is no doubt that at Helles in April and at Suvla in August, the Commander-in-Chief was less than well served by some of his senior officers.

Concerning Hamilton's ignorance of the Turks and of the Peninsula itself, our sympathy rather than condemnation should be drawn in view of his surprise appointment and precipitate dispatch to the Dardanelles.

There is certainly room for criticism over the separation of Sir Ian's Administrative Staff from his small GHQ Staff leaving the latter to plan the entire landing operations. One of the most tragic results of this was the inadequate provision for the collection, reception, first treatment and evacuation of wounded. The harrowing experience of wounded awaiting attention in the first days of the landing provides grim condemnatory evidence of a serious administrative blunder for which the ultimate responsibility falls upon the Commander-in-Chief's organizational decision.

There will always be debate over Hamilton's breaking of that cardinal tactical principle, the avoidance of the dispersal of your forces. There were two diversionary shows, one separate landing intentionally to be withdrawn, a further separate two-division landing and finally five separate landings for his main division the 29th. There is however strong argument in defence of the plan from an impeccable source: the instructions given to Hamilton which specifically directed him to assist the fleet in its passage through the Narrows. Commanding Cape Helles could be said to be not merely the best way but the only way of doing this, diversionary attacks being necessary to draw Turkish reinforcements away from Cape Helles. Here the beaches were each too small to take a full division in an opposed landing but by using several adjacent beaches opportunity could be taken to force the Turk to disperse his own defence resources. In parenthetical support of this may be noted the irony of the fact that the Navy from 18 March assumed a subordinate role and neither on 25 April nor on any subsequent date except in the form of submarine effort was the Navy to force the Narrows and vigorously attempt the necessary mine clearance for a co-ordinated attack to reach the Marmora. Was it entirely Hamilton's fault that his tactical appraisal had been based on a premise, the naval fulfilment of which, lay outside his control?

25 April itself presented the Commander-in-Chief undeniably with an opportunity which he chose to ignore. Despite defective signalling he was informed that the ground inland of Y beach towards the village of Krithia nestling beneath the 700 foot brooding eminence of Achi Baba was empty of opposition on the morning of the landings. He knew of the dreadful losses being suffered at the two major landings further south, W and V beaches. He invited his 29th Division Commander, Hunter Weston to divert his reinforcements to Y beach. Hunter Weston's response makes unhappy reading today: "Admiral Wemyss and Principal Transport Officer state that to interfere with present arrangements and try to land men at Y beach would delay disembarkation."[29]

Had Hamilton overruled this negative response a prospect of success might have been earned. With Krithia and Achi Baba taken, Turkish defence of Cape Helles would have been rendered impossible. If such consequences of intervention were to be judged matters of speculation, then the fact that no intervention was made when the situation surely invited it, is still irrefutable.

Evidence on all sides shows that Hamilton was saddled with a deferential complex before Kitchener and it drastically influenced his calls for reinforcement and his reports on the true state of affairs on the Peninsula. The utility of his optimism, an attractive quality in many ways, decayed as his attitude slid out of touch with reality. Sadly he lost the respect even of those members of his small GHQ Staff upon whom he had so heavily relied. As Haig had his Charteris, Hamilton had his Braithwaite as Chief of Staff and Braithwaite contributed to the isolation of the Commander in Chief from the harshly depressing evidence of failure and potential disaster.[30]

Hamilton's August plan was imaginative but his own travails from dysentery might have warned him of the excessive physical demands he was placing upon weakened troops committed to the night-marching and climbing exertions before battle on the heights above the Anzac position. There is little doubt that his delay in intervening at Suvla on 7 August to secure a vigorous push towards the encircling heights was disastrous and when events had overtaken the opportunity and he acted, his orders made the situation worse. Hamilton had waited on the island of Imbros too long during the critical hours, waiting, always waiting for information and never being sufficiently close himself either to Suvla or Anzac to make his own appraisal and issue new or reinforced or changed orders. As Hunter Weston of the 29th Division had failed him in April, Stopford, Commander of the 9th Corps and several Brigade Commanders at Suvla and one at Anzac were to fail him in August.

On the whole the Dardanelles Commission Report did not treat Hamilton unfairly: "We are of the opinion that with the resources then available, success in the Dardanelles, if possible, was only possible upon condition that the Government concentrated their efforts upon the enterprise and limited their expenditure of men and material in the Western theatre of War. The condition was never fulfilled."

"We recognize Sir Ian Hamilton's personal gallantry and energy, his optimistic disposition and his determination to win at all costs, but it would in our opinion, have been better if he had examined the situation after the first landings in a more critical spirit, impartially weighed the probabilities of success and failure and reported his judgement as to whether or not the force should be withdrawn."[31]

It is unfair, indeed unsound, totally to deride the temptations through which the Dardanelles lured the War Council into its extraordinary gamble. An awareness of the Government's sense of strategic imprisonment and the high cost in resources and in time should temper judgement made with hindsight, but one historian, John North, seem accurately to have judged that Britain: "drifted into the Gallipoli campaign and muddled through it."[32] A Royal Naval Division sapper wrote to his parents soon after the evacuation: "I expect you are feeling fairly disgusted at home at our magnificent bunk from Gallipoli. As a matter of fact we aren't sorry to leave. I think we could have stuck it alright, though it was getting a bit warm but I suppose they thought we should never do any good by staying there."[33] It seems to the author of this article that before one begins to consider *how* they were led, it must be emphasized that the circumstances surrounding the dispatch of the Gallipoli venturers cruelly cut out any likely dividend from their being on the Peninsula at all. If this were to be true, then the greater tragedy lies not in any failure to accomplish their mission but in being sent out to attempt it in the first place.

Notes

1. Public Record Office, Cab.22/1 3623. January 8, 1915.
2. *Ibid.*
3. Public Record Office, Cab. 22/1 3623. May 14, 1915.
4. *Ibid.* Haldane had been a member of the War Council from January 7, 1915.
5. *What of the Dardanelles?* G. Fortescue. Hodder and Stoughton, London 1915 (p. 23).
6. The Dardanelles Campaign. H.W. Nevinson. Nisbet & Co. London 1918 (p. LVII).
7. *Decisive Battles* J.F.C. Fuller, Eyre and Spottiswoode, London. Vol. III published 1956 (p. 235).
8. *From the Dardanelles to Oran* A.J. Marder. O.U.P. 1974 (p. 32).

9. Public Record Office, Cab. 19/1 3623. The Final Report of the Dardanelles Commission. Part ii. Conduct of Operations. General Conclusions (i).
10. Public Record Office, Cab. 22/1 3623. November 25, 1914.
11. *The Supreme Command 1914–18.* Lord Hankey. George Allen and Unwin, London 1961, Vol. 1 p. 249.
12. Public Record Office, Cab. 22/1 3623. January 8, 1915.
13. Public Record Office, Cab. 22/1 3623. January 13, 1915.
14. *Ibid.*
15. Public Record Office, Cab. 22/1 3623. February 16, 1915.
16. Public Record Office, Cab. 22/1 3623. February 19, 1915.
17. Public Record Office, Cab. 22/1 3623. February 24, 1915.
18. *Ibid.*
19. Public Record Office, Cab. 22/1 3623. February 26, 1915.
20. Public Record Office, Cab. 22/1 3623. March 3, 1915. This total includes the projected Russian Army Corps.
21. *Ibid.*
22. Public Record Office, Cab. 22/1 3623. March 19, 1915. Without prior intimation Hamilton had been appointed on 11 March and had been immediately hurried out to the Dardanelles.
23. *Ibid.* The fact that on 10 March Kitchener had authorized the embarkation of the 29th Division from Avonmouth for the Eastern Mediterranean is a further indication that the taking of certain sensible steps had not been supported by the reasoned cancellation of others i.e. the naval attack on 18 March. With Vice-Admiral S.H. Carden having fallen ill on the eve of the 18 March bombardment, Command of the Eastern Mediterranean Squadron had fallen to Vice Admiral J.M. de Robeck.
24. Public Record Office, Cab. 22/1 3623. April 6, 1915.
25. General Fahrettin Altay: letter 7.5.15. Peter Liddle's 1914–18 Personal Experience Archives, presently held within Sunderland Polytechnic.
26. H.K.L. Shaw (H.M.S. Minerva): letter of 10.5.15. Peter Liddle's 1914–18 Personal Experience Archives, presently held within Sunderland Polytechnic.
27. The Western Front. J. Terraine published by Hutchinson, London 1964, p. 195.
28. The Official History of Australia in the War of 1914–18. Vol. 1. The Story of Anzac. C.E.W. Bean. Angus and Robertson, Sydney 1921. p. 461.
29. Official History of the War: Military Operations, Gallipoli. Vol. 1. Brig. Gen. C.F. Aspinall-Oglander. William Heinemann, London 1929. p. 205, note 2.
30. Major General W.P. Braithwaite. Chief of Staff, Mediterranean Expeditionary Force.
31. Public Record Office, Cab. 19/1 3623. The Final Report of the Dardanelles Commission Part II Conduct of Operations. General Conclusions (IX).
32. John North, *The Fading Vision.* Faber and Faber, London 1936.
33. E.F. Wettern (Spr. R.N.D., letter 15.1.16). Peter Liddle's 1914–18 Personal Experience Archives, presently held within Sunderland Polytechnic.

9

The Navy and the Naval War Considered

COLIN WHITE

As several of the papers delivered at the Sunderland Conference have confirmed, the old negative attitudes towards the conduct of the First World War are, very largely, oversimplified and, indeed, in some cases quite clearly wrong. I think that it is fair to claim that no service has suffered more from this patronizing negativism than the Royal Navy. There are no stirring phrases such as "England Expects" or "Damn the torpedoes: go ahead!" to fill the more romantic history books. Instead, the one quotation that everyone remembers is Beatty's famous remark at the height of the Battle of Jutland: "There's something wrong with our bloody ships today".

Interestingly though, it is clear that at least so far as the Navy is concerned, this negative feeling is not solely the result of the misuse by armchair theorists of their advantage of hindsight. There is plenty of evidence that it was present very strongly in 1918 – even among the victorious allies. On 21 November, in accordance with the terms of the armistice, a significant portion of the German High Seas Fleet sailed into the Firth of Forth to surrender. They were met by an armada of some 370 British ships, together with a small French squadron and the American Sixth Battle Squadron. It was a fine, sunny misty day; the British ships were all flying their huge battle ensigns and bands were playing as the crews lined the railings to see the German ships steam forlornly by. It should have been a moment of enormous triumph and, certainly, there were some cheers for the British C-ir-C, Admiral Sir David Beatty, from the allied ships. But the triumph was marred by a deep sense of disappointment. Signalman Corbyn, hard at work on the signal bridge of the Grand Fleet flagship H.M.S. *Queen Elizabeth*, heard Beatty say as the German ships hove into sight: "This is very nice: but I would give them three salvoes start for a fight."[1] And this sense of frustration that the High Seas Fleet had not been defeated in a full-scale fight was felt throughout the Grand Fleet: "... all of us," wrote Commander Ian Sanderson, "... resented it that Waterloo should precede Trafalgar and that Trafalgar should never happen at all."[2] Linked with this very understandable disappointment, was a rather unreasonable contempt for the Germans who

HF–E

had been confidently expected to put up at least a show of a fight before surrendering. Beatty's flag lieutenant, Ralph Seymour wrote: "I must confess, it was a painful and morbid sight, which was somewhat distasteful";[3] Beatty himself, in a speech to the men of the First Battlecruiser Squadron three days later called it ". . . a pitiable sight . . . a horrible sight . . . a humiliating end . . .";[4] while Hugh Martin of the *Daily News* who was watching from the battleship H.M.S. *Royal Oak* noted, "The sailors watch the phantom ships with an odd look of contempt and pity and mourning in their eyes."[5]

Why was there such enormous disappointment – so universal that it occurs again and again in the memoirs of the officers and men of the period and so powerful that it still colours our perception of this more than usually tragic war? Partly, of course, it was due to weariness. Victors and defeated alike were exhausted: emotionally as well as materially. Moreover, by 1918, the unprecedented loss of life had had plenty of time to sink home and servicemen and civilians alike had begun to realize the horrible price which had been paid. So far as the Royal Navy is concerned, however, the main key to the cause of the depression lies in Ian Sanderson's remark quoted earlier: ". . . all of us resented it . . . that Trafalgar should never happen at all".

Trafalgar and Nelson. These two names dominated the minds of sailors of all ranks during the First World War. Beatty's flag captain, Ernle Chatfield, recalled later how in 1914 Beatty "longed" for war: "We had not fought for a century: it was time we repeated the deeds of our forefathers."[6] and "Jacky" Fisher – who always thought either in biblical or Nelsonian terms – was the first of many to cast the diffident, reserved, cautious and thoroughly unglamorous Jellicoe in the unlikely role of the new Nelson. All very well. High morale is a great battle-winner and, certainly, the Navy had a quite extraordinary and sometimes overpowering confidence in its own abilities. But traditions need to be based on true facts or else they can be misleading and dangerous and, by 1914, the tradition had become so oversimplified and romanticized that it bore very little resemblance to the truth at all. For example, Nelson was portrayed – quite wrongly! – as an aggressive genius who relied for his success upon flashes of inspiration in the heat of battle and whose invariable policy had been: "Never mind manoeuvres; always go at 'em." Naval history, when it was studied at all, had become merely a string of decisive battles such as Quiberon Bay, the Saints, Camperdown and Trafalgar. Little mention was made of the numerous indecisive battles with which naval history is strewn; there was little real appreciation of the long tedious periods of waiting in between battles and, most damaging of all, there was a tendency to believe that naval battles on their own could win wars. Even the works of the great and influential American naval historian Alfred Mahan were used to support the notion that the first and over-riding object of the fleet should be the annihilation of the enemy's forces.[7] And, of course, in 1918, the enemy's fleet had not been annihilated. The North Sea Trafalgar had not happened: in fact in the only major clash between the two main fleets, the Germans had managed to inflict such heavy losses on the Grand Fleet that they had been able to claim at least a moral victory. No wonder then, that there was such disappointment in the Firth of Forth on that misty day in November 1918.

And yet, although they could not appreciate it at the time it is – as I hope to be able to show – quite clear that British seapower had triumphed; that, moreover, it had made an indispensable contribution to the eventual allied victory. My aim in this paper is to examine some of the more important aspects of that triumph; to try to distinguish where British seapower succeeded and why; and to give some idea of what it actually felt like to be a sailor in the First World War, using some personal reminiscences from the Royal Naval Museum's archives and library.

First, however, we need to give ourselves a theoretical yardstick against which to measure the events of 1914–18. We need to ask: what are the basic principles of seapower?

Now, needless to say, such a huge subject cannot be adequately covered in a few moments; nor, indeed, in a single paper. There are so many different theories – and I certainly feel neither competent nor inclined to add to their number. I should like instead to take as my yardstick the principles formulated by Sir Julian Corbett. Corbett was certainly the greatest of all our British naval theorists and he is a particularly appropriate choice for us because he was at the height of his powers in the years immediately preceding the war and, through his teaching of naval history at the Royal Naval College, Greenwich, had an influence on the younger officers of the Grand Fleet. He also wrote the first three volumes of the Official History of the Naval War. At the risk of over-simplifying his very close-knit and wide-ranging theories, I would venture to suggest that he made three important points about seapower which are particularly relevant to any study of the naval aspects of the First World War.

Firstly, he argued that there was far more to naval warfare than the seeking out and destruction of the enemy battlefleet. By his careful use of historical examples, he demonstrated that: "The dramatic moments of naval strategy have to be worked for and the first preoccupation of the fleet will almost always be to bring them about by interference with the enemy's military and diplomatic arrangements."[8] Secondly, he showed that seapower could never, by itself, obtain a complete victory and so he emphasized the need for full co-operation between the Navy and the Army and urged the importance of the study of and planning for combined operations. Thirdly – and perhaps most important of all – he distinguished between the securing of the command of the seas and the exercising of that command. These, he argued, were two entirely separate and distinct functions that required different methods and thus different types of ship.

So let us look first at the all-important question of how command of the seas was to be secured. Corbett pointed out that, in the wars of the sailing era, one of the most effective methods had proved to be close blockade. Such a strategy had two beneficial results: firstly, it denied the sea to the enemy's fleets, thus leaving them free for one's own ships to move at will. It therefore, effectively, gave one command of the seas, although that command was constantly at risk while the enemy's fleet remained undefeated. But, secondly, by denying free use of the sea to one's enemy, the strategy of close blockade often compelled a reluctant enemy to give battle and so command of the seas could be decided. Mahan – always more subtle and deep-searching in his analysis than many of his disciples realized – also laid emphasis on the importance of the blockade during the French Revolutionary and Napoleonic Wars. Indeed, it was he who coined the memorable phrase about "those far-distant, storm-beaten ships" which so vividly sums up the effect of the British blockade upon the course of those wars.

However, by 1914 it was clear to all naval experts that mines, torpedoes, and submarines – not to mention the problems of keeping a fleet of coal- or oil-burning warships constantly at sea – had rendered close blockade impossible. But here Britain's geographical position came to her rescue. She lay directly astride Germany's main lines of communication; cutting off one – the Channel – and dominating the other – the northward route past Iceland. When war with Germany began to appear likely in the early years of the century, the Royal Navy had shifted its attention from the naval ports in the Channel and had begun to concentrate its operations in the North Sea. Plans had been made for a new base at Rosyth as early as 1903. When, on 28 July 1914 the Grand Fleet sailed to its war station, it was to Scapa Flow in the Orkneys that it went and after some months of searching for greater security from U boats there it remained until the closing year of the war when Beatty, who succeeded Jellicoe as C-in-C in the autumn of 1916, brought the fleet south to the Firth of Forth. By these means, the High Seas Fleet was effectively bottled up in the North Sea and could have no direct influence upon the course of the war in other theatres. It is all too easy simply to ignore or dismiss this aspect of the war, since it was unglamorous and almost entirely unseen. But for thousands of men this was their main experience of war: admittedly not the squalor and ever-present danger of the trenches, but a different kind of endurance, the acute monotony and brain-searing boredom of constant "sweeps" or patrols in all kinds of weather. Here is a vivid description by Hilton Young, who served in Jellicoe's flagship H.M.S. *Iron Duke* as a sub-lieutenant:

"But no rattling of the buzzers ever did break the weariness of those long night watches in the starboard shelter, nor any other adventure; and how long they were and how weary words cannot tell. To sit motionless on a stool for four hours and gaze into the blustering dark!. . . . . We were then lost in a blank eternity; moments seemed ages, and the mind struggled painfully through cycle after cycle of nothingness towards a goal that receded as it was approached, until hope died that the end would ever come. The body ached with lack of movement and the brain with monotony and emptiness. To look at a watch was a most fatal thing; give it as long as one liked between looks, wait until undoubted centuries had passed since the last look, and its lying hands would taunt one with the passage of a few miserable minutes. There was nothing for it but to sit and ache and struggle with drowsiness, nodding and starting and bracing oneself to resist the heavy clouds that drifted across the brain, as a half-tipsy man braces himself against the fumes of drink."[9]

So, thanks to the endurance of the seamen of the Grand Fleet, command of the worldwide seas was almost completely in British hands. The only threat to that command in the early stages of the war were isolated German ships and squadrons and by December 1914, nearly all of these had been eliminated or rendered useless. Most notable, of course was von Spee's gallant squadron which, after its initial success at Coronel over Cradock's outmatched cruisers, was in its turn wiped out by Fisher's darlings, the battlecruisers, at the Battle of the Falklands on 8 December 1914. There were further sorties by surface raiders in 1916/17, timed to coincide with the stepping-up of the U-boat campaign, but, when measured against the achievements of the U-boats themselves, or indeed the surface raiders of the Second World War, the raiders' achievements were negligible: Britain's command of the worldwide oceans was almost total.

In the North Sea, however, command of the seas was still, technically, in dispute and remained so until that day in November 1918 – although the High Seas Fleet spent most of its time in harbour and never attained the same degree of seagoing experience achieved by the Grand Fleet. What the Germans did achieve, however, were a number of very successful pin-pricks: above all, the famous raids on the East Coast of England, which caused so much outrage at the time but which have now paled into insignificance alongside the horrors of London, Coventry, Dresden and Hiroshima. In fact the Germans' main target was not civilian lives at all: the raids were part of a deliberate strategy designed to goad Jellicoe into detaching a section of his fleet to deal with the nuisance. The plan was that any such sections would then be cut off by the main body of the High Seas Fleet (which almost invariably went to sea in support of the raids) thus, gradually, unit by unit, reducing the British superiority in numbers of dreadnoughts.

This strategy might well have worked but for an extraordinary stroke of luck that favoured the British. Very early on in the war, the Russians captured the German cypher signalbooks and separately, a set of German confidential charts of the North Sea, complete with the operational grid used to identify location, also fell into Allied hands. These, together with the wireless direction-finding techniques perfected by the naval intelligence department enabled the now-famous "Room 40" to anticipate almost every major sortie by the High Seas Fleet, especially since the Germans were not nearly so strict as the British about preserving wireless silence.[10] So it was that, whenever the Germans mounted an attack, the Grand Fleet was usually steaming to intercept it even before the last German ships had put to sea. But no system was perfect and, all too often, attempts to meet with the High Seas Fleet were frustrated by bad visibility, incomplete or misunderstood intelligence, incompetence, sheer bad luck – or a combination of all four.

A combination of all four. This of course brings us neatly to the great set-piece of the naval war: the Battle of Jutland, fought in the late afternoon and evening of 31 May 1916 and through the ensuing night. I think that it is fair to say that more has been written about Jutland than about any other battle in naval history, including Trafalgar. It was so huge in its scale; so complex in its many bewildering phases; and so infuriatingly indecisive from the point of view of both the combatants; that it has eluded all attempts that have been made to come to any firm or lasting conclusions about it. In giving some emphasis to the battle, it is not because I believe that I have any startling new answers to offer to the many riddles of Jutland. Rather, I would suggest that it deserves close study because it highlights the reasons why the war at sea was so devoid of decisive clashes between the two main fleets and also because it spotlights dramatically for us the enormous practical and theoretical problems that were faced by both sides. Sadly, time does not permit me to deal with the other main clashes of the surface war – Heligoland Bight and the battle of the Dogger Bank – nor with the frequent operations which nearly ended in battles. But Jutland, in all its infuriating elusiveness, can fittingly stand for all.

First of all, let us get out of the way the tiresome and distracting question of who won. Neither side did. It is far more helpful to see Jutland as one more in that long line of indecisive battles that I mentioned earlier, rather than to try to contort it so that it appears to be a victory for either side. I do not intend to give a blow by blow account of the battle but I think it would be helpful to have a very broad outline in mind in order to appreciate some of the points I am going to make.

Contact was first made between the opposing battlecruiser squadrons and their respective supporting light forces and, in a fierce fight, two of Beatty's battlecruisers were sunk as the Germans drew their opponents southwards into the jaws of the High Seas Fleet, which was coming up fast in support. To the Germans, it looked at this stage as if their long-nurtured plan of cutting off a portion of Jellicoe's force and overwhelming it was about to be put into successful operation. Unknown to them, however, Jellicoe's Grand Fleet was also in close proximity and, as soon as he sighted the main German battlefleet, Beatty turned to northwards and began to lead the enemy towards his Commander-in-Chief. At this point, the Grand Fleet was still in open cruising order but, almost at the last minute in a manoeuvre which has been much discussed but which is now generally agreed to have been masterly, Jellicoe deployed in line ahead, steaming almost directly south-eastwards thus neatly crossing the enemy "T", so that, as German eyewitnesses later testified, the High Seas Fleet came racing through the gloom in hot pursuit of the battlecruisers to find the whole northern horizon ringed with fire from 28 British battleships. From this seemingly inescapable trap, the German Commander-in-Chief Admiral Scheer managed brilliantly to extricate himself by a most complicated manoeuvre known as the battle turn-away – difficult enough to achieve in peacetime conditions, but a miracle of seamanship when under heavy fire amidst the smoke and confusion of battle. He then tried to break away to the east, only to find that the Grand Fleet was still in front of him so that his "T" was crossed a second time; extricated himself again by another more scrappy turnaway covered by a torpedo attack and a seemingly suicidal assault by his battlecruisers, the former of which forced Jellicoe to turn his entire fleet away from the threat, thus losing contact a second time. By now, night was falling and, thanks to the lack of British training in night fighting and bad communications (a consistent failure in the Grand Fleet throughout the battle), the High Seas Fleet managed to escape during the night of 31 May/1 June, leaving the British in possession of the field of battle.

Such then, much simplified, was the Battle of Jutland. From the British point of view, they had confirmed the verdict of their blockade and had retained their command of the seas: to use a picturesque phrase of the time, the German fleet had assaulted its jailer and returned to prison. From the German point of view, an inferior fleet, lacking a long and proud naval tradition, had taken on the world's major naval power and had quitted itself well. Above all, the Germans based their claim to victory on the fact that they had sunk three British capital ships – the battlecruisers H.M.S. *Queen Mary* and *Indefatigable* in the battlecruiser action and the battlecruiser H.M.S. *Invincible* during the main fleet action – for the loss of only one main unit, the battlecruiser S.M.S. *Lutzow*. Losses of smaller craft had been in similar proportions. But, in fact, the tally of actual sinkings gave a false picture, since the overall damage suffered by the High Seas Fleet was far more serious than that sustained by the Grand Fleet. On the morning of 1 June, Jellicoe still had 28 capital ships in a battleworthy condition; the Germans had only 10.

The British, however much they may have claimed a victory later, were very much disappointed with the result at the time. As we have seen, public and servicemen alike had expected another battle as decisive as Trafalgar and no amount of propaganda could turn Jutland into a Trafalgar. And yet, I would suggest, the battle highlights clearly for us why it was so unreasonable to expect a Trafalgar in the vastly changed conditions of 1916.

First of all, the Germans were – quite understandably – not seeking a stand-up fight, ship against ship. Bearing in mind that Jellicoe had 37 modern battleships and battlecruisers with him at Jutland to Scheer's 21, the Germans would have been foolish in the extreme to have accepted battle on these terms. When faced with superior numbers, their tactics, inevitably, were to escape as quickly and as painlessly as possible. In such circumstances, it was extremely difficult for the British to force a decisive battle. As Professor Marder has pointed out, "... if the French had retreated instead of fighting, at Trafalgar, even Nelson could not have made a battle of it".[11]

Secondly, when comparing the battles of World War One with those of the sailing era, it is important to remember that Nelson and his contemporaries were fighting with well-tried vessels and weapons, which had remained essentially unchanged for centuries and, moreover, that they were building upon an accumulation of experience and expertise that had been built up by generations of seamen. By comparison, the men of 1914–18 were fighting in new ships and with weapons whose true potential could only be guessed at. At Trafalgar, the *Victory* was 40 years old and differed little in essentials from her predecessor of the same name; at Jutland, Jellicoe's flagship H.M.S. *Iron Duke* was only 4 years old and her predecessor less than 50 years before, had been a sail-and-steam broadside ironclad. Only 15 years before Jutland, battle practice had been conducted at ranges of 5,000 yards and less; at Jutland, Beatty's battlecruisers opened fire when they were nine miles distant from the enemy – and Beatty was later criticized for not opening fire sooner.

Thirdly, in these days of highly-developed technology, we are all too apt to forget that the ships of the First World War represented a halfway house in technological development, where technical advantages were often nullified by continuing limitations in other fields. They had guns which could fire projectiles distances of up to 13 miles: but they had no radar with which accurately to spot their target. They had ships which could reach speeds of over 25 knots: but they had no electronic computers to give them speedy calculations of the bewilderingly fast alterations in ranges. They had wireless with which to communicate with their home base but it was primitive and slow and so most manoeuvring orders were still given by signal flags and lamps.

We need to enter into this strange world in order fully to understand the problems that Jellicoe and Scheer faced. Before we condemn Jellicoe for excessive caution in the face of torpedo attacks, we need to remember that, in peacetime trials, the torpedo had appeared to have a power far in excess of its actual wartime performance. Before we condemn the poor effects of the British gunnery and the extremely inefficient signalling of the Grand Fleet, we need to remember that everything was so new and untried that no one had any idea beforehand of what a modern naval battle would be like. Listen to a few first-hand accounts of what it felt like to be there.

Lieutenant-Commander Rudolph Verner, gunnery officer of H.M.S. *Inflexible* at the Falklands, noted with some amusement that, when the German shells began to fall around them, one of his party in the director control cried out in surprise "They're *firing* at us!"[12] – an eloquent witness to the essential difference between peacetime practices and real battle conditions! Engineer Lieutenant William Rosevere, of the light cruiser H.M.S. *Galatea*, which first sighted the German battlecruisers at the beginning of Jutland, wrote home ". . . then ensued the most awful battle one could imagine. I don't think anyone had pictured a naval action like it and at one time I saw not less than 30 big projectiles falling into the sea around us."[13] And here is Julian Corbett's masterly description, based on eyewitness accounts, of the critical moment when Jellicoe made his historic deployment into line ahead:

> "There was not an instant to be lost if deployment were to be made in time. The enemy, instead of being met ahead, were on his starboard side. He could only guess their course. Beyond a few miles everything was shrouded in mist; the little that could be seen was no more than a blurred picture, and with every tick of the clock, the situation was developing with a rapidity of which his predecessors had never dreamt. At a speed higher than anything in their experience the two hostile fleets were rushing upon each other; battlecruisers, cruisers and destroyers were hurrying to their battle stations, and the vessels steaming across his front were shutting out all beyond in an impenetrable pall of funnel smoke. Above all was the roar of battle both ahead and to starboard, and in this blind distraction Admiral Jellicoe had to make the decision on which the fortunes of his country hung."[14]

Finally, we need to remember that the First World War was far more deadly than any preceding conflict. At Trafalgar, no ships were sunk during the action. One blew up later and others sank in the ensuing storm but the outcome of the battle was decided – as was usual in those times – by the number of ships which were captured, usually by boarding. There was an unwritten law that once a ship had suffered an undefined percentage of casualties, it was perfectly honourable to surrender. British captains who surrendered in this way were always court-martialled on their return home but, if they could prove that they had fought until resistance was no longer practical, they were always acquitted. No such gentlemanly rules applied in 1914–18. In each battle, ships of both sides went down with their colours still flying and on occasion with enormous loss of life. Sinkings not surrenders decided battles: and yet, at the same time, heavy armour and water-tight compartments coupled with the fact that even badly damaged ships often retained sufficient motive power to escape, meant that sinkings were difficult to achieve. A Nelson-style, annihilating victory was almost impossible in 1916, given the stage technology had reached at that time.

However, when all these allowances have been made, there is still much to criticize in the British conduct of the surface war. Firstly, despite the remarkable efforts made to modernize the fleet in the years immediately preceding 1914, there were still many defects of *matériel*, – defects which were revealed at Jutland. The British shells proved far less destructive than expected because of faulty fuses. British armour-protection, which had been quite deliberately sacrificed in order to gain more speed and heavier guns, was clearly inferior to that of the Germans. It is however worth underlining at this point the fact that most experts now agree that the dramatic loss of the battlecruisers at Jutland was not due to overthin armour but to faulty anti-flash arrangements in the magazines. British damage-control was also inferior to that of the Germans whose ships were honeycombed with water-tight compartments, which is why in several battles they remained afloat even after sustaining numerous hits from heavy shells.

Secondly, these *matériel* defects were matched by defects in training, particularly of officers. The gunnery of Beatty's battlecruisers was markedly inferior to that of the rest of the Grand Fleet and his flagship's signals officer made important mistakes at each of the three major North Sea battles. Indeed, Jutland showed that signalling – especially the sending of accurate enemy-sighting reports – had been neglected throughout the Grand Fleet. None of the scouting groups kept Jellicoe properly informed during the battle and, during the critical moments before the main action as the two fleets were approaching each other at a combined speed of some 40 knots, he was left almost completely in the dark. Incredibly, between 1700 and 1740, probably the most vital period of the daylight battle, while the battlecruisers were leading the High Seas Fleet northwards into the arms of the Grand Fleet, *no signals at all* were received in *Iron Duke* from any of the engaged ships. Hardly surprising then that the normally taciturn Jellicoe was heard to remark irritatedly: "I wish someone would tell me who is firing and what they are firing at!"[15]

This inadequate reporting was a symptom of a more wide-reaching problem: that of overcentralization. Jellicoe was not a delegator; nor did he believe in independence for the subordinate as Nelson of course under different circumstances, had done. His purpose, ever since taking command of the Grand Fleet in July 1914, had been to control as closely as possible the management of his force in every conceivable eventuality. The Grand Fleet Battle Orders with which he made his wishes known – a far cry indeed from Nelson's friendly dinner parties – had become a very thick volume by 1916 and it is clear that they had a stunting effect on initiative. There are many illustrations that one could use, but let Captain Arthur Craig of H.M.S. *Barham* speak for all. Defending the lack of signals during the crucial run to the north at Jutland, he wrote later: ". . . we came to the conclusion that the situation was known to the C-in-C . . . A stream of wireless reports from ships in company with the C-in-C seemed superfluous and uncalled for."[16]

In fairness to Jellicoe, it is right to point out that he was typical of his generation. Initiative and individual thought were not welcomed among the senior officers of 1914–18; only the more junior men who had received a more enlightened education thanks to the sweeping social reforms of 1902 were ready to question the "Father Knows Best" attitude that prevailed. As we shall see, many of their exploits when on detached duty had a distinctive verve and zest about them that was very different from the rigid control of the Grand Fleet. Winston Churchill, who as First Lord in the opening years of the war was able to observe the Navy at close quarters, summed up this defect in his usual pithy style. "At the outset of the conflict," he wrote later, "we had more captains of ships than captains of war."[17]

Lastly – again once all allowances have been made – there still remains a niggling feeling that in the North Sea and, indeed, elsewhere (though not as we shall see by any means everywhere) there was a lack of offensive spirit in the High Command of the Royal Navy. Not only were the conditions of war unfamiliar and disconcerting; so too, it would seem, was the actual cost of war. In a number of cases it is possible to find senior officers flinching from an otherwise desirable course of action because of the losses it was likely to bring. Jellicoe's turn *away* rather than *towards* the torpedoes at Jutland is the most notorious example, but he was not alone. At the very outbreak of war, Sir Ernest Troubridge allowed himself to be persuaded not to attack the admittedly powerful German battlecruiser S.M.S. *Goeben*, even though he had under his command four not insignificant armoured cruisers. His reason was that he considered that the *Goeben* would be able to use the longer range of her guns to keep him at bay, while she sank his ships one by one. Just how wrong his decision was, was proved at the Battle of the River Plate in 1939 when Commodore Henry Harwood, with a less powerful force than Troubridge's, managed to harry and seriously to damage the powerful German pocket battleship *Graf Spee*. Similar hesitation was also evident among the senior naval officers who had command of the early naval operations in the Dardanelles.

Again, to understand their caution, we need to enter their world. First of all, the large capital ships of the time were enormously expensive; there had been much debate in the last years of peace about their cost, and senior officers were very conscious of their value – perhaps over-conscious. "I suppose," said Beatty, at the beginning of the Battle of Heligoland Bight in August 1914, "I ought to go and support Tyrwhitt, but if I lose one of these valuable ships the country will never forgive me."[18] In the end, of course, he took the risk and so turned near defeat into the first British success of the war – but even Beatty hesitated! Secondly, every naval action of the war seemed to reinforce the lesson that, despite their size and power, these ships could be frighteningly vulnerable. Lieutenant William Chalmers, Beatty's biographer, who had served in *Lion* at Jutland, remarked of the loss of the battlecruisers, ". . . no one for a moment imagined that one of our ships would be sunk so soon",[19] and recorded that, because of this belief, sailors in other British ships cheered as they passed the wreck of a British battlecruiser, thinking that it must be a German ship. Signalman William Dawson, who witnessed the mining of British and French capital ships during the naval assault on the Dardanelles on 18 March 1915, wrote in his vivid diary,

> ". . . It is that awfully barbaric and in some way cowardly way of destroying ships that makes our work so dangerous. A good honest shell is almost welcome but to be struck and probably sunk by an unseen enemy as a mine or torpedo almost makes one mad with rage and sometimes more than rage . . ."[20]

So then, the greatly altered conditions of war, linked with important limitations in the performances both of ships and of men, robbed the British of a decisive victory at sea. But nonetheless Britain still retained her command of the seas. After Jutland, the High Seas Fleet made only two more abortive sorties before its final voyage to surrender in November 1918. Long range blockade had worked and Britannia still ruled the waves. Or did she?

Well, yes – strictly speaking. But only the surface of those waves. For, as is well known, the First World War introduced two new dimensions into conflict – the air and underwater. Now, air power had little significant effect upon the war at sea: partly because of conservatism, but mainly because the aircraft themselves and the means of launching and recovering them were still very primitive, submarines, however, came close to deciding the war – in Germany's favour.

Germany had been a pioneer in submarine warfare almost from their first introduction in the early 1900s. Like the torpedo boats of the 1880s, they were a most attractive proposition for a weaker naval power, since they were comparatively cheap to construct and maintain and they had an offensive potential that was quite out of proportion to their actual size. Although throughout the war the Germans tried to use their submarines against the Grand Fleet, their success in this area was very limited. It was in the war on trade that they really came into their own. To begin with, however, they were restricted by International Law which decreed that all targets should be stopped and the crew allowed to take to their boats before they were sunk. Such a limitation of course robbed the submarine of its main assets: concealment and secrecy. So, as the war progressed, successive German U-boat commanders broke the rules and as a result there were a number of international incidents, when ships carrying passengers of neutral nationalities were sunk – the most famous such incident being the sinking of the trans-Atlantic liner S.S. *Lusitania* on 7 May 1915.

To begin with, the diplomatic embarrassment of such incidents made the German High Command wary of endorsing the tactics of their subordinates. But, however much they might claim Jutland as a victory in public, they could see that the battle had confirmed that the battlefleet was unable on its own to break the British stranglehold. Accordingly, in a decisive switch of strategy, they authorized in February 1917 a second campaign of unlimited U-boat warfare in an attempt to starve Britain into submission. They even began to transfer some of the more experienced officers and men of the battlefleet into the U-boat service. The High Seas Fleet was going underwater.

And, while there, it almost succeeded, where the surface ships had failed. At that time, there were very few effective weapons that could be used against the submarines. Effective depth charges were finally introduced in 1916 but, still detection remained difficult and primitive though the use of airships and some aircraft was to provide an effective deterrent in coastal waters. Convoys were introduced belatedly and with seeming reluctance by the Admiralty. The preferred policy had been the organization of patrols by a number of destroyers of known U-boat hunting grounds and, linked with this policy, the most glamorous and dramatic of all the U-boat hunters, the Q ships. There were some remarkable acts of personal and collective gallantry associated with these ships; gallantry that was acknowledged by a large number of awards (5 VCs for example, compared with 4 for the entire Grand Fleet for Jutland) but they could not provide the answer to the U-boat threat.

Many factors combined to bring about the eventual introduction of convoys. The idea that any one person was mainly responsible has been largely discredited, rather, we should see it as an idea whose time had finally come. The protagonists of convoys were greatly helped in their campaign by the fact that by the spring of 1917, losses from U-boat action were becoming too huge to be ignored any longer. The most striking figure is the famous 870,000 tons sunk in the worst month of all: April 1917. At the same time, the Admiralty's own statistics were found to be seriously at fault. Arthur Marder, echoed by John Winton, in his excellent book *Convoy*, showed that one of the main arguments used against convoys was that it was believed that no less than 5,000 ocean-going ships called and sailed from the UK each week. Such a vast number, it was claimed, could not possibly be protected. But then, the figures were reassessed and it was discovered that arrivals and departures of truly *ocean*-going ships totalled only 140 a week and that the rest of the figure represented coastal vessels making frequent stops around the country. To convoy the far smaller percentage of ocean-going ships was clearly shown to be a more realistic proposition. 140 vessels, it was calculated, needed about 30 escorts to protect them compared with the 100 or more that would have been needed to protect 5,000. So it was that, in April 1917, the opponents of convoys finally gave way and the first convoy sailed to Scandinavia on 29 April, followed closely by the first Atlantic convoys on 24 May. By October the system was in full operation and the results could be clearly seen. The

September loss of merchant shipping was down to 345,000 tons and, after a brief upturn in October, continued to fall steadily.[21]

So, it is necessary to enter a caveat about Britain's command of the seas. Admittedly, the Grand Fleet did free the oceans by tying down the High Seas Fleet – although as we have seen, the North Sea remained technically in dispute up to the time of the German surrender. But, once Germany switched her efforts to unlimited submarine warfare, the battle for command of the seas had to be fought all over again and this battle was not really won until early 1918.

This then, was how command of the seas was finally secured by Britain: let us now examine how that command was used.

Corbett had shown in *Some Principles of Maritime Strategy* that one of Britain's most successful uses of seapower in earlier wars had been in the field of combined operations. The Cabinet and Naval Service Chiefs were fully aware of this tradition – but their problem was to find a suitable target for a naval-backed operation. Obviously, a direct attack upon Germany herself was a desirable aim but she had only 200 miles of coastline bordering the North Sea and these were covered by a complex maze of shoals and were very close to the bases of the still-undefeated High Seas Fleet. In the Baltic she was more exposed but the only way into that sea was by the land-dominated Skaggerak. Two British submarines – one commanded by the submarine-ace Max Horton – managed to penetrate into the Baltic where, in co-operation with the Russians, they harried German trade and even managed seriously to damage a German battlecruiser, thus threatening German fleet manoeuvres in the area. But it was recognized that surface ships could not go where the submarines had gone.

Nor, at first sight, did the Mediterranean seem to offer any targets. Germany's ally Austria-Hungary had a coastline in Dalmatia, but this was rough and impenetrable with very poor communications. So it was that, when Turkey finally entered the war, Churchill and the Admiralty, who were under considerable pressure both from the War Office and from public opinion to find a means of relieving the allied armies in Belgium, seized on the opportunity to attack the Central Powers by first eliminating Turkey. And this need for a target for a sea-borne offensive was the genesis of the ill-fated Gallipoli campaign.

The operation was, at least at the outset, sold to the War Council as purely naval – although doubts were voiced very early on, particularly by Fisher, about whether the objective could be achieved without the support of troops. "The Dardanelles," he wrote, with a characteristic mixture of capital letters, underlinings and exclamation marks, "Futile without soldiers!" And, more soberly, later, "Someone will have to land at Gallipoli sometime or other."[22] And, as so often before, he was right; the Navy proved unable on its own to force the Dardanelles and yet another campaign settled down to a bloody stalemate.

However, even after the soldiers had been called in, the work of the Navy was by no means over; the fleet organized (or perhaps improvised would be a more appropriate word) the landings of 25 April and covered them with supporting fire; it kept the troops supplied and ferried the wounded and reinforcements and, finally, in a miraculously smooth operation, evacuated the entire invasion force almost without loss. The Navy also did invaluable work behind the Turkish lines, for British submarines penetrated into the Sea of Marmora and caused havoc there, sinking a total of 205 vessels – 101 of which were sunk by Lieutenant-Commander Martin Naismith's E.11 alone. The exploits of the submarine crews in the Baltic and the Dardanelles provide a welcome corrective to the rather gloomy view of excessive caution that I painted earlier when referring to the surface war – and we shall find the same kind of dash and verve in other operations elsewhere in the world. But it is worth pausing just for a moment to remember the extraordinarily foul and difficult conditions in which those early submarine crews worked:

> "Only those who have actually experienced the horrors of sea-sickness can have any conception of the agony men who served in submarines suffered when they were sick as a result of a combination of bad weather, foul air, improper food, and breathing an atmosphere saturated with the fumes of crude-oil and gassing batteries. Imagine trying to work out problems in navigation when your stomach was in such revolt that you worked with a pail beside you and cold, clammy sweat, trickling down from your forehead and dripping off the end of your chin, smeared the pages of the work book in which you tried to figure. The greatest agony of all was that one couldn't always be sick. We had to use every ounce of will-power to get on our feet and do our work."[23]

That account was written by Lieutenant William Carr who served in the North Sea, but it can stand as typical of the experiences of submariners of that period. As another officer put it: "... The story of the North Sea operations was as much a story of men sealed in unsavoury tin cans, wallowing around a shallow ocean and continually at war with Nature, as it was a story of dramatic encounters between craft of opposing navies ..."[24] Very true: and yet, when Max Horton was recommended for the post of Senior Naval Officer, Baltic in 1915, the Second Sea Lord commented "I understand Commander Horton is something of a pirate and not at all fitted for the position."![25]

To return to the Navy's support for the Army: the traditional use of seapower had failed at Gallipoli and, indeed, throughout the war, the Navy was able to do very little directly to relieve the pressure on the Western Front by diverting German troops elsewhere. But its direct contribution to the land war was by no means negligible. Right at the outset, the so-called "race for the sea" was decided in the allies' favour very largely by the intervention of a force of monitors under the command of Sir Horace Hood, one of the brightest of the senior naval officers of the time, who was killed when H.M.S. *Invincible* blew up at Jutland. Their highly accurate bombardments held up the German right wing at Nieuport and, thereafter, vessels from the Dover Patrol kept up regular shellings of the German right flank whenever it was in range. The Dover Patrol was also responsible for maintaining the vital lines of communication across the Channel and, as a result of the constant work of their 400 assorted vessels, over 5 million men passed in safety across the potentially dangerous stretch of water – at the height of the war between 12 and 15,000 men were making the crossing each day.

To modern eyes, the most unusual contribution made by the Navy to the Allied effort was the sterling service rendered by the Royal Naval Division. At the outbreak of war, the naval reserve system worked so well that there was an excess of some 20 to 30,000 RFR, RNR and RNVR men available for whom places could not be found in ships. In fact, in 1914, the concept of sailors fighting ashore was not at all strange – indeed, as I have shown elsewhere,[26] during the preceding 100 years, the average British bluejacket had seen more action ashore in the naval brigades in the numerous colonial wars of the period, than afloat in the ships! So two naval brigades and a Royal Marine brigade were formed in the summer of 1914 and these first saw service during the attempted defence of Antwerp in October of that year. They were organized along army lines, with Royal Marine sergeants and instructors and with retired army officers commanding – although for the first months of the war they fought in their naval uniforms and they had no divisional engineers or other support units until 1915 and no divisional artillery until 1916.

As the numbers grew, the two brigades were merged to become the Royal Naval Division, with 8 battalions each named after a naval hero. Gradually, the men with previous sea service were transferred to the Navy and so, by the time the Division took part in the Gallipoli campaign, scarcely any experienced sailors were left – a fact that was finally recognized officially on 29 April 1916, when control of what was thereafter known as the 63rd (RN) Division was transferred to the War Office. After Gallipoli, the Division returned to the Western Front in time to take part in the Battle of the Ancre on 13/15 November 1916 and it remained at the front until the end of the war. It suffered some 48,000 casualties and won over 1,000 decorations – including 3 VCs, 137 MCs and 555 MMs. Seamen – or, to be strictly accurate, seamen-on-paper – had managed to make a major contribution in the principal theatre of the war, where seapower itself had been almost powerless to assist.

You will remember, however, that I outlined earlier one other most important way in which Corbett believed that seapower could affect the course of the war. As I mentioned, he made a clear distinction between the securing of command of the seas and the actual exercise of that command. In this field, I think it is fair to claim a large measure of success for the Royal Navy for Britain's exercise of her command of the seas had a most profound effect which, because of the ubiquity of seapower, was felt at all corners of the globe.

It was felt, for example, as far afield as Lake Tanganyika, where an Anglo-Belgian operation against German East Africa was held up because the Germans controlled the lake with 3 tiny gunboats. Two small motor-launches, armed with three-pounder guns and powered by two 100 horsepower engines which gave them a speed of 19 knots were shipped out to Cape Town from whence they were transported some 3,000 miles overland to the shores of the lake. *Mimi* and *Toutou*, as they were rather feyly called by their commanding officer, Lieutenant-Commander Spicer-Simpson, made short work of two of the German boats and so established sufficient British control of the lake for the invasion to go forward in safety. King George V sent by wireless his personal congratulations to "... his most remote expedition ...".[27]

A little nearer home, – but just as far distant from the glare of publicity – was the major campaign in Mesopotamia, which resulted in the capture of Baghdad in March 1917. This was a type of campaign in which Britain had plenty of experience, for it followed the lines of so many of the classic colonial campaigns of the Victorian period. The fighting centred on the River Tigris up which a British Army advanced, supported by a flotilla of gun-boats which gave covering fire and also kept the lines of communications open. But this was no mere "sideshow": from first to last nearly 900,000 British and Indian servicemen took part and its successful conclusion secured for Britain the crucial oil supplies in the Persian Gulf. And, unusually, the naval C-in-C, Vice Admiral Wilfrid Nunn, was able to bear witness to the fact that "... the Navy, Army, Air and Political Services always pulled happily together ...".[28]

Coming close to home, the umbrella of the Grand Fleet enabled the variegated forces of the Dover Patrol and the more homogeneous destroyer and light cruiser forces based at Harwich under Commodore Reginald Tyrwhitt constantly to harry the Germans. Tyrwhitt's force, in particular, was regarded by the Navy as an élite, very much like Beatty's battlecruisers – and with perhaps rather more justification. When Lieutenant Hilton Young was appointed to Tyrwhitt's flagship. H.M.S. *Centaur*, a fellow officer said enviously "Tyrwhitt's ship! You will be in everything that's going on, he always is."[29] – and, sure enough, he was. A typical example of Tyrwhitt's style occurred early on in Young's service in the *Centaur* when, while out on a routine patrol, a force of battlecruisers was spotted on the far horizon. So far as Tyrwhitt knew, there were no other British ships in the area, so it seemed certain that his force had stumbled across Hipper's squadron. He did not hesitate for a moment: hoisting the signal "General Chase" he increased speed and led his puny cruisers and destroyers into an attack – hoping, presumably, to damage the enemy with torpedoes. The strange ships turned out to be British but, as Young remarked, ". . . the Commodore would take every legitimate risk rather than let slip the least chance of injuring the enemy."[30]

So far as the Dover Patrol was concerned: besides its regular duties guarding the Channel crossing, once Roger Keyes was in command, it also carried out the full-scale raid on the important destroyer and submarine bases at Zeebrugge and Ostend on St. George's Day 1918. Once again, a long-standing tradition of naval warfare was being observed since hit-and-run attacks upon enemy ports and shore installations had been an important element of the Navy's contribution to the Napoleonic War. The argument still simmers over how effective the raids were in purely practical terms: the balance of the evidence would seem to suggest that neither port was damaged or blocked severely enough to affect operations for more than a few days or weeks at the most. But the psychological effect was considerable. As Professor Marder says:

> ". . . the whole Allied cause received a lift. No incident in the war on sea or land, had more deeply touched the imagination in Britain. It restored faith in the Navy. The country enthused over the magnificent skill and audacity of the exploit and hailed it as a rebirth of the spirit of Nelson and Drake."[31]

These are just a few of the more dramatic and therefore the most easily identifiable effects of Britain's use of her seapower – there were others of equal dash and decisiveness. But beneath the protection provided by the constant vigilance of the Grand Fleet, the aggressive defence of Tyrwhitt's force and of the Dover Patrol and the intricate monotony of the convoy and anti U-boat service, there, unseen and almost unsung, seapower was working even more powerfully to assist in Germany's eventual downfall. For the naval blockade was not aimed solely at the High Seas Fleet: it was above all an offensive against the German sea-borne trade. And here, its effect was truly deadly. By the spring of 1918 there was country-wide distress in Germany: food and clothing shortages, the closing of factories or drastic reductions in working hours because of acute lack of raw materials, the breakdown of the transport system because of shortages of spare parts, above all, the lack of any hope of improvement. All these factors combined to break the will of the German people. By the autumn of 1918, there was open revolution in the streets and mutiny in the High Seas Fleet and submarine service.

And this is only half the story. For, as the Central Powers grew steadily weaker, so the allies were gaining in strength with every month that passed. The advent of the American forces did much to ease the acute shortages of manpower and supplies – and they came by sea. The plentiful quantities of weapons and machines made the final offensive of the summer of 1918 possible – and all of this came by sea. In Britain, robust industries, fully geared by then to wartime production, were plentifully supplied with raw materials – much of it coming by sea. As a result, the civilian population was protected from severe hardship. Certainly, there were privations and queues – but they were in no way comparable to the terrible sufferings of the German people and their allies.

To sum up. On the one hand, were crippled industries, a demoralized and starving population and acute lack of supplies and manpower. On the other, were prospering industries, sound morale, plentiful supplies and new sources of manpower. And, when all due and just credit has been given to the skill of the allied generals and the enormous courage and fighting efficiency of their men, it must surely be allowed that the factors which I have just listed contributed significantly to the sudden German collapse in the summer of 1918. Each of these factors can be attributed either directly or indirectly to British seapower. Trafalgar had not been refought. A second Nelson had not arisen. But all the same, unobtrusively, undramatically, almost unnoticed – even by many historians – the seamen of the Royal Navy and their comrades of the Mercantile Marine had fulfilled their primary function. They had created the conditions in which the army could do its work.

To paraphrase the famous words of Mahan: those ever-present mist-shrouded ships upon which the Kaiser had looked so enviously in times of peace had stood – as he had always feared they would stand – between Germany and her coveted "place in the sun".

Notes

1. Notes kept by Signalman Corbyn, RNM 239/84.
2. A. Marder, *From Dreadnought to Scapa Flow*, (OUP 1961–70 5 vols) London, Vol. v, p. 193.
3. Marder *op. cit.* v. p. 193
4. Marder *op. cit.* v. p. 193
5. Marder *op. cit.* v. p. 192
6. E. Chatfield, *The Navy and Defence*, (Heinemann, London, 1942) p. 120.
7. *Vide*: D. Schurmann, *The Education of a Navy*, (Cassell, London, 1965) especially Chapters 4 and 7.
8. J. Corbett, *England in the Seven Years War* (Longmans, London 1907 2 vols) vol. 1, pp. 3–4 see also: J. Corbett *Some Principles of Maritime Strategy* (Longmans, London 1911).
9. E. Hilton Young, *By Sea and Land*, (Jack 1920) pp. 52–3.
10. *Vide*: P. Beesly, *Room 40*, (Hamish Hamilton, London, 1982).
11. Marder, *op. cit.* vol. iii, p. 186.
12. R. Verner, *The Battlecruisers at the Falklands*, (Bale and Danielsson, 1920) p. 8.
13. Letter from William Rosevere to his family, RNM 160/76.
14. J. Corbett and H. Newbolt, *Naval Operations*, (Longmans, London, 1920–31, 5 vols) vol. 3, p. 361.
15. J. Winton, *Jellicoe*, (Michael Joseph, London, 1981) p. 188.
16. R. Hough, *The Great War at Sea*, (OUP, London, 1983) p. 281.
17. W. Churchill, *The World Crisis* (Butterworth, London 1923–9, 5 vols) vol. 1, p. 93.
18. Chatfield, *op. cit.* p. 124.
19. W. Chalmers, *The Life and Letters of David, Earl Beatty*, (Hodder and Stoughton, London 1951) p. 235.
20. Journal of Signalman William Dawson, RNM JD15 82/80.

21. *Vide*: J. Winton, *Convoy*, (Michael Joseph, London 1983).
22. A. Moorehead, *Gallipoli*, (Hamish Hamilton, London 1956) p. 79.
23. E. Gray, *A Damned UnEnglish Weapon*, (Seeley, Service and Co., London 1971). p. 188.
24. Gray, *op. cit.* p. 189.
25. Gray, *op. cit.* p. 89.
26. C. White, *The End of the Sailing Navy 1830–1870 (Mason, 1980) The Heyday of Steam 1870–1910* (Mason, 1983).
27. P. Shankland, *The Phantom Flotilla*, (Collins, London 1968) p. 167.
28. W. Nunn, *Tigris Gunboats*, (Melrose, 1932) p. 281.
29. Young, *op. cit.* p. 174
30. Young, *op. cit.* p. 194.
31. Marder, *op. cit.* v. p. 58.

10

The British Soldier on the Western Front

KEITH SIMPSON

In terms of British folk history, the Western Front *is* the First World War. Images of that war invariably include trenches, barbed wire, mud, lice, rats, the lunar landscape of the shell holes around Passchendaele, the gaunt faces of British soldiers weighed down by the medieval style "dish" steel helmets, the continuous attritional battles and seemingly mindless slaughter of hundreds and thousands of young men – the "Lost Generation" – incompetent and insensitive generals and their red-tabbed staff officers, Bairnsfather cartoons, the evocative sounding names of Mons, Ypres, Arras and the Somme which will forever link the British army and a generation of British men and women with the battlefields of Belgium and northern France.

Popular British perceptions of the First World War are based almost entirely on the memoirs, diaries, prose and poetry of those who served on the Western Front, dominated by such literary giants as Wilfred Owen, Siegfried Sassoon and Robert Graves. R.C. Sheriff's influential play, *Journey's End*, written in 1928 and based upon the author's personal experiences during the First World War, is set in a British dug-out on the Western Front in the winter of 1918. A more recent stage musical, which was then adapted in 1969 for the cinema, was *Oh, What a Lovely War*, and was itself a caricature of many anti-war and anti-military attitudes associated with the First World War and centred upon the Western Front.

Even the traditional British acts of remembrance, including the ceremonial Remembrance Sunday, the medals and berets of the British Legion, and the symbolic red poppy, are part of a collective national memory of the Western Front. All these images have been reinforced through the close proximity of the Western Front battlefields and the extent of the war cemeteries – over five hundred – which overwhelm and move even the most casual sightseer.[1]

During the First World War, British soldiers and civilians regarded the Western Front as *the* decisive theatre of military operations, and other fronts, including Mesopotamia, Salonika, Palestine and even Gallipoli, were seen as "sideshows", and those who had served on them were thought to have had a "cushy" time. Such highly subjective opinions failed to take into account the fact that both the general conditions of campaigning and some of the fighting in these "sideshows" were just as arduous, and in certain cases more so, than those on the Western Front. Furthermore, service in the combat arms in these "sideshows" was frequently more dangerous than service with the support arms on the Western Front. Seen from the perspective of Australian national consciousness, Gallipoli is much more important than the Western Front.[2]

The largest single proportion of British troops serving overseas at any given time during the First World War was on the Western Front. (Table 1) In the month before the armistice, on the 1 October 1918, the theatre strength of the British army on the Western Front was 1,763,980, whilst the combined other theatre strengths was 546,333. Although there were 1,427,079 troops stationed in the British isles, many of these were drafts for overseas, and the Western Front during the war absorbed the majority of such drafts.

TABLE 1. *Distributed Strength of the British Army 1914–18*[1]

	1914	1915	1916	1917	1918
Home	990,489	1,308,972	1,542,342	1,495,615	1,427,079
Colonies	55,522	23,327	27,598	26,537	16,995
India	68,444	49,744	79,074	82,946	83,878
France	212,917	906,777	1,378,663	1,800,705	1,763,980
Mediterranean[2]		179,067	269,654		
Mesopotamia		5,399	35,961	73,034	111,283
East Africa		2,478	10,505	9,828	8,737
Salonika				207,809	149,189
Egypt[3]				185,783	199,842
Italy				760	73,735
Russia					3,547

[1] On the 1 October for each year
[2] Includes Egypt and Gallipoli for 1915, and Egypt and Salonika for 1916
[3] Includes Palestine
Source: *General Annual Reports on the British Army for the Period from 1 October 1913 to 30 September 1919* Cmd. 1193, HMSO 1921
Tables 5A–E, pp. 52–56

The importance of the Western Front in relation to other fronts for the British army during the First World War can also be assessed by a comparison of total war casualties. The total war casualties for the Western Front was 2,271,726, whilst the next largest total of 73,341 was for Gallipoli, an active theatre of operations for less than eight months.[2A] The total war casualties for other theatres were relatively insignificant in comparison to those of the Western Front. (Table 2)

Naturally, casualty figures by themselves do not necessarily indicate the importance of one particular theatre of operations. But the overall intensity

TABLE 2. *Summary of War Casualties in the British Army between 4 August 1914 and the 30 September 1919*

	A^1	B^2	C^3
France	510,821	1,523,332	236,573
Italy	2,071	4,689	344
Dardanelles	18,688	47,128	7,525
Salonika	9,668	16,837	2,778
Mesopotamia	15,230	19,449	3,581
Egypt	14,763	29,434	2,951
East Africa	1,269	534	62
Afghanistan	120	152	2
North Russia and Vladivostock	359	453	143
Other Theatres	508	461	217

[1] Killed in action, died from wounds, and died from other causes
[2] Wounded
[3] Missing including prisoners
Source: *General Annual Reports on the British Army 1913–1919*
        Table 1G pp. 71–72

of fighting and firepower in each theatre may be judged by comparing the proportion of battle casualties to the total number of men employed in each theatre of war. (Table 3) Whilst variations of danger existed equally between all theatres, a British soldier serving with a combat arm stood a much greater chance of becoming a casualty on the Western Front than on any other front.

What this deployment of British military manpower and the comparison of casualties between theatres meant in practice can be seen in the war effort on one British regiment during the First World War. The Black Watch, a distinguished old Scottish infantry regiment, raised some fourteen battalions for war service between 1914 and 1918.[3]

Of the two regular battalions, the 1st served on the Western Front throughout the war, whilst the 2nd served there until November 1915 before being transferred to Mesopotamia, and then Palestine. The 3rd Special Reserve Battalion remained at the regimental depot. Of the Territorial battalions, the 4th served on the Western Front from February 1915 until March 1916, when it was amalgamated with the 5th Battalion which had been on the Western Front from November 1915. Both the 6th and 7th Battalions served on the Western Front from May 1915. Of the New Army battalions raised as part of the Kitchener Armies, the 8th Battalion served on the Western Front from May 1915, the 9th Battalion served there from July 1915 until May 1918 when it was amalgamated with the 4/5th Territorial Battalion, to become the 2/9th Battalion. The 10th Battalion served at Salonika from November 1915 until July 1918 when it was sent to the Western Front. The 11th Battalion remained on Home Service throughout the war, whilst the 12th Battalion saw Home Service

TABLE 3. *Percentages of Battle Casualties to the Total Numbers of Men Employed in Each Theatre*

	A^1	B^2	C^2	D^4
France	12.06	37.56	6.37	55.99
Italy	0.84	3.40	0.52	4.76
Salonika	2.76	5.25	0.59	8.60
Egypt	1.93	4.20	0.40	6.53
Mesopotamia	5.94	8.36	1.49	15.79
Dardanelles	6.32	14.93	1.58	22.83
East Africa	5.25	2.86	0.15	8.26
Other Theatres	2.77	3.45	3.45	9.67

[1] Killed and died
[2] Wounded
[3] Missing and prisoners
[4] Total battle casualties

Total Per Cent of Battle Casualties and Deaths

France	55.99 . . . 5 casualties to every 9 men sent out
Dardanelles	22.83 . . . 2 casualties to every 9 men sent out
Mesopotamia	15.79 . . . 2 casualties to every $12\frac{1}{2}$ men sent out
Other Theatres	9.67 . . . 1 casualty to every $10\frac{1}{2}$ men sent out
Salonika	8.60 . . . 1 casualty to every 12 men sent out
East Africa	8.26 . . . 1 casualty to every 12 men sent out
Egypt	6.53 . . . 1 casualty to every 15 men sent out
Italy	4.76 . . . 1 casualty to every 21 men sent out

Source: Statistics of the Military Effort of the British Empire 1914–1920
HMSO 1922 p. 248

until May 1916 when it was sent to the Western Front until its disbandment in May 1917. The 13th Battalion was a curious and quaint result of an amalgamation between the 1st and 2nd Regiments of Scottish Horse, which was sent to Salonika in October 1915, and then to the Western Front in June 1918. Finally, the 14th Battalion, formed from the Fife and Forfar Yeomanry in Palestine in January 1917, served in that theatre until April 1918, when it too was sent to the Western Front.

This brief outline of the war services of the Black Watch, a not untypical regiment of the British army during the First World War, reveals that out of a total of fourteen battalions, eight served almost continuously on the Western Front, whilst another five battalions completed some service in that theatre. An analysis of the war casualties of each battalion once again shows the lethality of the Western Front in comparison to other fronts. (Table 4) This was undoubtedly the result of a combination of a series of major offensives and the greater continuous attritional intensity of fighting.

The Western Front remained the most important theatre of operations throughout the war for the Anglo-French High Command. Before 1914, the British general staff had conducted a series of detailed military

TABLE 4. *Summary of Total War Casualties of The Black Watch 1914–1918*[1]

	Killed	Wounded	Missing	Total
1st Battalion	1,633	2,985	803	5,421
2nd Battalion	1,077	2,147	274	3,498
4th Battalion	423	599	116	1,138
5th Battalion	283	255		538
4/5th Battalion	511	1,279	216	2,006
6th Battalion	1,009	1,725	667	3,401
7th Battalion	269	1,252	645	2,166
8th Battalion	1,191	1,766	518	3,766
9th Battalion	691	2,117	231	3,029
10th Battalion	130	321	2	453
13th Battalion	180	381	1	562
14th Battalion	253	507	17	757

[1] Except in the case of the regular battalions, these figures do not include casualties other than those suffered in major actions

Source: Major-General A. G. Wauchope (ed.) *A History of The Black Watch* in the Great War
1914–1918   The Medici Society 1925–26
Volume One   Regular Army pp. 130 and 322
Volume Two   Territorial Force pp. 28, 56, 111, 216 and 324
Volume Three   New Army pp. 186, 261, 306 and 335

conversations with the French general staff which resulted in the preparation and organization of an Expeditionary Force which in the event of a future conflict between France and Germany would be deployed in northern France. In August 1914 there was no alternative plan to that of sending the BEF to that theatre of operations to support the French. The overwhelming majority of senior British army officers was convinced throughout the war that the decisive theatre of operations for the allies was on the Western Front. The British War Office and GHQ in France were sceptical about the relevance of "sideshows" such as Gallipoli and Salonika, arguing that they were diversions of military effort away from the Western Front where the bulk of the German army in the west was deployed. Thus the strategic debate in the First World War in Britain was dominated between the "westerners" and the "easterners". The "westerners" were personified by Haig and Robertson and the "easterners" by Churchill and Lloyd George.[4]

This strategic debate over the deployment of the British army was to continue after the armistice with some of the main protagonists using their memoirs to attack each other. Robertson, the former C.I.G.S. argued a formidable case for the "westerners",[5] whilst Lloyd George in his memoirs,[6] and then the military thinker Liddell Hart through a series of articles and books continued the case for the "easterners".[7] The debate concentrated not only upon the strategic question of where the decisive point had been to defeat Germany but also included the painful question of whether the very high casualties suffered by the British army on the

Western Front could have been avoided by what Liddell Hart was later to describe as the "Indirect Approach".[8]

From the French perspective, the British debate during and after the war between the "westerners" and the "easterners" was something of an intellectual military luxury. For the French, both civil and military, the Western Front was the decisive theatre of operations for the simple but important reason that the German army was occupying a significant number of France's northern départments and posed a direct threat to national survival. At various moments of crisis during the First World War, the French had serious doubts as to the British determination to stand by their ally. Field-Marshal Sir John French's erratic behaviour during the great summer retreat in 1914 was the first of such events that were to culminate in the crisis of March 1918.[9] Gallic suspicions of "perfidious albion" and the belief that "the British would fight to the last Frenchman" were in the event to be proved wrong, but it was a factor that was always present in Anglo-French military relations and was to reach a new and bitter intensity in the summer of 1940.[10]

The British are prone to forget that during the First World War their military contribution was significantly smaller than that of the French until 1917. It is easy to exaggerate the military importance of the BEF in the first year of the war, when in fact it made up less than 10 per cent of the French army mobilized on the Western Front. Haig was very conscious of this imbalance and the need to prove to the French that the British army was pulling its weight. After 1916 the strength of the British army on the Western Front was significantly more important, and by the autumn of 1917 the British army by itself had to undertake the main offensive operations, a consequence of the mutinies in the French army, a situation that was to last until the spring of 1918.[11]

A cursory glance at photographs of the Western Front or at contemporary memoirs and diaries might give a superficial impression that from 1914 until 1918 the British soldier spent a continuous existence locked in trench warfare. In fact there were several distinct periods of warfare on the Western Front with variations between each period depending upon such factors as terrain, the aggressiveness of local and higher commanders, and the tactical importance of certain areas. In August and early September 1914 there was large-scale open warfare with traditional manoeuvre. In September 1914 there was a degree of limited trench warfare along the Aisne and further to the east, particularly in the Vosges, that was a consequence of operational stalemate and mutual exhaustion. But the British, the French and the Germans regarded this as a temporary respite with the use of field fortifications to enable each side to seek new opportunities for manoeuvre. This was found to exist in Flanders, and in October and early November 1914 the British, the French and the Germans attempted to manoeuvre around what each believed was the other's exposed flank, before resorting to major offensives to batter a way through the other side's hastily prepared field entrenchments. The failure of the Germans to break through the allied position in Flanders resulted in a new stalemate which saw the regularization of semi-permanent field fortifications and defensive positions from the Channel coast to the Swiss frontier and the establishment of what became known as "trench warfare".[12]

Neither side believed that the stalemate of trench warfare was permanent, and each side was convinced that it would be possible to regain the initiative by breaking through their opponent's defensive position and thus reverting to the war of manoeuvre. Despite the increase in set-piece major offensives by the British army from the spring of 1915 which were to culminate in the battle of the Somme from July to November 1916, warfare for the British soldier on the Western Front became an institutionalized and industrialized form of trench warfare. This pattern of warfare, which was a mixture of major offensives and a continuous and fluid form of trench warfare was to last until the spring of 1918. Then the German March offensive attempted to break through the allied line and re-create the circumstances for open warfare. Although the Germans failed in their objective, they did as a result of this failure create the circumstances for a form of cautious open warfare which saw the allies gradually push them back from one defensive position to another until the armistice in November 1918.

The British soldier's experience of warfare on the Western Front not only varied from one part of the war to the next, but also from one part of the line to another, with terrain and climate having a significant influence. With the gradual expansion of the British army on the Western Front, the extent of front line held increased from 24 miles in November 1914, 36 miles in April 1915, 85 miles in June 1916, 105 miles in February 1917, 123 miles in February 1918 and a reduction to 88 miles in May of the same year.

There were important differences between the various areas of the trench system held by the British army on the Western Front. Between Nieuport near the Belgian coast and Armentières in France, the trenches meandered across the flat and usually flooded fields of Flanders, with dykes and raised roads assuming considerable tactical importance. At the southern end of the Flanders sector was the notorious Ypres Salient, where from the relatively high ground to the northeast, east and southeast the Germans were able to dominate the British position. For some twenty miles south of Armentières the land was fairly flat farming country, but then between Givenchy and Lens it became an area of slag-heaps, pitheads and mining villages. The final seventy miles between Lens and Lassigny was largely rolling chalk downland, apart from the marsh valley of the river Somme. Each of these areas varied in terrain and climate which in turn produced variations of trench warfare.[13]

For the British soldier on the Western Front there were different types of front line and trench systems and a complex and changing situation with regard to the so-called "quiet" and "active" sectors. Other theatres also were characterized by the development of trench warfare, whether it took the form of the haphazard and close proximity of the system on Gallipoli or the more temporary nature of the field fortifications in Mesopotamia and Palestine. Although other theatres had variations of trench warfare, none was as complete or so extensive as those found on the Western Front.[14]

It is unwise to make generalizations about the British soldier on the Western Front. There were considerable differences in social and educational background, professional expertise and military experience between the officer class and the majority of NCOs and other ranks in the pre-war regular army. Although these distinctions were to blur as a result of casualties and the expansion of the army which brought in a massive influx of men from a wide variety of social and educational backgrounds, including many who served in the ranks and who were considered at the time to be "officer material", there still remained a considerable distinction between officers and other ranks throughout the war. This divide was both social and professional and was encouraged by the military authorities who invested the holder of the King's Commission with special powers, privileges and responsibilities.

Although the experience of war on the Western Front was generally the same for all ranks at regimental level, especially in the front line or during the course of a battle when danger and fear were foes to all and friends to none, nevertheless, the officer was able to maintain certain comforts and privileges not available to other ranks over questions of rations, dug-outs, leave and freedom of movement. This was not a situation that was unique to the British army, nor for that matter to the Western Front. Certainly a regimental officer below field rank in an infantry battalion had these privileges weighed against the probability that he stood a greater chance of being killed than did his soldiers.[15] Given the rapid expansion of the British army and the complicated organizational structure available to absorb manpower combined with Kitchener's decision to graft the volunteers onto the regular army rather than utilize the Territorial Force, there were at least initially, a number of distinctions between the regular, territorial and volunteer soldiers, and after 1916 between them and the conscripts.

The pre-war regular soldier lived in a very narrow environment, and his experience of war was limited to colonial soldiering. His service was very much related to economic circumstances, and in 1914 many regulars would have cheerfully fought the French as they would have the Germans. The original BEF was drawn mainly from units of the regular army supplemented by large numbers of reservists. It was this force which fought in Belgium and northern France between August and November 1914, gradually being reinforced by other regular units recalled from colonial garrisons, and also by a steady flow of units from the Territorial Force. The rapid expansion of the army and the heavy casualties in the period 1914–1915, meant that the pre-war regular army had all but disappeared by 1916. Even so-called regular battalions retained only a small cadre of their pre-war regular soldiers. But one cannot avoid thinking that as a result of heavy casualties and the nature of trench warfare many pre-war regular soldiers came to believe that they had "done their bit" by 1916 and as survivors sought a "cushy" billet in the rear areas behind the lines or back in Britain with a training battalion on Home Service.[16]

During and after the First World War, as part of British folk history, the Kitchener volunteers were lionized as patriotic citizen soldiers, over-shadowing the not inconsiderable contribution of the unfashionable Terri-torials. Not only were Territorial units sent to the Western Front within a few weeks of the despatch of the BEF in August 1914, but they steadily reinforced it throughout 1915. Furthermore, the War Office would have been unable to have withdrawn so many regular units from colonial garrisons and sent them to the Western Front in the autumn of 1914 without the availability of the Territorial Force which provided formed units as replacements.[17]

But there can be no doubt of the social as well as the military significance of the Kitchener volunteers who provided the manpower to create new divisions for the regular army. The majority of those divisions were sent to the Western Front, and there was grave disappointment amongst those sent to other theatres. The significance of the Kitchener volunteers and the Western Front lies in their special spirit of enthusiasm, camaraderie and a belief that they would succeed where the old army had failed. The journey to the Western Front was "the great adventure" and the "supreme test" of manhood for a whole generation of British civilians who had never experienced war. So Loos, and more importantly the Somme came as something of a shock, and as a result of heavy casualties and the reorganiza-tion of many units the unique volunteer atmosphere of the New Armies was diluted or disappeared completely.[18]

After 1916 the conscript became the main reinforcement for regular, territorial and New Army units of the British army on the Western Front. There is no real objective evidence that the conscript *per se* was a worse soldier than either the regular, territorial or volunteer soldier, but it was perceived that he lacked the volunteer spirit and made an unwilling contribution to the British war effort. This ignores the fact that there were many complex reasons which drove men to volunteer in 1914 and 1915, including unemployment, family and business imperatives, the influence of family and friends, the desire to experience "the great adventure", as well as simple, honest patriotism. There was a feeling amongst many officers and soldiers who had joined the army before 1916, that the reinforcements the British army received on the Western Front after the introduction of conscription were far from adequate. But this was probably as much a result of general war weariness and poor training as the fact that the replacements really were "the bottom of the barrel".

By 1917 the distinctions between what had been regular, territorial or New Army units had blurred or disappeared. Although many soldiers clung to their distinctive identity, for all intents and purposes the British soldier on the Western Front had become a "National Serviceman". But even to speak of the "British" soldier on the Western Front is something of a misnomer. Throughout the war tens of thousands of ex-patriot British citizens returned from overseas and enlisted in the British army. Then there was the imperial and dominion contribution to the British military effort on the Western Front. In September 1914 the BEF had been reinforced by the Indian Corps which helped to relieve the strain in Flanders. In fact the two Indian infantry divisions were withdrawn from the Western Front by the end of 1915 because it was recognized that Indian soldiers were not suited to the climate, became stressful with the loss of their British officers, and were a liability under the conditions of trench warfare. They were usefully employed on other fronts.[19]

After January 1916 the British army on the Western Front was substantially reinforced by divisional contributions from the dominions, which at its height represented one sixth of the total available British divisional strength on the Western Front. (Table 5) Furthermore, many of these dominion divisions came to be regarded both by British soldiers, GHQ and the Germans as élite formations to be used for difficult offensive and defensive operations.[20] The extent of this dominion contribution to the British military effort on the Western Front can also be considered in terms of the manpower and casualties of the Canadian Expeditionary Force. The strength of the CEF on the Western Front increased from 200,000 in January 1916 to over 250,000 in January 1917 and to over 300,000 in 1918. Total casualties for the CEF during the war amounted to 191,217.[21]

The experience of the British soldier on the Western Front also depended upon the arm or branch of the army in which he served. As

TABLE 5. *Divisional Distribution of the British Army on the Western Front 1914–1918*

---

3 British Cavalry
2 Indian Cavalry until February 1918
57 British Divisions for a period of three months or more consisting of 12 Regular, 18 Territorial and 27 New Army (Out of a total of 75 British Divisions)
4 Canadian Divisions after 1915
5 Australian Divisions after 1915
1 New Zealand Division after 1915
2 Indian Divisions until 1915 (Out of a total of 18 Indian Divisions)

Source: Statistics of the Military Effort of the British Empire
Divisional Distribution Chart between pp. 28–29

with the French and German armies on the Western Front there was a substantial increase in the proportion of non-combatant to combatant troops. This reflected not only the static nature of the war and the specific requirements of trench warfare, but also the amount of human and material effort required to sustain the combat soldier in modern warfare. By 1918 hundreds of thousands of British soldiers were undertaking jobs which were far removed from the front line and in many cases directly related to civilian occupations, but which gave them the status of service on the Western Front.

A study of the statistics relating to the comparative strength and percentages of other rank British soldiers on the Western Front shows that the percentage proportion balance between combatant and non-combatant troops had altered from 83.37 per cent to 16.63 per cent on the 1 September 1914 to 65.72 per cent to 34.28 per cent on the 1 September 1918, and by the 11 November 1918 this balance had shifted further from 64.84 per cent to 35.16 per cent. (Table 6).

TABLE 6. *Comparison of Percentage of Arm or Branch to Total Other Rank Strength of the British Army on the Western Front*

Combatant	1914[1]	1915	1916	1917	1918	1918[2]
HQs	—	—	—	—	1.10	1.15
Cavalry	7.72	3.20	2.55	2.15	.98	1.01
RH & RFA	15.26	11.79	13.09	10.54	11.54	11.40
RGA	1.09	2.25	3.58	4.82	6.23	6.47
RE	4.92	6.56	9.20	9.54	7.72	7.71
RFC[3]	.49	.36	.97	1.49	—	—
Infantry	53.89	57.56	52.17	45.61	33.25	31.90
Army Cyclist Corps	—	.64	.80	.39	.34	.35
M.G. C	—	—	2.09	2.77	3.72	3.87
Tank Corps	—	—	.04	.39	.84	.98
Total	83.87	82.36	84.49	77.70	65.72	64.84
Non-Combatant						
ASC	10.55	11.47	10.19	10.02	9.93	10.38
RAMC	5.25	4.53	3.37	4.50	3.47	3.44
AVC	.26	.99	1.09	1.03	.97	.96
AOC	.53	.60	.77	.85	1.16	1.18
APC	.04	.05	.04	.03	.04	.07
Labour Corps	—	—	—	5.83	14.28	14.37
Transportation	—	—	—	—	4.04	4.37
Miscellaneous	—	—	.05	.04	.39	.39
Total	16.63	17.64	15.51	22.30	34.28	35.16

[1] On 1 September for each year
[2] On 11 November 1918
[3] After 1 April 1918 the RFC became the Royal Air Force
Source: Statistics of the Military Effort of the British Empire pp. 65–66

The most significant growth in the non-combatant arms was through the formation of the Labour corps in 1917, which by the end of the war accounted for 14.37 per cent of the other rank strength on the Western Front, and 40.88 per cent of its non-combatant strength. The Labour Corps undoubtedly relieved combatant troops, particularly the infantry, from labour tasks behind the lines and at the base, and in theory released more troops for combat duties.

Within the combatant arms the most significant change in the strength of arm on the Western Front was in the infantry. On the 1 September 1914 the infantry made up 53.89 per cent of the BEF, and within the combat arms 64.64 per cent. By the 11 November 1918 this proportion had declined to 31.90 per cent and 49.20 per cent respectively. However, the combat strength of the Army Cyclist Corps and the Machine Gun Corps should really be added to the infantry strength. But this decline in the strength of the infantry on the Western Front was due to the introduction of new weapons, such as the Lewis gun, which resulted in a smaller requirement for "bayonet strength" and the substantial casualties amongst the infantry which resulted by 1918 in the combat strength of the average battalion in the line being as much as three hundred below an establishment of eight hundred.

Reflecting the siege-like nature of trench warfare on the Western Front was the increase by almost 30 per cent in the strength of the Royal Engineers, and the shift in balance away from the Royal Horse and Royal Field Artillery to the heavy artillery of the more socially despised Royal Garrison Artillery. The effect of firepower and the attritional nature of trench warfare is reflected in the quite dramatic decline in the strength of the cavalry from 7.72 per cent in September 1914 to 1.01 per cent in November 1918, and the formation of the Tank Corps in 1916 which reached a strength of 3.87 per cent by November 1918.

The uniform, weapons and equipment of the British soldier changed quite dramatically between 1914 and 1918. In 1914 the majority of British soldiers were in the infantry, were armed with a rifle and bayonet and marched into battle. By 1918 not only had the proportion of soldiers in the infantry declined in relation to other combat arms, but the majority of infantry soldiers were specialists acting as bombers, snipers, machine gunners. Wearing a steel helmet and carrying a gas mask, the soldier looked more like an industrial worker as he went into action after a journey to the front by lorry, supported by armoured cars, tanks and aircraft.

Trench warfare on the Western Front and the increasing centralization of bureaucratic control by GHQ produced a variety of tensions and stresses at different levels within the organization of the British army. Some of these were traditional ones which had gradually become more significant in the evolution of modern warfare, including the antipathy between the combat soldier and the non-combatant soldier, between the front line and the base. This antipathy was not new, it had been apparent in the Crimean and South African Wars. But it was the vast extent of the war on the Western Front and the presence, really for the first time in the British experience of war, of large numbers of articulate civilians as combat soldiers which highlighted these differences. This antipathy could also be found in the French, German, Russian and American armies during the First World War, was a characteristic of the Second World War, the Korean and Vietnam Wars, and on a smaller scale amongst British soldiers on the Falklands in 1982.

The group loyalty of the British soldier on the Western Front usually did not extend beyond his own battalion, battery or squadron, and in practice, did not go much further than his "muckers" in his section or platoon. Institutional loyalty can be created remarkably quickly, and the British army had an excellent vehicle for this through the regimental system. The horizon of the average regimental officer and soldier was limited to the operations and movements of his battalion. Higher formations were seen as impersonal authorities who were liable to threaten the regimental soldier's sleep, leave, comforts, and ultimately his life. Although battalions were often to spend many months in the same brigade and division, increasingly there was a roulement system brought about by military necessity and manpower shortages which meant that loyalty to higher formations became a matter of chance. Regimental soldiers judged a higher formation by very practical criteria that included efficiency, and whether its commander had a reputation for being a sensible soldier or a "thruster". Corps and armies were impersonal institutions, although soldiers took a keen interest in who they were attached to for operations. Plumer's Third Army enjoyed a good reputation amongst soldiers because its commander was seen as an avuncular figure who had an efficient staff, despite the fact that the army area was around the notorious Ypres Salient. Gough's Fifth Army stood in stark contrast and soldiers believed he was a "thruster" and his staff incompetent.[22]

What was unique for the British soldier serving on the Western Front was the close proximity of Britain. Although English armies had been compaigning in Flanders from at least the fourteenth century, in the past soldiers had had little opportunity to correspond with their families even if they were literate and would have found it physically difficult to have returned for leave even supposing such a radical scheme had existed for the rank and file. But in the First World War things were radically different with so many educated and articulate civilians amongst the rank and file who regularly corresponded with their families and friends, read newspapers and magazines and may have crossed the Channel on holiday. This proximity of the Western Front to the soldier's home and family was both a comfort and a stress. For other ranks, the allocation of leave was fairly infrequent, but it did give a soldier the opportunity to return and see his family and friends, and many gained moral strength from this to bear the strain and discomfort of soldiering on the Western Front. Others were distressed by leave, because they found it difficult to adjust, sometimes within twenty-four hours of travelling from combat duty at the front to family life at home. Many soldiers were unable to explain to their family and friends what life was really like at the front and had no desire to distress them with descriptions of death and mutilation. Civilians frequently had a romantic view of war and the soldier's life and did not understand why so many soldiers were uneasy and irritable on leave. Ironically for some soldiers, after having looked forward for months to a few days leave, they were hardly home before they were eager to return to the Western Front and their "muckers". As the war continued the home front appeared to be selfish and greedy.

The close proximity of Britain for the soldier on the Western Front was also maintained through letters and parcels which brought news, sometimes censored, of another world. Soldiers, and more particularly officers, attempted to maintain "home comforts" at the front with gramophones, magazines and "Fortnum and Mason" hampers especially prepared for duty in the field. The nature of military operations on the Western Front changed between 1914 and 1918, and even the commonality of experience of trench warfare varied from one period of the war and from one sector of the front to another. The early months of static warfare after November 1914 was a period of informality and improvisation as the soldiers of all the combatant armies learned to fight under conditions for which they had not been trained, armed or equipped. It was during this period that the tactics of trench warfare were developed, particularly the concept of raids, which began at a local level, and at least initially was left to enthusiastic battalion commanders to organize and execute. The requirements of trench warfare produced a greater degree of specialization amongst the soldiers of an infantry battalion with the formation of special sections of snipers, bombers and Lewis gunners. After 1915 the firepower of a British infantry battalion on the Western Front continually increased which compensated for a decline in both its establishment and actual strength.[23]

Following the appointment of Douglas Haig as C-in-C of the British Armies on the Western Front in December 1915, there was a much greater degree of professionalism and centralization of control by GHQ, and the army and corps headquarters. Far less initiative for the planning and execution of "active" trench warfare was left to regimental officers.[24] In that sense, the war on the Western Front for the regimental soldier became more bureaucratic and more impersonal. This is one explanation for the increased tension between the regimental soldier and the staff.

A great deal of attention has been given to the major offensives undertaken by the British army on the Western Front, but far less attention has been given to the rituals of trench warfare which were just as important in Haig's operational planning as well as for the experiences of the British soldier. The trench systems of the British, French and German armies on the Western Front had developed from the improvized linear trenches and ditches of 1914 to the complex trench system in depth which had been established in most sectors of the front by 1916. This trench system was frequently an impressive defensive position of trenches, strong-points, observation posts and communication trenches established in depth over an area from two to six miles. For the regimental soldier, moving in and out of the front line involved hard physical exertion as well as danger, and within and behind the trench system were established the necessary support arms such as the artillery, engineers and heavy trench mortars, as well as the services of transport, medical facilities, ordnance and supply.

Trench warfare did not necessarily involve the British soldier who served within the front line in a continuous bloody battle with the Germans. There were "active" and "passive" sectors and these varied from one part of the line to another and changed even over a short period of time.[25] Sometimes a "live-and-let-live" system developed between the British and the Germans because the terrain and weather made active hostility extremely difficult if not impossible. Each side was only too aware of how it could make life uncomfortable for the other, and therefore restraints in aggression were established. These complex and intricate local truces, frequently understood and rarely formally agreed to, were, nevertheless, the objects of suspicion by higher command who viewed all such tacit agreements as dangerous to the fighting power of the army. Forcing front line units to mount raids or using artillery directly under the command of a higher formation were two methods by which the "live-and-let-live" system could be disrupted.

It would be wrong to assume that the majority of British battalions or for that matter British soldiers were passive victims of trench warfare. Some battalions, such as the 2nd Battalion The Royal Welch Fusiliers, earned a reputation for aggressive trench warfare, including bombing and active raids and the determination to dominate the misnomer of "no-man's-land". Such battalions were popular with brigade and divisional commanders, but this was not just because the battalion commander was a "thruster" hoping for promotion and the acquisition of red tabs. Within battalions, many junior officers, NCOs and soldiers relished the prospect of small unit combat against the enemy, and were willing to volunteer to go on raids or take part in bombing parties. It was rather ironic that a subaltern serving under Captain Siegfried Sassoon in the 25th Battalion The Royal Welch Fusiliers on the Western Front in June 1918 noted that Sassoon "spent a large part of his nocturnal watches crawling through the deep corn in no-man's-land with a couple of bombs in his pocket and a knobkerrie in his hand".[26] Trench warfare continued during major offensives, not only in the same sector of the line whilst the battle was in progress, but also in other sectors well away from the offensive. "Active" trench warfare and continuous raiding all formed part of Haig's attritional strategy to wear the Germans down and to prevent an otherwise dormant British army from becoming affected by the malaise of trench warfare.

The British soldier on the Western Front faced a variety of dangers which were always present in trench warfare, and were intensified on larger scale during major battles. Many of these dangers were indirect and impersonal and related to the lethality of modern weapons systems which could kill without warning and over a much greater distance than had been the case in previous wars. There was a danger from all types of artillery fire, from trench mortars, enemy mines, machine-gun fire, gas and sniping. Even in a quiet sector of the line there was a steady dribble of casualties every day from the stray shell, the sniper or an accidental discharge.

The First World War was the first major war in which casualties from combat were in excess of those from disease amongst soldiers. This was the result of a much greater awareness by military authorities of the need to teach soldiers personal cleanliness and to provide them with the opportunity to wash and exchange old and filthy clothing, and greater advances in medicine. Nevertheless, the filthy conditions of trench life meant that there were always a significant number of soldiers who became casualties as a result of the effect of cold and damp and the diseases spread by lice and rats.

Recently, considerable attention has been given to the social life of the British soldier on the Western Front, from his bowel movements to his political opinions. It is interesting and relevant to study the social background, political opinions, humour, creativity and philosophical outlook of what was basically Britain's civilian army on the Western Front. But sometimes one suspects that social historians are unaware or do not want to consider the rather distasteful fact that the British army was deployed on the Western Front to wage war and the British soldier to fight. It is vitally important to study the British soldier in the context of his capability as a fighter. This does not mean an old fashion "fife and drum" analysis of battle and soldering, the "war is fun" school of military history, but a study of such unfashionable but vital questions as training and tactics.[27] The motivation of the British soldier on the Western Front and the methods by which the War Office and GHQ maintained discipline and inculcated fighting spirit are of paramount importance, and here the work of the sociologist, the psychologist and the military historian complement one another. It could be argued that the simplest criteria for assessing the fighting capability of the British soldier on the Western Front is by the fact that the British army won the war and the German army lost the war. At the time many British soldiers, and subsequently some military historians, believe that the German army was beaten on the field of battle by the British, with the assistance of the French, and better late than never, the

Americans. But this defeat came about not as the result of one single, decisive battle, but after a long attritional war which involved material and psychological factors. This war was wider than the Western Front, and the German defeat came about as a result of a physical and spiritual collapse and exhaustion. But for soldiers on the Western Front, the decisive factors were morale, discipline, confidence in their leaders, and the necessary supply of weapons, equipment and rations to sustain a fighting capability.

There is a danger that the study of the British soldier on the Western Front will become sharply divided between two broad schools of thought. The "patriotic" school who are concerned to demonstrate that the British soldier was an idealistic volunteer who fought for "King and Country", and that Haig and GHQ conducted a realistic strategy under the circumstances, [28] and the "revisionist" school, who believe that the British soldier was a poor dupe who was sacrificed due to the incompetence of Haig and GHQ. [29] The "patriotic" school is offended by any study which attempts to denigrate the motivation of the British soldier and the competence of GHQ, whilst the "revisionist" school is concerned to publicize the dreadful conditions of service for the British soldier on the Western Front, the unnecessary casualties and the high level of indiscipline and the number of "mutinies" in the army.

What is needed is a more objective study of the British soldier on the Western Front. There is now an abundance of contemporary oral and written evidence to show the peculiarites relating to the First World War, and the similarities of experience from other wars. The British soldier on the Western Front was motivated by a variety of factors, which included patriotism as well as the fear of the consequences of disobeying orders. Recent scholarship has shown that incidents of indiscipline were frequently widespread amongst British soldiers on the Western Front. But this indiscipline varied from the trivial, through the military to the criminal.[30] It is hardly surprising that discipline was frequently a problem for the British military authorities who were faced with maintaining discipline amongst over one million men, the majority of whom were civilians and reluctant soldiers.

The problem of motivating men to fight and sustain casualties and conquer fear was not unique to the British army on the Western Front, but has been an historical problem for all armies.[31] Ultimately, the British soldier obeyed his officers and military authority out of a combination of habit, social deference, the fear of the consequences of disobedience, and personal loyalty and respect. Disobedience and mutiny were frequently the consequence of administrative incompetence and insensitivity by military authorities. But they were also likely to occur under the continual stress of front line service, in battle or when faced with the prospect of being sent into battle. Even veteran soldiers with an excellent *esprit de corps* could become mutinous at a sudden change of orders which sent them back into the line after they had reckoned to have "done their bit", particularly if they came under the command of unfamiliar officers and NCOs.

The study of command and leadership in the British army during the First World War frequently has been trivialized to the level of competing personalities. But the personalities, leadership and competence of individual commanders like French and Haig have to be placed in the broader context of the evolution of the machinery of high command and the ability of the staff to plan and conduct operations and simultaneously analyse and absorb tactical lessons and the potential of new weapons.[32] Although the British regimental soldier on the Western Front may not have been aware or even interested in the strategic debate, he was keenly conscious of the quality of planning, preparation, training and leadership which went towards a "good show". Social deference and military discipline by themselves were insufficient in motivating soldiers in battle, and many articulate and intelligent civilians who served in the ranks were resentful and angry about what they believed were the frequent examples of military incompetence by the professional soldiers of the regular army who dominated the staff and senior command appointments on the Western Front.

The most powerful images of the British soldier on the Western Front come from contemporary literature and through photographs, paintings and film. For any significant assessment of the literary legacy of the British soldier on the Western Front, it is necessary to consider what was published during the First World War. At the time there was a plethora of patriotic books written which attempted to show what fun it was to be a soldier on the Western Front, and even those books which came near the truth in revealing the real conditions at the front excluded many explicit details. The British public learnt about the war through newspapers such as the *Daily Mail* and magazines such as *The Illustrated London News*. Some of these were so bad that the troops invariably treated them with derision, and were placed in the same category as some military broadsheets under the heading "Comic Cuts". Although some newspapers and magazines had included photographs before 1914 from the South African and Russo-Japanese Wars, it was during the First World War that the civilian population were made aware of what war was really like and the conditions of soldiers on the Western Front. There was also the impact made by the official government film, *The Battle of the Somme 1916*, which in many cases shocked the audience.[33] Equally influential were the many commercial films produced in Hollywood which gave highly dramatized views of the war.

The unpublished contemporary literature consisted of the letters and diaries of soldiers serving on the Western Front, and although these were seen by families and friends at the time, many soldiers kept their diaries to themselves until prompted to reveal them in the great upsurge of interest in the First World War in the 1920s and then again in the 1960s. One of the more poignant literary legacies of the First World War are the numerous privately published and posthumous collections of letters or extracts from the diaries of dead soldiers. These were usually lovingly edited by the parents or the wife of the dead man, the majority officers, in a proud attempt to place the sacrifice of the loved one in the context of patriotism and duty. Published during the war they provide a simple testimony to the ethos of the Victorian and Edwardian era.

During the war, many soldiers had been unaware of the rivalry between senior military officers such as Haig and French, and the disputes between the "frocks and the brasshats". But the ghosted memoirs of Lloyd George, the revealing biography of Henry Wilson and the polemics of William Robertson made many veterans disillusioned with their experiences on the Western Front. With the publication of the first volumes of the "Official History of the Great War", the most controversial of which covered operations in Belgium and France, there was strong criticism that they avoided controversy and massaged the truth. Certainly, they made dull reading and lacked the skilled commentary to be found in the Australian official history.[34]

Many veterans were politicized by the war and the disappointments of its aftermath. Some joined socialist ex-servicemen's organizations, whilst others were motivated eventually to join the British Union of Fascists. But the majority were encouraged to join the establishment-organized British Legion, which was formed precisely to prevent veterans becoming radically politicized or forming pressure groups to put their case in strong terms for better pensions and conditions to the government. Haig took a leading role in the formation of the British Legion.[35]

Although the period 1929 to 1935 is usually associated with the period of the anti-war and anti-military books, the most important of which were written by former soldiers of the Western Front, it would be wrong to assume that they were representative of a collective opinion.[36] The authors of a number of classic anti-war books, such as Siegfried Sassoon and R.C. Sheriff show an ambivalent attitude towards both the war and the army. But the experience of the Western Front and the literature of this period were undoubtedly influential in promoting pacifist sentiment amongst the electorate and the search to find any alternative to that attritional trench war which scarred the national memory.

The experience of the Western Front also influenced the doctrine and organization of the British army in the postwar period. Within a few months of the armistice, the conscript wartime army had been reduced to the small regular army, which despite all the military and social changes brought about by the war, bore a striking resemblance to the pre-war army. It was hardly surprising that for most of the next two decades the regular army was dominated by officers who had held senior command and staff appointments during the First World War, particularly on the Western

Front. Lessons from the First World War, which largely meant from the Western Front, were studied, but in a narrow way and were dominated by fractious disputes between former senior officers, and the debate, marked more by passion than reason, between the advocates of mechanization and their opponents. British military policy after 1918 was largely determined by the political intention not to repeat the pre-war decision to send an Expeditionary Force to the continent.[37] However, many officers who had served in subordinate positions with their regiments or on the staff on the Western Front were determined not to make the mistakes of their seniors if they ever held command in a future war. Regular officers like Montgomery, Alanbrooke and Alexander had learned a lot about how *not* to plan operations, motivate civilian soldiers and exercise command. In the Second World War, British military leadership reflected this experience of the Western Front and there was considerably less friction between regimental soldiers and the commanders and their staffs.[38]

In certain political and military ways the Second World War was a continuation of the First World War. Despite some mechanization and re-armament, the BEF which went to France in September 1939 was remarkably similar in uniforms, weapons and tactics to the British army on the Western Front in November 1918. The Second World War was dissimilar to the First World War because air power and mechanization made mobility easier to obtain, but although there was no static trench system established in a semi-permanent way over a period of several years, some of the characteristics of the fighting on the Western Front could be found in the battles for Cassino, Normandy and the Reichswald Forest.[39] And at least for the British army, the casualties in the Second World War were significantly smaller.

Since the Second World War, the major revival of interest in the Western Front began with the publication in 1959 of Leon Wolff's *In Flanders Fields* which was about the Third Battle of Ypres. But it was the fiftieth anniversary of the outbreak of the First World War in 1964 which saw a major re-appraisal of the British soldier on the Western Front through the work of such military historians as John Terraine, Correlli Barnett, Alan Clark and Anthony Farrar-Hockley.[40]

This was combined with the publication of hitherto unseen diaries and letters and a spate of new memoirs and autobiographies by veterans from the Western Front. The war poetry of Owen, Sassoon and Graves became part of the English Literature syllabus in schools. In the 1970s the British soldier on the Western Front attracted the attention of social and local historians who were concerned to use the oral and written evidence to document the life of the British soldier and the impact the First World War had had on British society.[41]

Today there is a need to consider the continuities and discontinuities of the experience of the British soldier on the Western Front. There is a tendency amongst many military and social historians of the First World War to see this as a unique experience, not only in the context of British history but also in relation to European history. Most of the discomforts, trials and tribulations, fears, anxieties and sufferings were part of the wider experience of all soldiers in war.[42] British historians must break away from their narrow historical approach to the Western Front and consider the French and German experience in comparison.[43] Before 1914 British society had not been directly affected by the impact of war, and only a limited proportion of the population had undertaken military service. Kitchener's appeal for volunteers and then the introduction of conscription brought into the army hundreds of thousands of men who would not under normal circumstances have ever considered taking the "King's Shilling". Military life as well as active service at the front made a profound impression on those men and in turn upon British society.

At least some of the disillusionment experienced by the generation of 1914 can be explained by the contrast between their enthusiastic naivety both about military life and war which helped to motivate the volunteer spirit, and the subsequent realities they endured on the Western Front. Far from the war being a romantic game, it became for the British soldier, as well as the French and German soldier, an industrialized and impersonal conflict which was symbolized by the Western Front.[44]

There is a tendency sometimes to place too much emphasis on the horrors faced by the British soldier on the Western Front. Danger and fear were not necessarily the continuous or universal experience of all British soldiers, and many of them thought at the time, and later, that it had been "the great adventure".[45] Many of them were young men who were exhilarated by the danger, remembered the laughter and the camaraderie and indeed the love they had experienced as temporary soldiers on the Western Front.

Notes

1. See Rose Coombs *Before Endeavours Fade* Battle of Britain Prints International 1976, which is a very good illustrated guide to the battlefields and war cemeteries of the Western Front.
2. See Patsy Adam Smith *The Anzacs* Hamish Hamilton 1978.
2A. The Gallipoli figures do not include sick and evacuated from the Peninsula.
3. Major-General A.G. Wauchope (ed.) *A History of the Black Watch* in the Great War 1914–1918 3 volumes The Medici Society 1925–26. This is a particularly detailed regimental history with very useful information divided between the Regular, Territorial and New Army battalions.
4. See Paul Guinn *British Strategy and Politics 1914–1918* Oxford Clarendon Press 1965.
5. Field-Marshal Sir William Robertson *Soldiers and Statesmen* 2 volumes Cassell 1926.
6. David Lloyd George *War Memoirs* 6 volumes London 1933–36.
7. B.H. Liddell Hart *The Real War 1914–1918* Faber 1930 and *A History of the First World War 1914–1918* Faber 1934.
8. See Brian Bond *Liddell Hart: A Study of His Military Thought* Cassell 1967. This is a scholarly analysis of the development of Liddell Hart's military thought. The author

shows that Liddell Hart moved from almost uncritical admiration of Haig during the war to becoming one of his most outspoken critics by 1930.

9. The best account is in Richard Holmes *The Little Field-Marshal: Sir John French* Jonathan Cape 1981 pp. 225–236.

10. B.H. Liddell Hart *Foch: Man of Orleans* Eyre & Spottiswoode 1931. Although Foch was the most anglophile of French generals, even he had momentary doubts about British determination during periods of crisis.

11. Haig's views about the French army, and particularly his growing concern about French morale and military efficiency can be seen through his diary in Robert Blake (ed.) *The Private Papers of Douglas Haig 1914–1919* Eyre & Spottiswoode 1952 pp. 51–58, 91, 96, 112, 234–235 and 265–266.

12. A general account of this period of the war and the origins of "trench warfare" seen from the perspective of the BEF and illustrated with contemporary photographs is Keith Simpson *The Old Contemptibles* A Photographic History of the British Expeditionary Force August–December 1914 Allen & Unwin 1981.

13. Too few military historians bother to "walk the ground", and it really is necessary to do this, during the different seasons over the battlefields of the Western Front. A useful modern guide which gives the reader some feel for the ground is Nigel H. Jones *The War Walk* A Journey Along the Western Front Robert Hale 1983.

14. Some interesting contemporary accounts can be found in Peter Liddle *Men of Gallipoli* Allen Lane 1976.

15. On the British army officer during the First World War see Keith Simpson "The Officers" in Ian Beckett and Keith Simpson (eds.) *A Nation in Arms* A Social Study of the British Army in the First World War Manchester University Press 1985. For the contrast between officers and other ranks see Denis Winter *Death's Men: Soldiers of the Great War* Allen Lane 1978.

16. The effect this had on a regular battalion can be seen in the semi-official history of the 2nd Battalion The Royal Welch Fusiliers, a book based on the compilation of interviews, letters and diaries. *The War the Infantry Knew 1914–1919* A Chronicle of Service in France and Belgium with The Second Battalion His Majesty's Twenty-Third Foot, the Royal Welch Fusiliers P.S. King & Son Ltd 1938. This excellent book is now almost impossible to obtain, but the author has obtained permission from the Regimental Committee of The Royal Welch Fusiliers to edit a reprint.

17. For the role and importance of the Territorial Force during the First World War see the chapter by Ian Beckett in this volume.

18. Until recently, there was no scholarly account of the raising, training and deployment of the New Armies, apart from the somewhat dated and romanticized accounts by Ian Hay *The First Hundred Thousand* 1916 and Victor Germain's *The Kitchener Armies* 1930. However, Peter Simkins's new study *The Kitchener Armies* should be available by 1986.

19. Philip Mason *A Matter of Honour* An Account of the Indian army, its officers and men. Jonathan Cape 1974 pp. 412–425.

20. An argument sustained by Bill Gammage *The Broken Years* Australian Soldiers in the Great War Australian National University Press 1974.

21. Colonel G.W.L. Nicholson *Official History of the Canadian Army in The First World War: Canadian Expeditionary Force 1914–1919* Queen's Printer Ottawa 1962 Appendix "C" Tables 2 & 3 pp. 547–548.

22. Charles Carrington makes some interesting comments about this in *Soldier From the Wars Returning* Hutchinson & Co. 1965.

23. A good general account of trench warfare is John Ellis *Eye-Deep in Hell* The Western Front 1914–1918 Croom Helm 1976. Sidney Rogerson's *Twelve Days*, Arthur Barker n.d. is a moving description of one of the many twelve day periods spent by the 2nd West Yorkshire Regiment in the line during 1916.

24. See the important study on this subject by Tony Ashworth *Trench Warfare 1914–1918 The Live and Let Live System* Macmillan 1980.

25. *ibid.*

26. Vivian de Sola Pinto "My First War" in George A. Panichas (ed.) *Promise of Greatness* Cassell 1968 p. 81.

27. Recently this has been undertaken by military historians such as Shelford Bidwell and

Dominick Graham *Firepower* British Army Weapons and Theories of War 1904–1945 Allen & Unwin 1982 and T.H.E. Travers in a series of stimulating articles including his important "Learning and Decision-making on the Western Front 1915–16: The British Example." *Canadian Journal of History* April 1983 pp. 87–97.

28. At the risk of labelling him unfairly, John Terraine has established his reputation as the "doyen" of what the author would call the "patriotic" school.
29. See Alan Clark *The Donkeys* Hutchinson 1963.
30. J. Brent Wilson *The Morale and Discipline of the B.E.F. 1914–1918* M.A. Thesis University of New Brunswick, Canada 1978.
31. See in particular John Keegan *The Face of Battle* Jonathan Cape 1976 and Richard Holmes *Firing Line* Jonathan Cape 1985.
32. An important point brought out by Travers in "Learning and Decision-making on the Western Front" *op. cit.* This is also the conclusion of Timothy Lupfer in his excellent analysis *The Dynamics of Doctrine: The Changes in German Tactical Doctrine During the First World War* Leavonworth Papers No. 4 Combat Studies Institute Fort Leavonworth Kansas July 1981. Lupfer stresses the importance of the collective and consultative process by the Germans.
33. Kevin Brownlow *The War, The West and The Wilderness* Secker & Warburg 1979 pp. 61–62.
34. On the background to the writing of the official history see Jay Luvaas "The First British Official Historians" in Robin Higham (ed.) *Official Histories* Kansas State University Press pp. 488–502.
35. See S.R. Ward "Intelligence Surveillance of British Ex-Servicemen 1918–1920" *History Journal* xvi, L 1973 pp. 179–188 and by the same author *The War Generation: Veterans of the First World War* Kennikat New York 1975.
36. See Hugh Cecil's chapter in this volume.
37. For the postwar army and the strategic and tactical debate see Brian Bond *British Policy Between the Two World Wars* Oxford University Press 1980.
38. Montgomery dwelt on these points in his *Memoirs* Collins 1958, and his views are supplemented by Nigel Hamilton's biography *Monty; the Making of a General 1887–1942* Hamish Hamilton 1981.
39. For an analysis of combat conditions as they affected the British army in the Second World War see John Ellis *The Sharp End of War* David and Charles 1980 and Carlo d'Este *Decision in Normandy* The Unwritten Story of Montgomery and the Allied Campaign Collins 1984.
40. John Terraine has been a very important interpreter of the controversies surrounding the British soldier and the Western Front and seminal works include *Mons* The Retreat to Victory Batsford 1960; *Douglas Haig* The Educated Soldier Hutchinson 1963 and *The Western Front* Hutchinson 1964. He also wrote the scripts for the very influential BBC television documentary series *The Great War* 1964. Since then he has tended to re-state his opinions in a number of books, the most revealing of which is *The Smoke and the Fire* Myths and Anti-Myths of War 1861–1945 Sidgwick & Jackson 1980. Although Correlli Barnett has not written a major work about the British soldier on the Western Front he has also been influential and has placed the British experience into his own historical context in *Britain and Her Army* Allen Lane 1970. Alan Clark's *The Donkeys* Hutchinson 1963 is a contentious and sloppily argued book criticizing British generalship on the Western Front which provoked a spirited debate with John Terraine. Anthony Farrar-Hockley was a distinguished British army officer who had experienced combat as an infantry soldier in the Second World War and the Korean War, and he brought that experience to bear in *The Somme* Batsford 1964 and *Death of an Army* Barker 1967.
41. "War and Society" has become a new intellectual industry in the past 20 years and has touched the Western Front. Arthur Marwick's *The Deluge* British Society and the First World War Bodley Head 1965 started its own deluge of literature, and since then there has been a steady flow of books such as Denis Winter's *Death's Men* Soldiers of the Great War Allen Lane 1978, and Lyn Macdonald's impressive output based on interviews with veterans, the first of which was *They Called It Passchendaele* Michael Joseph 1978.
42. The author was struck by the number of his former students who had served in the Falklands who recounted experiences of soldiering which came straight from those of

Private Wheeler of the Peninsula War and Private Frank Richards from the Western Front.

43. There is virtually nothing available in English which even begins to examine this subject. Accounts of trench warfare by Ernst Junger *The Storm of Steel* Chatto & Windus 1929, and Erwin Rommel's memoir of the Western and Italian Fronts, *Infantry Attacks* US Army 1943, are a useful introduction. The military historian Anthony Brett-James was completing his research on a comparative study of the experiences of French and German soldiers on the Western Front, but sadly died in 1984 before his efforts bore fruition. However, his papers are to be lodged with the Imperial War Museum.

44. Correlli Barnett argued in "A Military Historian's View of the Great War" *Essays by Divers Hands* Royal Society of Literature 1970, that life for the British soldier on the Western Front was not noticeably much worse than in previous wars, or for that matter much worse than the everyday living conditions of the British working class in Edwardian Britain. He suggested that many of the outspoken literary critics of the war and the army were not typical of the broad mass of the men who served between 1914 and 1918. For the contrast between the aspirations of those who went to war and the realities of industrialized modern warfare on the Western Front, see E.J. Leed *No Man's Land* Cambridge University Press 1979.

45. See for example the cheerful correspondence of Graham Greenwell *An Infant in Arms War Letters of a Company Officer 1914–1918* Lovat Dickson & Thompson Ltd. 1935.

11

Britain and the Middle East in the Great War

BRIAN PORTER

Turkey in 1914 was still the Ottoman Empire, which, although it had lost the bulk of its remaining European territory in the Balkan Wars of 1912–13, yet comprised not only Asia Minor but also the non-Turkish lands of Syria, Palestine, Mesopotamia, and the western flank of the Arabian peninsula down to and including the Yemen. It claimed, too, suzerainty over Kuwait, Hasa, and most of the interior of Arabia, and held title to Cyprus and Egypt, even though these territories had been under British occupation for more than 30 years. The Sultan, moreover, was also Caliph, or spiritual head of the whole Muslim world, able to proclaim *jihad* or holy war against the infidel – a factor not without influence in British official circles, given the large number of Muslims within the British Empire, and especially in India, whose loyalty in such an eventuality might prove problematic.

Furthermore, the Ottoman Empire was an acknowledged Great Power, governing vast territories with a total population in 1914 of some twenty-five millions, and possessing an army which had a war strength of nearly a million men, making it the fourth largest in the world, inferior only to the Russian, German and French.[1] Yet politically the Empire had long been moribund, the proverbial "sick man of Europe", governed by a corrupt and effete despotism capable neither of internal reform nor of effective resistance to foreign pressure and ambition. In 1908, however, a coup of the sort which has since become commonplace in the world, brought to power in Constantinople a group of young nationalistic reformers, or "Young Turks" as they came to be known. These reformers did not intend to abolish the Ottoman Monarchy, but to work through it, fastening Turkish rule upon its minorities even more stringently than before, and, with popular support behind them, favouring more thrusting, modernizing policies than the Sultans had been able or willing to pursue.

The situation, in those years of feverish jockeying for position amongst the Great Powers up to 1914, was one which the Germans felt they could profitably exploit. Unlike the French, British and Russians, they had not taken part in the grab for the Ottoman Empire, nor had they any territorial ambitions towards what remained of it. Indeed they were sympathetic to

Turkish nationalism, and, with a need for markets, saw the Ottoman domains as being ripe for economic penetration. The Berlin to Baghdad railway, latterly a largely German enterprise, was designed materially to aid this process. Turkey, hitherto something of a buffeted object amongst the Powers, was glad of this help, and turned moreover to the German Army, the most professional and self-confident in Europe, for a supply of experts in training her own. Enver Pasha, leader of the Young Turks, himself had had a German military training.

These, though powerful reasons why the Turks should gravitate towards the German orbit, would not have been sufficient without a dramatic change in Great Power relationships. Enmity between Turk and Russian has been one of the constant features of modern European history. Through much of the nineteenth century, Britain usually, France occasionally, had supported Turkey against Russian ambitions and incursions. But in the first years of the twentieth century, fear of growing German might, or of a possible continental coalition against her, brought Britain out of her isolation and led her to make common cause with her two traditional rivals, France and Russia. Where did this leave Turkey?

In July 1914 Turkish counsels were divided as to what to do in the deepening European crisis. Were they to side with Britain and France? But neither Power was prepared to risk alienating Russia. Were they to stay neutral? And there were many of the old Ottoman establishment who favoured this. Or were they to throw in their lot with Germany? This certainly appeared to offer tempting advantages. The Young Turks, and notably Enver, were pan-Turk in sentiment. The Muslim parts of the Russian Caucasus, as well as Turkestan – the original homeland of the Turkish race – should, they felt, belong to Turkey. The defeat of Russia by Germany would make these otherwise far-fetched ambitions capable of fulfilment. But perhaps even more important was the fact that Russia had long coveted the Straits and the Turkish capital, Constantinople, the source and symbol of the Russian religion, Orthodoxy. And if Britain and France were now unwilling to defend Turkey against Russia (as they had done in the Crimean War) to where else was she to turn for support, if not Germany? On 2 August 1914 Turkey signed a secret defensive and offensive alliance with Germany against Russia. The pro-German party among the Young Turks had prevailed.

Yet for nearly three months Turkey hesitated to enter the war. Partly this was owing to lack of preparation and money, partly to her minimum naval needs and the diplomatic complications these posed. In July 1914, two Turkish battleships, needed in any war against Russia, were on the verge of completion in British yards. On 28 July, Churchill, as First Lord of the Admiralty, requisitioned them. This action caused a wave of public anger in Turkey, the warships having been paid for by public subscription, but it also left Turkey vulnerable and so nearly induced neutrality. Not until the arrival in the Bosphorus in August 1914 of the German battlecruiser and cruiser, *Goeben* and *Breslau*, following a providential escape from the Royal Navy, and their transfer to the Turkish flag, was the way clear for a war against Russia. By October, failing to make a breakthrough in France, the Germans were impatiently pressing the Turks to act, a massive German loan being made conditional upon Turkey's entry into the war. On 29th October, the *Goeben* and other units of the Turkish navy, on the instructions of Enver, although under German command, bombarded Odessa and Sebastopol. In consequence of this strike against an ally, Britain declared war upon Turkey on 5th November.[2] And so, somewhat tardily, from the Sinai Desert to the Red Sea, from Aden to the Persian Gulf, wherever the Ottoman and British Empires touched, war came to the Middle East.

For the British, the key to success or failure in a war against Turkey lay in Egypt. To protect the naval base of Alexandria, and also the Suez Canal, so important for the transport of troops from India and Australasia, it was necessary to secure the British position there. And that position could not be taken for granted. Following over 30 years of British military occupation, and despite, or indeed because of, the financial and administrative reforms carried through by Lord Cromer and others during that period, there was much anti-British feeling in Egypt, particularly amongst the ruling, professional and student classes. The khedive, Abbas II, resentful of British power, was avowedly pro-Turk, and when war broke out was in Constantinople. He was promptly deposed, and after some weeks' hesitation while the British Government contemplated outright annexation, Egypt was declared a Protectorate under the nominal rule of Abbas's more tractable uncle, Hussein. Cyprus, meanwhile, on lease from the Ottoman Empire since 1878, was annexed by Great Britain on the outbreak of war.

With these political moves, the British Government sought to end the uncertainty and ambiguity which had long been associated with the British presence in the area. But how would a Muslim population respond to the call of *jihad*? During November 1914 the Sultan and his chief religious dignitaries formally proclaimed a Holy War against the Allies, a call to arms binding upon all Muslims.[3] The effect was to explode a Victorian myth, for, apart from some spasmodic uprisings in Morocco against the French, very little happened. More might have been achieved had the Sultan been supported by the Sharif of Mecca. As guardian of the Holy Places and descendant of the Prophet, the Sharif enjoyed great prestige and influence throughout the Arab world, but, despite Turkish urgings, that astute dignitary singularly failed to lend his authority to the call for *jihad*. Awaiting an opportunity to overthrow Turkish rule in the Hejaz, he cleverly played for time, professing his entire sympathy, but pleading that his country's vulnerability to British command of the Red Sea made an open declaration of support inopportune.

Of more material concern to the British was the threat the Turkish Army posed to Egypt and the Suez Canal. By striking at the Canal, the Turks aimed both to sever a vital British sea-route and to encourage the Egyptians to rise against their British masters. By mid-January 1915 they were ready to move, advancing out of Palestine with a force of 20,000 men and ten batteries, one of heavy guns. But not for the first, nor for the last time, were the wastes of Sinai to prove an advantage to the defender. The invading force had to reach fresh water quickly or fall back, and adequate fresh water was to be found only on the Egyptian side of the Canal. The main body of Turks reached the central section of the Canal on 1st February and attacked it on the 3rd, even managing to get three pontoons across it before those manning them were either killed or captured. But, facing a force of 30,000 supported by the guns of warships, they lacked the strength to proceed. And with the hoped-for Egyptian rising, which alone might have sufficiently diverted the defence, failing to materialize, the Turks prudently withdrew their main force to Beersheba, thereafter limiting themselves to occasional raids against the Canal and associated targets.

The British, for their part, proceeded to turn Egypt into an immense transit camp, supply base and training ground. Large contingents of troops began to arrive from India, Australia and New Zealand, as well as from the United Kingdom, raising the strength of the Imperial forces there from 70,000 at the beginning of 1915 to something approaching 300,000 at its end.[4] Little use was made of this heterogeneous army during the first half of the War, other than the employment of part of it in the Gallipoli campaign, discussed elsewhere in this volume, but it was held to constitute a vital Imperial reserve, to be drawn upon at need, either for service on the Western Front or for use in one or other of the minor campaigns which developed in the Near and Middle Eastern theatres. One of these was the defence of Aden, successfully maintained throughout the War against a Turkish force from the Yemen. Another was a series of minor operations undertaken in the Western Desert between 1915 and 1917 against the Senussi, a religious sect whose leader, Sayed Ahmed, at last succumbed to persuasion by the Turks and Germans to attack Egypt following the accession of his chief enemy, Italy, to the Allied cause. A concerted rising was staged by Ali Dinar, the Sultan of Darfur, in the far west of the Sudan, with the capture of Khartoum as the ultimate goal, but it was put down by a British-led force during the course of 1916 – surely amongst the most remote and marginal of all the campaigns constituting the Great War.

One use to which an army based in Egypt might have been put was advocated by Kitchener in January 1915. This was a landing in the Gulf of Alexandretta, the north-eastern "corner" of the Mediterranean, where Turkish communications both with Mesopotamia and with Syria, Palestine and Arabia, and in particular a nearly completed railway link, lay at no great distance from the coast. If the Dardanelles may be likened to the throat of the Turkish Empire, then the Gulf of Alexandretta was the groin, and an effective blow there could paralyse the Turkish war-effort throughout the Middle East. The Gallipoli campaign while it lasted ruled out any such alternative, but the idea was revived in 1916 after that ill-fated enterprise had been abandoned. Telling arguments, however, were raised against the Alexandretta scheme. It was calculated that 100,000 to 150,000 troops would be required, and an expedition of this magnitude, apart from using up much needed shipping, was anathema to the "Westerners" – that school of thought which held that any serious diversion of men and resources from the Western Front was a misdirection of effort. Moreover, the French, having earmarked Syria for themselves, raised objections, claiming that the proposed scene of operations lay within their own sphere of interest. In such ways, at least as far as the Western Powers were concerned, far more than in the Second World War, did inter-Allied jealousy in the First impair the strategical direction of the conflict.

Following the repulse of the Turkish attack on the Suez Canal, fighting died down on the Egyptian Front. At first the Canal itself was used as a moat, inviting the gibe, attributed to Kitchener: "Is the garrison of Egypt defending the Canal, or the Canal defending the garrison of Egypt?"[5] On Kitchener's orders strong defensive lines were therefore constructed along the Canal some six miles to the eastward of it, Egypt being drawn upon for the huge labour force required.

Thus was one vital Imperial interest safeguarded. Another in the Middle East remained. This was the refinery at Abadan and the pipelines linking it with the oilfields of the Anglo-Persian Oil Company, a company in which the British Government, on behalf of the Admiralty, had a 51 per cent holding. As the Royal Navy was in process of equipping itself with oil-burning ships – including the latest and most powerful class of battleships, the five *Queen Elizabeths* – British security might be imperilled if these installations should fall to the enemy. In consequence the Admiralty continually pressed the Government of India to send troops to guard the oil. On 6 November 1914, the day after Britain declared war on Turkey, a brigade of the 6th Indian Division, which had waited in the Gulf for a month, was landed on Abadan Island.

The Government of India, however, was at best indifferent, at worst hostile, to the defence of Persian oil.[6] It had its own motives for waging a campaign in the area. The Persian Gulf, in fact, had been regarded as a sphere of interest of British India since the days of the East India Company. An elaborate system of Residents, Political Agents and treaties with native rulers had been built up during the nineteenth century, so that when, only a decade earlier, in 1903, Lord Curzon had made an official tour of the Gulf, he did so as though it were a Viceregal lake. Given this view of its own Imperial interests, the Raj could not regard an enemy-controlled Mesopotamia with indifference. Turkey was bad enough, Germany would be worse, and Russia, even though temporarily an ally, should her Caucasian army prove victorious and pour southward into the plains, could ultimately prove the greatest threat of all. It was therefore necessary in order both to inspire confidence in the Gulf rulers, and for longer-term political reasons, to acquire at least the head of the Gulf and preferably as much of Mesopotamia as could be secured.

With this strategy London agreed, and an almost unopposed landing near the mouth of the Shatt al-Arab (the great waterway formed by the confluence of the Tigris and Euphrates) was soon effected by the remaining three brigades of the 6th Indian Division. The Turks had clearly been caught off balance, and so, with Cabinet sanction, the force was ordered to advance on Basra, the main port of Mesopotamia, some seventy-five miles from the sea. This it took on 22 November, and then, on 9 December, Qurna, some fifty-five miles farther on, near the junction of the two rivers.

Here might have been a suitable place to halt, for further progress upstream not only meant dividing the invading force, but required an adequate number of shallow-draught vessels of which too few had been provided. But the Government of India in April 1915 raised the expeditionary force to Army Corps strength under General Sir John Nixon, and, being encouraged by the success achieved, that summer ordered advances to be made up both rivers. On 29 September, having advanced over 200 miles beyond Qurna, the Tigris division, under General Townshend, captured Kut al-Amara after heavy fighting.

Baghdad was now but a hundred miles distant, and the temptation to take it was strong, even though hitherto both London and Delhi, harbouring misgivings, had forbidden the attempt. On 23 October, however, the Cabinet put the onus on Nixon by sanctioning a march on Baghdad "if he is satisfied that the force he has available is sufficient for the operation".[7] Encouraged by the promise of two further Indian divisions from France, Nixon ordered Townshend to proceed. Twenty-five miles from Baghdad he found the main Turkish force, some 20,000 strong, barring his way at Ctesiphon, and here, within sight of the great arch of the Sassanids, he attacked them on 23 November 1915.

The Turks were strongly entrenched and the fighting was fierce. Townshend's Anglo-Indian army of 12,000, although outnumbered, took the enemy front-line and repelled a counter-attack, but lost 4,500 men in so doing. Indeed the casualties were so heavy that, pessimistically, *both* armies withdrew from the field. The Battle of Ctesiphon, given its situation, was like a miniature Borodino which just failed to come off. And as with Napoleon's retreat from Moscow, Townshend's retreat from Baghdad had both nature and the natives against it. Across the flat, dreary plain of mud which is Mesopotamia – aptly "Mespot" to the British – exhausted by forced marches, to drop out from which was to risk murder and mutilation, the little army retired to Kut, which it reached on 3 December, and here, in a fortified bend of the Tigris, Townshend elected to stay. His army was in no state to retreat further, but he had every confidence of being relieved.

By this time, however, the Turks were beginning to transfer to Mesopotamia their battle-hardened veterans from Gallipoli. And with the final British evacuation there in January 1916, the flow became a flood. There was a flood, too, in the form of the winter rains and the rising river. Kut became a quagmire and Turkish machine guns turned it into a Passchendaele under the palms. A number of desperate attempts were made to relieve the starving garrison, with even the Russians launching an offensive in Armenia to take off the pressure. But all was to no avail. After the relieving forces had suffered 23,500 casualties – about twice the number of the beleaguered army – and at one time approached to within seven miles of their goal, the effort was given up. Townshend and his 12,000, having endured a siege of nearly five months' duration, in which they had to provide not only for themselves but also for the inhabitants of Kut, were compelled to surrender.

Shortly before they did so a strange business occurred. The War Office adopted the suggestion that an attempt should be made to bribe the Turkish commander, Khalil Pasha, to let the Kut garrison go free.[8] In consequence T.E. Lawrence and Aubrey Herbert, MP (a Turkish speaker) were sent secretly to Basra to act as emissaries. Learning of their mission and scandalized by it, some of the generals there gave them a cool, even hostile, reception, and Sir Percy Cox, the Chief Political Officer for Mesopotamia, condemned the move as likely to have an effect worse than defeat. Herbert and Lawrence were led blindfold through the Turkish lines, met Khalil Pasha, and offered him first one million sterling, then two. These offers he curtly rejected, and Turkish and German propaganda fully exploited the whole affair.[9]

That same day, 29 April 1916, Townshend surrendered. He was well treated by his captors, his officers adequately, his men atrociously, over two-thirds of the British other ranks dying on the march or in captivity.[10] They had fought with great bravery and had endured unparalleled sufferings. They deserved better than to receive such callous treatment at the hands of the Turks, a possible presentiment of which fate may explain, and arguably even excuse, one of the most dishonourable proposals ever to have emanated from a British department of state.

Thus the first Mesopotamian campaign ended in defeat and humiliation. What had gone wrong? Aubrey Herbert returned to England determined to bring to book the authorities in India he alleged were chiefly culpable. To this end he raised the matter several times in the House of Commons, pressing for an enquiry, a demand which got widespread support. Meanwhile, Lloyd George, newly appointed to the War Office following the death of Kitchener, had taken a similar view, and promoted a Mesopotamia Commission which first met in August 1916 and reported in May 1917. Its findings were damning: the Mesopotamian campaign had been grossly mismanaged from the start. Indeed, it recalls the Crimean War in the lack of adequate preparation, the complete breakdown of the medical services, the ignorance of the nature of the country (the rivers had to be the chief means of transport, but in the dry season they were too shallow for the vessels ordered), the plethora of authorities (the C.-in-C. Mesopotamia, the C.-in-C. India, the Viceroy, the India Office, the War Office, and the Cabinet War Committee), the absurd over-confidence, and finally the attempt to fight a campaign on the cheap. These faults and failures were compounded by the notorious amount of red tape characteristic of Indian administration. So might the Circumlocution Office have gone to war – with Mr. Micawber as Chief of Staff.

As for the actual handling of the campaign, General Nixon was optimistic to the point of irresponsibility in not awaiting the reinforcements promised, but Sir Percy Cox was equally sanguine and the British Government itself cannot wholly be absolved from blame. It allowed a political desideratum to override logistical and strategical realities. In a bleak year of frustration on the Western Front and failure at Gallipoli, the magic name of Baghdad was too great a lure.

Whereas Mesopotamia had been Delhi's "show", the Arab Revolt was Cairo's, in the sense that the British authorities there had shown a keen interest in the possibility of it, and once it had begun were materially to assist it. To close observers it had become apparent that within the Arab population of the Ottoman Empire a situation was developing which might well lead to a successful independence movement. Arabs were the largest ethnic group within the Empire, outnumbering even Turks, but they were treated as second-class citizens, especially after the rise of the Young Turks with their unpopular centralizing policies and notions of Turkish racial and cultural supremacy.[11] The politically conscious among the Arabs reacted by forming secret societies, engaging in agitation, and deploying propaganda, with Arab autonomy or even independence as their goal. But if war were to break out between Great Britain and Turkey, which way would the Arabs jump? Would they be loyal to their fellow Muslims the Turks? Or would their desire for independence be sufficiently strong for them to ally themselves with the Christian Powers of the Entente? These were questions which much exercised the minds of representatives of the British Government in Cairo, and in particular Lord Kitchener, who, as Agent and Consul-General there in the years immediately preceding the War, looked to Arab autonomy or independence as a means of keeping Turkish-German influence at a safe distance from the Suez Canal and the Persian Gulf.[12]

Sharif Hussein of Mecca, by descent and office the most eminent of all the Arabs, was alarmed by the regime's centralizing policies and aware that Constantinople was planning his removal. He thus had his own reasons for favouring a revolt, and so initially his prime concern was winning independence for his own province, the Hejaz. But he had to act with the greatest circumspection. The chief cities of the Hejaz, Mecca, Medina and Jedda, were garrisoned by Turkish troops, and a narrow-gauge line, completed to Medina in 1908, could rapidly bring reinforcements from Syria and the north. In these circumstances it would be necessary first to know what help could be obtained from Great Britain.

Between February 1914 and January 1916 a series of contacts took place between the Sharif Hussein, and his son, the Emir Abdullah, on the one hand, and a succession of high-ranking British officials – Kitchener, his Oriental Secretary, Ronald Storrs, and his successor, Sir Henry McMahon – on the other. The first exchanges were exploratory, each side seeking to discover the position of the other in the event of conflict with Turkey. The later exchanges, the so-called Hussein–McMahon Correspondence, were more important, because more specific, and sought to establish the actual conditions, especially relating to the future of the Arab lands, under which a revolt would be launched.

At first the British assumed that they were dealing only with the Sharif and the Hejaz, but in October 1915 they were suddenly made aware that a revolt would have much wider implications when a young Arab officer in the Turkish Army who had deserted at Gallipoli, revealed to them the existence of two important secret societies sworn to Arab independence: one of chiefly Mesopotamian army officers, and the other of mainly Syrian upper-class intellectuals. Both groups earlier that year had had contact with the Sharif, and had put to him their proposals, "The Damascus Protocol", for an independent Arab state. This was to be a huge entity, encompassing, with the exception of Aden, the whole of the Arabian peninsula, as well as the Fertile Crescent. It was to be in a defensive alliance with Great Britain, which for its part would enjoy economic preference. These far-reaching proposals, representing the terms under which important bodies of opinion in Syria and Mesopotamia would be prepared to support the revolt, were then communicated (14 July 1915) to McMahon by the Sharif as those of "the Arab nation". McMahon was reluctant to pledge large areas of territory with specified frontiers at a time when Turkey still controlled most of it, and before any of Britain's allies had been consulted; but upon the Sharif's dismissal of such a response as "lukewarm", and to obviate the danger that he might lose interest, or even go over to the Turks and Germans, McMahon obtained, and conveyed to him in the most important of the letters (24 October 1915), the British Government's approval of the boundaries of the proposed independent Arab state, subject only to certain reservations. These were: the exclusion from the proposed area of the Syrian–Lebanese coastal region, and of territories already in a treaty relationship with Great Britain (Oman and the Gulf sheikhdoms); and the acknowledgement of special British interests in the Basra to Baghdad region, and of any special interests that France might have.

The trouble was that France did have interests, indeed claims, and considerable ones. The French held that the whole of Syria – and then Greater Syria included Palestine – should be theirs, or at least under their influence, by historical right. It is an interest which goes back to Napoleon, to the protection of Catholics by the Bourbons, even to the Crusades, in which the French took the leading part. Indeed, in the Arabic of the region, *Franji* (Frank) was a term applicable to any European.[13]

For the British Government, therefore, the problem was how to secure the Arab Revolt while not falling foul of their chief ally in any promised settlement of territory. In consequence an attempt was made to meet French claims in the so-called Sykes–Picot Agreement, negotiated by the representatives of both Powers, ratified by the War Committee on 23 March 1916, and later submitted to the Russians for their approval. By this arrangement Palestine, because of its international religious significance (and, for the British, as a way of pre-empting the French) was to be placed under international administration; the French were to control the Syrian-Lebanese coastland, and the British the Baghdad–Basra region together with the ports of Haifa and Acre. However, the whole of the area lying between, including what is now northern Iraq, was to be recognized and upheld as the new independent Arab state or states, although divided into French and British zones for purposes of enterprise and the provision of advisers on request. From the point of view of Arab advantage, this now notorious document is not nearly as bad as it has been painted.[14] It allotted to the new state the cities of Amman, Damascus, Homs, Hama, Aleppo, Mosul and Kirkuk; it stipulated the Sharif's agreement to the international arrangements for Palestine; it guaranteed, with the sole exception of Aden, indigenous rule for the entire Arabian peninsula; and it represented, through Sir Mark Sykes' efforts, a considerable reduction in the French demands. Yet these arrangements clearly fell short of the type of Arabian kingdom Sharif Hussein had supposed in his own mind that he was going to get, and, not surprisingly, he was not informed of what had been decided.

Whether, had he been apprised of the Sykes–Picot settlement, the Sharif would have launched the Revolt, must remain an open question. The fact that he was prepared to leave for future negotiation those reservations in the McMahon correspondence with which he disagreed, suggests he feared that if he pushed them too hard the Allies would simply ignore him. The McMahon promises had at least given him a moral claim on Great Britain; the success of the Revolt would add to this the irrefutable claims of a victorious ally.

On 10 June 1916, Hussein, Grand Sharif of Mecca, raised his standard of revolt, his forces first attacking the Turkish garrison in Mecca itself. The Arabs having no artillery, Wingate rushed two guns, with some companies of Egyptian gunners, across the Red Sea from the Sudan, and, after holding out for three weeks, the main Turkish force in the city surrendered. Jedda and other coastal towns also fell, with the help of shellfire from British warships.

The story of how the British supported the Revolt involves the names chiefly of three men: Sir Reginald Wingate, Governor-General of the Sudan and Sirdar of the Egyptian Army, who furnished the Arabs with equipment, instructors and specialized units; Admiral Sir Rosslyn Wemyss, who rendered invaluable aid by sea; and T.E. Lawrence. The last, half genius, half charlatan, whose enigmatic personality has a fatal attraction for biographers, was a member of the Arab Bureau in Cairo, a collection of British orientalists, formally under the Foreign Office, engaged on intelligence work (as in the surrender at Kut). Lawrence's role in the Arab Revolt was initially one of liaising between its leaders and Cairo. Sharif Hussein and his four sons were a curious and complex family. None of them had the outsize physique and personality of Abdul Aziz ibn Sa'ud, the heroic desert chieftain who was later to displace them from the Hejaz. The Sharif himself was exquisitely mannered, subtle, shrewd and, having so long survived at the Ottoman Court, adept in keeping his own counsel. Of all the sons, the one who seemed most cut out for military leadership was the third, the Emir Feisal, an intelligent, highly-wrought, frail, yet energetic prince, with an instinct for handling men and wholly unsparing of himself. With Feisal, Lawrence worked in close association, welding, with liberal supplies of British gold, the desert tribes into a coherent military force, and making frequent raids upon the Damascus-Medina railway. The Arabs were unable to dislodge the strong Turkish garrison in Medina, nor did the British particularly wish that they should, both because the vulnerability of the line was a constant drain on Turkish strength, and because its survival made the Sharif more dependent upon British help.

From mid-1916 two factors combined to make a more dynamic prosecution of the war against Turkey possible. First was the immense accession of manpower that had become available from the various countries of the Empire. The second was the increasing part played in the direction of the war by Mr. Lloyd George, culminating in his rise to the premiership in December 1916. It was largely through him that offensives were pushed forward in Mesopotamia and Sinai.

Already in July 1916, on his going to the War Office, a new spirit entered into the Mesopotamian theatre. It showed itself first in the transfer of responsibility for the campaign from the Indian to the home government. General Cowans, perhaps the best organizer in the British Army, was sent out to bring order to the hitherto chaotic state of transport and supplies. Reinforcements arrived, so that the enemy were outnumbered by possibly four to one, and a new commander-in-chief was found in the person of General Sir Stanley Maude, an exceptionally competent soldier, thorough in preparation, although with an inability to delegate verging on fussiness.

The Government wanted a forward policy on two grounds: to redeem the Kut disaster, and to assist the Grand Duke Nicholas who, on the Armenian front, was about to launch the last offensive of Czarist Russia. Maude began his advance in December 1916 and on 24 February following, reoccupied Kut. By this time the Grand Duke had informed London that he intended to send a force through Persia and on to Mosul and Baghdad – news which caused the War Office to urge Maude forward.[15] On 11 March 1917 a victorious British army at last entered Baghdad.

A parallel series of developments was meanwhile taking place on the Sinai front. In the spring of 1916 a Turkish force of 18,000 under Kress von Kressenstein, the same enterprising German commander who had masterminded the 1915 attack on the Suez Canal, again advanced towards it, but after an initial success at Katia in April, was defeated in August some twenty miles eastward of the Canal near the Mediterranean coast at the Battle of Romani. As in Mesopotamia, the British now outnumbered the enemy by four or five to one, but such was the nature of the terrain that to follow up this success required thorough preparation. During the autumn and winter of 1916 the Egyptian Expeditionary Force (EEF) advanced across the Sinai Desert, building a railway and a twelve-inch water pipeline as it went. By the spring of 1917 it had crossed the desert and reached Gaza, but here it was repulsed in two successive battles, the first of which failed through faulty staff-work, and the second through lack of surprise. This led the Government to recall the Commander-in-Chief of the EEF, General Murray, and to cast about for a replacement. Jan Smuts, the South African soldier-statesman was first approached, but he declined. The next choice was General Sir Edmund Allenby, commander of the Third Army on the Western Front.

Allenby plays so large a part in the final phase of the war in the Middle East that some mention should be made of his character. His outstanding qualities were professional competence and drive. In many ways he brought to the EEF that same extra dimension of leadership that Montgomery brought to the Eighth Army a generation later. But there the resemblance ends: Montgomery was an eccentric; Allenby was a stickler for discipline and form. An inspection by Allenby was marked by angry bellows whenever he spotted inefficiency or contravention of orders. He once erupted in wrath when he discovered that a dead soldier had not been wearing his helmet, and Australians who tended to be less formal than troops trained in the British tradition, especially those given to stripping off in the heat of the Jordan Valley, aroused his particular ire. Whenever he was coming the signal would go out, "The Bull's on the loose". But with all this went a man in whom exceptional ability, and strength and generosity of character – he never bore a grudge – quite overshadowed such foibles.

Like Maude, Allenby had an army that was greatly superior in numbers to the enemy's, but one whose sheer heterogeneity probably required a man of his stamp to give it fighting unity. It was made up of British, Australians, New Zealanders, Indians, South Africans, Jews (three battalions of Royal Fusiliers were all Jewish), French, Italians, two battalions of West Indians, the Egyptian Labour Corps, and even some Polynesians to run boats ashore on to those harbourless, surf-breaking beaches.[16] Like Maude, too, Allenby had an historic city to capture: Lloyd George wanted Jerusalem as a 1917 Christmas present for the British people.

In November 1917, just as Allenby was poised to take Jerusalem, two startling political developments occurred which caused perturbation in Arab circles. The first was the issuing of the Balfour Declaration in which the British Government viewed with favour the establishment in Palestine of a national home for the Jewish people. The second was the "blowing" of the Sykes–Picot Agreement by the Bolsheviks when, on seizing power in Russia, they published all secret treaties.

The British were hard put to explain away these two set-backs to Arab hopes. Allenby refused to allow the Balfour Declaration to be published in Palestine, and Hogarth, of the Arab Bureau, was sent to smooth matters out with the gravely concerned Sharif (now King) Hussein. The Foreign Office acted similarly, playing down Sykes–Picot to Hussein as merely an *ad hoc* arrangement between allies, something which had since been overtaken by events.[17]

The Arab army of Feisal and Lawrence, having taken Aqaba on 6th July for use as a supply base, was then keeping pace with Allenby's army as it advanced north, acting as a flank guard and harrying the left flank of the retreating enemy. Hussein could have reined in the whole Arab Revolt, and indeed, exploiting the Sykes–Picot revelation, the Turks made overtures to him, but these he curtly dismissed and informed his British allies of them. Aside from questions of honour, he must have realized that, with Allenby's advance, the British were going to be in possession, and that his best course was to be in possession too. It was for this same reason that Lawrence hurried to get Feisal and his Arabs into Damascus before it could be handed over to the French.

Despite the Sykes–Picot Agreement the British and French were still manoeuvring for position in the closing stages of the war against Turkey.

Through military success, however, the British held the stronger hand. After taking Jerusalem on 9 December 1917, Allenby continued his advance northwards, and, even though obliged to relinquish all but one of his British divisions – some 60,000 of his best men – to help stay the German spring "push" on the Western Front, went on to win his greatest victory at the Battle of Megiddo (19–21 September 1918), an action in which, by a bold and imaginative plan, two Turkish armies were cut off and destroyed. By this time, however, the Turks were not only heavily outnumbered but also demoralized, and not even the skill of their German commander, Liman von Sanders of Gallipoli fame, could save them from largely disintegrating as an effective force. On 1 October, the same day as Damascus was entered by Australian cavalry, Haifa fell to an Indian division which went on to take Beirut a week later. The Arabs, meanwhile, who were given the administration of Damascus, kept abreast of the main advance and were the first to enter Aleppo on 25 October.

At the same time a parallel success had been achieved in Mesopotamia. Maude having died of cholera in Baghdad in November 1917, his successor, General Sir William Marshall, continued his offensive strategy, pursuing the main Turkish force in the direction of Mosul. On the last day of the Turkish war, 30 October 1918, he captured the entire enemy army some fifty miles south of the city.

Before these actions in the field had been concluded, virtually on the frontiers of Turkey itself, the Turks, made vulnerable by the collapse of Bulgaria at the end of September, had made overtures for peace. They hoped for a negotiated settlement which would help them to save face, but the British Government insisted that only a surrender would be permitted, and that at the signing of this – aboard the British battleship *Agamemnon* – the British alone would represent the victors. The French objected, but Lloyd George was adamant, being prepared, if need be, to "split the Entente" over the matter. The reason for this somewhat high-handed behaviour is not hard to define. If British prestige and influence were to be preserved throughout the large parts of the Muslim world which Britain now controlled, then Turkey must be seen to be vanquished, and the British victorious. The world must be left in no doubt as to who were the new masters of the Middle East.[18]

Moreover, in the wake of Allenby's conquest, there was now no more talk of an international regime for the Holy Land. The new dispensation was neatly revealed when Allenby received the surrender of Jerusalem. Georges Picot, co-author of the notorious Agreement, who was attached to his staff as French Political Representative, said to him: "And tomorrow, my dear General, we will take steps to set up an administration in this city." Wavell records that Allenby's chin went up and out just a little farther than usual as he replied that Jerusalem was, and would remain, under martial law.[19] This echoed the Government's view. For a variety of reasons, apart from the prestige of acquiring so famous and historic a country, they wanted a British Palestine. Indeed they came to see that if the French were to get Syria, then it might best suit British Imperial interests if they were kept as far from the Suez Canal as possible. As for Lawrence's championship of the Arab Revolt, this, too, had an anti-French aspect. It was an Arab nation under British tutelage and protection that he dreamed of, and French ambitions in Syria, if fulfilled, would shatter that dream.[20]

It is in the light of this Great Power rivalry that Lloyd George's so-called side-shows must in part be seen. His critics have held that, being a devious man, he naturally chose devious, back-door methods for getting at the enemy. But this ignores much. The Palestine and Mesopotamian offensives were undoubtedly launched partly to raise morale, to achieve fairly cheap victories with glamorous prizes like Jerusalem and Baghdad to offset for the British public the grimness of the War at home and on the Western Front. Nonetheless they were also undertaken with an eye to the future. Great Britain and France had been brought together by a common fear of Germany only since 1904, and there was no compelling reason why that friendship should long outlast the War. But history is rich in irony, and today these imperialistic calculations and schemings strike an odd note indeed. The future of the Middle East lay ultimately not with the players of Kipling's "Great Game", but with the nationalisms so irresponsibly encouraged, or so unthinkingly thwarted, which the experience of the Great War, its fighting and its politics, did so much to advance and to ripen. Out of that four years' struggle for the Ottoman inheritance the modern Middle East was born; but of the Empires whose ambitions and rivalries determined the scope and course of that struggle – all are now at one with Nineveh and Tyre.

Notes

1. The Turks are reported to have called up 2,700,000 men in the War, yet, owing to losses and desertions, Wavell doubted that the Turkish Army ever exceeded 650,000 men. A.P. Wavell, *The Palestine Campaigns*, London: Constable, 1931 edn., p. 21.
2. Hostilities began earlier. At 5-5 p.m. on 31 October the Admiralty signalled all ships to commence hostilities against Turkey; on 1 November a Turkish minelayer was destroyed at Smyrna; and on 3 November British and French warships bombarded the Dardanelles forts. W.S. Churchill, *The World Crisis 1911–1914*, London: Thornton Butterworth, 1923, pp. 495–6.
3. The call came in three stages. See George Antonius, *The Arab Awakening*, London: Hamish Hamilton, 1938, pp. 140–2.
4. C.R.M.F. Cruttwell, *A History of the Great War*, Oxford: Clarendon Press, 1934, p. 352, note 1.
5. Wavell, *op. cit.*, p. 32.
6. Marian Kent, *Oil and Empire*, London: Macmillan, 1976, pp. 118–19.
7. Sir James Edmonds, *A Short History of World War I*, London: Oxford University Press, 1951, p. 382.
8. General Robertson's telegram sanctioning this (P.R.O., FO, 882/13) is quoted in P. Knightley and C. Simpson, *The Secret Lives of Lawrence of Arabia*, London: Nelson, 1969, p. 46.

9. This astonishing proposal was originally to be part of a "package deal", involving exchange of prisoners (the British and Indians to be parolled for the duration), payment of the money, and the surrender intact of Townshend's artillery. Khalil Pasha instead demanded unconditional surrender and Townshend thereupon destroyed his ammunition and guns. The most Herbert and Lawrence were able to arrange was the exchange of Townshend's wounded for an equivalent number of able-bodied Turkish prisoners. Accounts are given in all major Lives of Lawrence and in *The Man who was Greenmantle*, London: Murray, 1983, a biography of Herbert by his grand-daughter, Margaret Fitzherbert. See also Ronald Millar, *Kut: the Death of an Army*, London: Secker & Warburg, 1969, pp. 252–9, 270–6.

10. Of the British O.Rs., about 1,700, or 70 per cent of them, died as prisoners, but of the total force of about 12,000, a majority of whom were Indians (Muslim Indians were better treated), about 4,000, or a third, died in captivity. See Millar, *op. cit.*, p. 284. The Memorial tablet in St. Paul's records 5,746 as having died in the siege or in captivity, of which number 1,746 are known to have died in the siege (Millar, p. 263).

11. The total population of the Ottoman Empire (excluding Egypt) in 1908 was about 22 million, of whom about $10\frac{1}{2}$ million were Arabs and $7\frac{1}{2}$ million Turks. Antonius, *op. cit.*, p. 104, note 1.

12. *Ibid.*, p. 129.

13. For example, as applied to the English explorer Doughty: C.M. Doughty, *Travels in Arabia Deserta*, London: Jonathan Cape & Medici Society, 1926 edn., Vol. 1, p. 412.

14. See, for example, Antonius, *op. cit.*, pp. 248–51, for the Sykes-Picot Agreement as seen from the point of view of Arab nationalism: i.e. imperialistic greed at its worst.

15. P. Guinn, *British Strategy and Politics*, Oxford: Clarendon Press, 1965, p. 220.

16. General Sir Archibald Wavell, *Allenby: A Study in Greatness*, London: Harrap, 1940, pp. 262–3.

17. Antonius, *op. cit.*, p. 257.

18. See V.H. Rothwell, *British War Aims and Peace Diplomacy 1914–1918*, Oxford: Clarendon Press, 1971, chap. VI, esp. pp. 240–4.

19. Wavell, *Allenby*, p. 236.

20. Lawrence's dislike of the French was unconcealed, and when Allenby took on to his staff a French Political Adviser, he asked to be sent home. The French have reciprocated: Aldington's Life of Lawrence, when published in Paris in 1954, bore the title, *Lawrence l'imposteur*.

12

The Government of the Home Front and the "Moral Economy" of the Working Class

BERNARD WAITES

It is commonplace that the First World War involved a massive intrusion of the powers of government into the lives of the common people. It is a mistake to think this intrusion was entirely unprecedented: the introduction by the pre-war Liberal ministry of labour exchanges, National Insurance, Wage Boards for "sweated trades", the increasing tempo of official arbitration in labour disputes, and other measures, all involved government having a greater presence in working-class life. Especially in the sphere of labour policy, where the power of government impinged most directly on wage earners as producers, there was a considerable degree of continuity in terms of institutions and personnel between the Liberal state and the wartime state.[1] In certain respects, therefore, the most *novel* intrusions of government into working-class life after 1914 were those affecting wage earners and their families as consumers: the introduction of rent control in 1915, of price control of basic commodities in 1917 and 1918, the control of food distribution and rationing, the nationalization of part of the liquor trade, the regulation of working-class drinking habits, the dilution of beer were unprecedented acts of government, and scarcely less palpable (or palatable) than the dilution of labour.

There were significant differences in the ways government intruded into production and consumption, and into the everyday life of producers and consumers. The regulation of production originated from within government, and – as far as wage earners were concerned – was sanctioned by the coercive powers of munitions tribunals and (after 1916) the threat of conscription. Workers certainly believed that employers in the engineering and other trades colluded with the Ministry of Munitions to represent truculent "hands" as industrially dispensable before military tribunals.[2] Whether this were the case is difficult to substantiate or refute.[3] But when we add this belief to the powers of government to direct certain workers to the War Munitions Volunteers, to restrict labour mobility by means of the Leaving Certificate [4] and labour embargoes, and consider the official backing given to the stricter industrial discipline of wartime, then we can understand why wage earners felt that as producers they were helots or industrial serfs.

The regulation of consumption, on the other hand – particularly with respect to rent and price control, food distribution and rationing – resulted from the often tardy response of government to working-class demand, voiced indirectly through national and local Labour organizations, the co-ops, tenants' associations, and more directly in rent strikes, angry food queues and, in the latter phase of the war, absenteeism from work, partly as a protest against shortages, partly in order to join queues.

In its relations with working-class consumers, government was not only responsive to demand but was itself frequently a supplicant. During the war, working-class incomes for the first time had a sufficient disposable margin for the state to tax them directly, but because of married men's allowances the numbers actually paying tax were a fairly select minority and they were mostly working-class bachelors.[5] If the government wanted working-class consumers to put some of their disposable margin into war-savings, or to alter their patterns of consumption by eating less bread, observing meatless days, and generally conserving scarce resources, then it had to persuade them. Hence, the increasing sophistication with which after late-1916 government turned to the modern media to communicate with its own citizens. Later, I will describe in some detail how government used the popular pictorial press to placate working-class consumers and give an example of government's awakening to "the immense possibilities of films as educational and propagandist agents".[6] But it is worth noting here that films were produced for the Treasury in connection with the war thrift campaign, for the Ministry of Food for the food economy campaign. The Cinema Branch of the Ministry of Information invented entirely new types of films and entirely new ways for distributing and showing them. Film-tags – two minute shorts with some useful moral like "Save Coal" or "Buy the War Loan" – were made by the Ministry for tagging on to features. Each tag was seen by an estimated ten million individuals.[7]

Although it is essential for the purposes of analysis to distinguish wage earners as producers and consumers, this should not lead us to suppose that they lived their lives in discrete compartments or that popular attitudes and values were not carried over from one sphere of life into the other. On the contrary; while the nation engaged in the common pursuit of a victory which wage earners desired as much as any other section of the community, individuals engaged in the private pursuit of profit in a way deeply offensive to certain social values wage earners held as both producers and consumers. In both social roles working people felt that illegitmate advantage was being taken of national needs for private ends, and in both roles they felt a class resentment which was actually strengthened by patriotic indignation. When America entered the war in April 1917, its government was warned by an official British delegation of the growing "tendency (in Britain) to revert to the pre-war method of industrial warfare" and the most important of the factors producing this was "the gradual awakening of the workmen to the fact that their employer is profiting from the war . . . of all the factors that have been contributing to the difficulty in handling the labour problem in this country, the most formidable has been what has been called "Profiteering by Contractors".[8] The contemporary warnings of the parallel abuse of the wartime consumer were equally explicit. In February 1917, Lord Devonport, a spectacularly incompetent Food Controller, told Lloyd George: ". . . profiteering is rife in every commodity – bread, meat, tea, butter, and the masses are being exploited right and left."[9]

In its dual relationship with wage earners as producers and consumers, wartime government was made acutely aware of what – borrowing a phrase from Edward Thompson – we can call the "moral economy" of the working class. In an article on the eighteenth-century crowd, Thompson traced the legitimizing notions behind food and price "riots" and related them to the popular moral consensus as to what the rights of the people were.[10] One hesitates to draw comparisons between a pre-industrial, agrarian society whose norms were still traditional, and a highly urbanized society where the rationality of the market had (supposedly) supplanted custom. Equally, one hestitates to generalize about the mentalities of an urban working class highly differentiated by skill, market rewards, work-life cycles, ethnicity, and aspirations to respectability. The concentration of staple, export trades in the North of England, the Clyde Valley and South Wales had led to a geo-political fissure within the working class and regional differences in the patterning of class relations.[11] Still, there is a good body of evidence suggesting that manual work for wages and the class-segregation of towns and cities which gave rise to the working-class community led to common life experiences (notably the family life-cycle documented in poverty surveys), a common style of life and the common mentalities of a distinct sub-culture.[12] Working-class education in the public elementary schools, working-class speech and dress all emphasized a sense of apartness from salaried white-collar work and the professional and business strata, although that apartness was not incompatible with the quite frequent movement of workers' children into clerical and other non-manual occupations. In contrast to their apartness from the rest of society was the social solidarism of the respectable poor. In York, in the case of illness in a working-class family, neighbours would almost always come in and render assistance by cleaning the house, nursing, and so on, while in Lambeth the very poor but respectable lived over such a mass of intolerable poverty, that they were said to unite instinctively to save those known to them from falling into it. What bound them together was a kind of "mutual respect in the face of trouble".[13] The experiences of apartness and solidarism meant that common social values were framed within a strong sense of society divided between "them" and "us". Few working-class people were class conscious in Marx's sense of being conscious of their class for itself. But nearly all knew who were "the likes of us". Furthermore, this self-identity was, by all accounts, becoming more distinct in pre-war years. Stephen Reynolds, a participant observer of Edwardian working-class life, asserted that, beneath the variety of popular opinions, the underlying feeling – the ethos – of the working class was "much the same everywhere". Meeting with working people from a distance and from the great towns, he and his west country working-class friends found them more in touch with "us" – more "like the like's of a fellow's self" – than people of other classes who had lived in the neighbourhood all their lives.[14] During the industrial unrest of 1911, George Askwith, chief labour arbitrator of the Board of Trade, made much the same point to the Cabinet: "The cheap press and the increase in all means of communication have made the workmen more homogeneous and more in touch with one another. They are more inclined to act in masses, and more conscious of their numbers and strength." It was a portentous change in social consciousness for industrial relations: a generation before the general strike had been a very shadowy proposal, now – he warned – it was a definite objective deliberately advanced.[15]

At the time Askwith was writing, popular economic nostrums were fluid; economic and social issues were becoming political matters under the influence of the Tariff Reform campaign, the government's welfare pro-gramme, and inflation. There persisted, however, an acquiescent, some-times fatalistic attitude towards an economic system which gave rise to stupendous inequality, with an insistence that social rules and conventions ensure fair dealing between man and man. Perhaps it is more accurate to say that the economy was not seen as a system at all, but that wealth and poverty were seen as matters of luck and good fortune. Throughout the south of England – we are told – labourers had no sort of animosity against the rich man; they inferred that labour would perish if there were no rich to be supplied and if a man spent his money freely, then the richer he was the better.[16] The attitude was, I think, particularly explicit where workers were close to a rural past, but we find it in music-hall song, in the dialect columns of industrial Lancashire's local press, and it was the despair of Robert Tressell's socialist hero. The too ostentatious display of wealth could disturb popular acquiescence towards it, but what jarred most with popular morality was profit made by "them" taking unfair advantage of "us". Fair play was the working man's chief standard of judgement: a moral notion reflected and reinforced in the huge popular following for organized games. The moral authority of the House of Commons rested upon the apparent "fairness" of its proceedings and elections which were imitated in working-class organizations and popular debating societies.[17] On the other hand, the law, the judiciary and the police were the devil in working-class ethics precisely because they were seen as not being "fair" towards "us". The worker brought a particular test of fairness towards his own and his workmates' wages; up to the First World War, wage rates and differentials were strongly influenced by customary comparisons which the skilled and the unskilled in one trade made with each other, and with men of similar levels of skill in other trades in their district. Though the influence of this customary standard was diminishing before 1914, the modern comparisons with the cost-of-living or the profits of capital had by no means displaced custom when war broke out.[18]

Now, this thumb-nail sketch of certain popular frames of mind is made in the absence of systematic evidence for public opinion and obviously entails generalizations whose connections with historical reality are tenuous. Still, this sketch is a necessary prelude to reviewing wage earners' responses to profiteering, inequalities of food distribution and shortage, and to examining the way their moral notions were articulated in the demand for a capital levy to help pay for the war. Workers' social consciousness in wartime combined an existing "design for living" in the Edwardian world of labour with the sense they made of the entirely new experiences of war industrialism. What I call the working-class "moral economy" was a set of attitudes which changed and developed under the impact of war.

The first six months of the war were a time of peace in the world of labour such as had never existed before and has probably not existed since.[19] The disruption of this harmony in the early spring of 1915 was coincident with (although not merely coincident with) the first public revelations of the extraordinary profits being made in wartime circumstances. In March, Josiah Stamp noted in an Inland Revenue memorandum on exceptional profits due to the war that if businesses had done well at all, they had very well.[20] Huge windfall profits had been made by those holding stocks of basic commodities (such as corn merchants, millers, sugar merchants) and by ship-owners the value of whose services was suddenly inflated. These excess profits very quickly became common knowledge in the Labour movement, in large part because they were publicized by the War Emergency Workers' National Committee formed to represent the common interests of organized workers when war broke out.[21] Knowledge of profiteering did not cause strikes, but it greatly strengthened the propensity to strike and legitimized strikes for the strikers when they did break out. Striking in wartime meant breaking with the national patriotic consensus and drawing on one's head the censure of both the popular press, and relatives and workmates in uniform. It was a difficult step to take without a frame of mind in which specific grievances over wages, dilution, the skilled man's trade card, and so on, were placed within a sense of overall, systematic unfairness. Resentment of profiteering created that frame of mind. This was powerfully demonstrated in the South Wales miners' strike of July 1915 when virtually all the miners struck in defiance of the proclamation on the strike by the government. The Miners' Federation was seeking both a pay award to match rising prices and a revision of the agreement covering wages.[22] But there can be little doubt that, in a coalfield noted for its patriotism, the striking miners saw their actions as morally justified by the well-founded rumours of huge profits being made by coal owners and merchants. Later in the war, the government's Commissioners of Enquiry into Industrial Unrest who reported on South Wales were to write: "... we believe (the 1915) strike to be largely due to the suspicion that employers of labour were exploiting the national crisis for personal gain". The Commissioners added that "the men were driven to strike by the belief on their part that the owners were 'exploiting' the patriotism of the miners, believing it would inevitably prevent them pressing home their claims by actually striking".[23]

Once the term "profiteer" re-entered common speech in the spring of 1915, it was constantly reiterated in the Labour press, at Labour organization conferences and meetings, and we have ample reason for believing that it was common currency amongst wage earners who were outside or only loosely tied to the Labour movement. In trade union newspapers and journals, the profiteer was vividly depicted as "The Vampire on the Back of Tommy", the "Brit-Hun" (it was the age of the bad pun), and in other images representing him as predatory and immoral. In his September 1916 presidential address to the Trades Union Congress, Harry Gosling drew the "contrast [between] the conduct of the workers who had toiled in the industries so necessary for the successful prosecution of the war [and] the conduct of shipowners, food exploiters, war contractors, and other profiteers who had scrupled at nothing so long as it secured their enrichment", which was to become a basic theme of Labour rhetoric.[24] "Profiteering" was a highly emotive slogan invaluable in maintaining some measure of unity in a Labour movement deeply divided in its attitudes to the war, but over the course of time it tended to strengthen the position of that minority of Labour leaders who accepted an anti-capitalist ideology and were class-conscious in something like Marx's sense. This minority was able to seize on the profiteering scandal as a breach of faith on the part of the capitalist class with the unwritten social compact of August 1914. While condemning the exploitation of the working class, they drew a bitter consolation from the fact that (as one put it) "... if this war has served no other good purpose, it has at least revealed and emphasized the selfishness and immorality of modern capitalism".[25] It is true that "the profiteer" was excoriated in the middle-class press quite as vehemently as he was by working-class representatives and it is worth emphasizing that the detestation of the "profiteer" by Labour arose as much from an affront to its patriotism, as it did from latent class consciousness, and the victim of capital was seen as the patriotic community no less than the working class. Still, organized workers are usually persuaded to organize because they see some sort of conflict of interests with their employers, and the effect of the "profiteering" scandal re-alerted them, after the lull of the industrial truce, to the antagonistic character of Capital-Labour relationships. (We must remember, too, that the number of organized workers, only about a quarter of the labour force in 1914, was growing rapidly despite enlistment.) Askwith, whose experience of industrial relations was unmatched, wrote that there was no greater cause for the waning of working-class patriotism than

> "the fact that some people were making money out of the War without any restraint upon their methods . . . A shipowner who stated that he had made profits, was going to make profits, and had a right to make profits, did more harm than a great naval defeat would have done. To name 'defeat' would rouse the nation to set their teeth and fight against an alien foe. The profiteer's statement would rouse class against class, and only tend to disruption within the nation itself".[26]

The extent of popular hostility to profiteering was underlined for the government when its Industrial Commissioners reported in the summer of 1917, following the widespeard engineering strikes of May. The strikes had arisen out of the sectional, somewhat narrow grievances of skilled craftsmen, angered by the threat of the spread of dilution to non-war work and by the withdrawal of the Trade Card which had given them exemption from conscription. But the Commissioners interpreted their brief as diagnosing the general causes of working-class discontent and with near unanimity they identified "profiteering" as having induced the wage earners' sourness of mind. The Commissioners from London and the South East reported that:

> "Statements of prices and profits in the newspapers, admissions made in Parliament, the workmen's own sources of information and their personal and family experience make them feel, to use their own language, they are 'being bled white'."[27]

Their colleagues for the Yorkshire and Midlands Area recorded a general

> "conviction that insufficient steps had been taken by the Government departments to prevent profiteering, exploiting and plundering, such as make the poor contribute heavily to the abnormal advantage of those traders and others, who by their selfishness secured immense gains from the sacrifices and sufferings of the poor".[28]

The Commissioners for the South West Area argued that the techniques of war finance (from which rentiers had profited) and the wartime excess profits duty, had tended to exacerbate popular resentments. They found witnesses insisting on the contrast between the common soldier, compelled to serve at a shilling a day, and the rentier who voluntarily lent his capital to the government at an inflated rate of interest, and the Commissioners themselves suggested that because the excess profits duty did "not take money out of the rich man's pocket in the same way that direct tax on his income would have done . . . it [had] consequently failed in its moral effect on the working classes as a symbol of equality of sacrifice".[29] (My purpose is to delineate popular attitudes, rather than establish the objective facts of the matter, but it is worth noting that the Inland Revenue thought it possible that up to 1917, the excess profits duty was taken into account by business-men in determining prices and was convinced that fiscal change during the war led to a great increase in account "cooking" and fraud.[30] Dissatisfaction with the attempts to tax abnormal profits was not simply based on popular indignation.)

Around the summer and autumn of 1917 the question of inequalities of food distribution, of shortages which reflected existing social class divisions (which the common enterprise of war made more intolerable) and of food prices took precedence over "profiteering" as the sources of working-class resentment. "Profiteering" remained a highly emotive slogan – if only because prices were believed to have been inflated by a species of "profiteer" – but the "food question" became much more prominent in expressions of popular discontent. However, the slogan had become embedded in working-class consciousness and it is worth examining how the resentments that clustered around it resurfaced in the de-mobilizing society of 1919. It was a year of extraordinarily high profits and witnessed what *The Economist* (no less) considered an "orgy of extravagance" on the part of the well-to-do.[31] It was also a year when workers were being constantly exhorted to raise their output to compensate for the widespread reduction of hours. What was called the "dead-weight of resistance to any suggestion that output should be increased" was analysed in several of the weekly Labour situation reports that went from the Ministry of Labour to the Cabinet and in October 1919 the three ideas then said to be "dominating the masses" were that "the more the working class produce, the more the 'idle rich' will waste", that "a man cannot work his best in a system run for private profit", and that "the landowners and capitalists should loose their stranglehold on land and money before they begin to lecture labour on restricting production". To counter these ideas, it was suggested that expenditure on luxuries should be restricted and more forceful action be taken by the Profiteering Tribunals set up to investigate excess profit-making.[32] We cannot, of course, be sure how accurately civil servants monitored phenomena as elusive as workers' attitudes and values, but there are reasons for believing that the popular ideology discerned by official-dom in October 1919 was not a figment of its imagination. Economic historians have established that British industry did fail to raise productivity to compensate for reduced hours so there is something to be explained, while in November 1919 Labour party candidates in the municipal elections campaigned with a new vitality, in close alliance with trade-union organizations, and often articulated these "ideas" said to be dominating the rank and file.[33] They achieved many notable successes. There can be no doubt that "profiteering" was the central ideological motif of local and national Labour organizations from the summer of 1919 through the spring of 1920; it was raised in numerous resolutions forwarded from trade councils, local Labour parties and trade unions, was the subject of a massive demonstration in Hyde Park in September when the government was violently denounced for sheltering profiteers, and was a major theme of the December Trades Union Congress. The argument that this motif was aligned with widely-felt resentment is greatly strengthened by a factor discussed in the Cabinet's Labour situation reports during July and August: working-class wages began to outstrip inflation in 1918 and 1919 and certain domestic consumer goods until recently rarely found outside the homes of artisan and labour aristocrats were now being regarded as prerequisites of a decent way-of-life by nearly all working-class families. A new sensitivity to prices and profits in consumer goods was made evident in mid 1919 when, as part of the measures to restore business confidence, the government simultaneously decontrolled several consumer goods industries and halved the rate of excess profits tax. Profits and prices soared, notoriously in wool where the prices rose by 30 per cent to 50 per cent within a brief time after decontrol, and there were similar rapid rises in the price of boots, furniture and most household utensils. It was reported:

> ". . . neither inflation nor the rise in labour costs due to increased wages and shorter hours will satisfactorily account in most cases for the prices now being charged. The effect of this on the minds of the working classes may easily be conceived. Every man and every woman is hit by high prices of domestic articles, which they know are largely due to excessive profits . . .".[34]

Somewhat later, a Labour situation report – noted with respect to failure to raise productivity: "The wage earner is . . . also a purchaser, and in him are combined resentment against being cheated as a purchaser, and disinclination to do his best in an industrial system which tolerates the 'profiteer'."[35] The comment sums up one of the fundamental shifts in the value-cluster of the working-class moral economy: industrial attitudes and behaviour and the seemingly more "visible" inequalities of society outside the workplace were brought into closer connection in wage earners' minds. A further shift, suggested by this and a great deal of other comment on the labour situation, was towards a more widespread perception of the economic system as a system and a greater receptivity to anti-capitalist ideology. The same Labour situation report quoted as an accurate assessment of this shift in popular thought the guild socialist journal, *The New Age*:

> "The popular adoption of the word '*profiteering*' and the application of it to particular abuses of profit-making, has . . . contributed to bring profit into wider disrepute. There has been a marked change during the war in the public attitude towards profit. The Socialist case has in consequence been much strengthened, and the view that the individual system of industry is iniquitous and intolerable has spread and intensified among working men . . . Profit . . . finds itself confronted with this new element, the spirit which denounces its former pretensions as immoral."

Resentment of "profiteering" did not simply express itself as a moral rejection of capitalism, it reinforced working-class sympathy for the closely related demands of the Labour movement that there should be conscription of wealth during the war and, after 1918, a levy on capital to pay for war-debt. The call for the "Conscription of Riches" was first heard in the wake of the outcry against "profiteering" and some time before the conscription of men. It was taken up by the WEWNC and the Triple Industrial Alliance and became a more plausible political demand as a corollary for the conscription of manhood after 1916.[36] The Workers' National Committee saw the imposition of a graduated levy on all capital wealth on the basis of the existing Death Duties as an alternative to the war loans raised by the wartime chancellors. Royden Harrison – in his essay on the Workers' National Committee – has shown how the "Conscription of Riches" slogan became a call for the public ownership and control of all the most vital sectors of the economy and transformed what had hitherto been the academic shibboleth of a minority in the Labour movement into an immediate issue, and into a practical demand of the organized workers as a whole. In the short term, the conscription of wealth served as a bargaining counter in relation to the Munitions and Military Service Acts. However, a full delegate conference of the Industrial Alliance of June 1917 called for the conscription of wealth in order to achieve a real equality of sacrifice between conscripted men and their employers, and increasingly the proposal became seen in terms of "fair play" and equal dealings between classes. Similarly with the call for a one-off capital levy to liquidate war debt which was demanded in the Labour party's document "The New Social Order" published in June 1918. In a lengthy memorandum on the Capital Levy proposal, Stamp commented:

> "The contention that 'life' has been conscripted and therefore that wealth should also be taken has been the most important *ad captandum* argument so far employed. Most writers and speakers make more or less use of it, and it lends itself in a special degree to appeals to class feeling, and to declamation according to individual taste, e.g. 'Lads and lasses have given work and service, why should wealth escape?'"

He warned that

> "if there is an active movement for the levy which has no effective result, the propaganda will leave the working classes (whether rightly or wrongly) with a sense of injustice on a point of sentiment."[37]

It is important to relate the conscription of wealth and capital levy proposals to the popular economic morality subsumed in the notions of "fair play" and "equality of sacrifice", both to shed light on the changes in Labour's ideology during the war, and to illuminate the social tensions of the Home Front. (The argument which we find in some recent historiography that Labour's adoption of a quasi-socialist programme and ideals in 1918 was a mere token of its independence and a sop to its middle-class intellectuals[38] seems to me to rest upon a totally implausible insulation of the Head Offices and national centres of the Labour movement from its rank-and-file.) But it is no less important to stress how popular support for such proposals was contained by being caught in the cross currents of class anger and conventional patriotism. The policies and proposals most clearly formulated on the basis of a "class" analysis of society came from men and women opposed to the war, although their opposition was usually a matter of renunciation, dissociation and withdrawal rather than of determined resistance.[39] The great mass of workers and trade union leaders were for it, many savagely and uncompromisingly so. For them, policies formulated on a "class" basis were easily tainted with a want of patriotism. Hence, the call for a capital levy, while it articulated attitudes and values widely held by wage earners, was easily drowned out as the war ended by the demand that Germany should pay for it. There is ample reason for believing that, in its electoral rhetoric in the run-up to the December polls, the government was following, not leading public opinion. Several weeks before Lloyd George first publicly spoke of making Germany pay for the war, it was reported to his Cabinet that in working-class circles even former advocates of a round-table conference with the enemy powers were not only determined to beat the Germans, but to make them pay for the war "even if it takes a 1,000 years to do it". Workers appear to have concluded for themselves that an indemnity was justified by the indemnity imposed on France in 1871, since this view was reported as being widely entertained, five weeks before Lloyd George made it a major theme of a speech at Newcastle.[40]

This last fact reminds us that the value-cluster of the working-class "moral economy" co-existed with a people's patriotism and a nationalist "mass" culture whose strength ebbed and flowed with the progress of the fighting. There had long been a flag-waving, peer-saluting, foreign-hating side to the plebian mind,[41] and it was given an immense fillip by victory. Before this, however, in the early days of 1918, the popular will to victory had been strained to breaking point and the conduct of the war imperilled by grievances over the distribution and shortage of the necessities of life, the industrial disruption to which these grievances gave rise, and the effect of these grievances on the morale of troops in France. In voicing these grievances, wage earners and soldiers brought home with unmistakable clarity to the government what they thought was "unfair" about the conduct of the Home Front.

High food prices were, with "profiteering", pre-eminent amongst the general causes of working-class unrest uncovered by the Industrial Commissioners of the summer of 1917. They also received extensive evidence that workers perceived their families' shortages as the result of social class inequality and the failure of the government to intervene forcibly in distribution. The Iron and Steel Trades Confederation, one of the most patriotic Labour organizations, submitted, for example, that:

"In matters of supply [the workmen] attribute their inability to obtain fuel and food not so much to the actual shortage as to the entire failure on the part of the Government to obtain control and to establish machinery for more equitable distribution. They point to the fact that the 'potato queue', 'sugar queue', etc. are practically confined to working-class people and working-class districts, and even so the foods they need are not obtainable, while stories of ample supplies and even waste so far as the well-to-do are concerned, are prevalent."[42]

To the discontent caused by the shortages localized to working-class districts was added what the Commissioners for the North East called the "deep-seated conviction in the minds of the working classes that food prices had risen not only through scarcity, but as a result of manipulation by unscrupulous producers and traders".[43] Only in Coventry, however, had food prices been the direct cause of the May strikes (where, it is worth noting both skilled and unskilled men downed tools) and the reason for this is easily suggested: Coventry was the fastest growing city in Britain and the influx of population created acute local shortages and correspondingly high prices.[44]

The first food queues had appeared in the spring of 1917, but were not a source of bitter and persistent social grievance (and government alarm) before October. Prior to then, however, the issue of food control had become enormously important to the Labour movement. This was chiefly because such Food Control Committees as had been formed under Devonport were unduly representative of local traders and middle-class voluntary workers inimical to working-class interests. In London much of their personnel was derived from local War Savings Committees, which had been the fief of charity organisers and promoters of patriotic thrift – people convinced that working-class shortages resulted from working-class waste.[45] We can trace the growing importance of food control to the working-class movement through the rise of Food Vigilance Committees representing local Labour parties, trades councils and co-operators.[46] In London such a committee was formed in June 1917 with the aim of achieving adequate Labour representation on Food Control Committees, placing these committees under municipal authority, and giving them powers to register distributors in each locality and to use the co-ops to ensure equitable distribution.[47] On the 1st August, representatives of the London Food Vigilance Committee – led by the Chairman of the London Trades Council – argued their case before Lord Rhondda, Devonport's successor. They said that only the desire not in any way to injure the men in the trenches was keeping working-class people quiet. Men and women had flocked from Battersea, Poplar, East Ham and other working-class districts to a Hyde Park demonstration in late July to protest against inequalities in distribution and unless something was done trouble of a serious nature would occur. Rhondda conceded nearly all of Labour's case with remarkable frankness. He admitted that when he took over his job the producers and wholesalers were over-represented, while the co-ops and retailers were not considered. He was even certain that a revolution was near if prices were not lowered. The government was wrong in allowing profiteering since the war began. The trades councils were encouraged to bring local pressure in order to get better representation and he expressed his disappointment with the small penalties magistrations were inflicting on traders convicted of selling at higher than the fixed prices.[48]

Class inequality in distribution was exacerbated by the Food Ministry's first measures of compulsory rationing, for its own civil servants conceded that the principle of alloting supplies of sugar, bacon and butter to districts on the basis of consumption in previous years had "the cardinal defect that it favours rich against poor districts".[49] But rather than a knowledge of these defects being a spur to more egalitarian methods, it was pressure from industrial workers, the example set by go-ahead municipalities such as Birmingham and the fear that food queues were stamping grounds for pacifist and revolutionary agitators which drove the government to a larger measure of collectivism.

In Birmingham, one of the cities most affected by the shortage of supplies, Saturday morning shopping queues became so serious a problem in the autumn of 1917 that the municipal authorities inaugurated a ration scheme to minimize queueing and "to introduce a more equitable method of distributing the available food supplies in the city".[50] Even so, the city faced a winter of serious social discontent. In mid-January 1918, queues were reported as beginning before dawn and by mid-day they had assumed such lengths in working class districts that the police were required to marshall and control them. Shortages were most evident in those shops which had a predominantly working-class custom, such as pork butchers, and the prices in the central market were such that the most moderate expression of resentment they aroused was "It's daylight robbery of the working classes".[51] In late January, munitions workers coming off night shifts were beginning to form queues when they left work, despite notices that shops would not be open until 10 or 10.30 a.m., and according to a Labour situation report of early February, several butchers shops were raided by munitions workers.[52]

Meanwhile, in Coventry – where the importance of the food question as a contributory cause of industrial unrest has already been noted – there occurred in November one of the first instances of a Saturday protest strike against food prices and food queues and the example set by the city's munitions workers of short protest strikes was later taken up throughout the country.[53] At Manchester on 16 January men and women in eight of the largest munitions factories in the Openshaw and Gorton districts ceased work for three hours and marched down to Albert Square to protest against the queues and to demand a national system of rationing with equal distribution of food amongst all classes. At Erith, on the 19th, all the engineers employed at Vickers, took the morning off to do their family shopping.[54] On the 29 January practically the whole of the munition workers in Bedford (about 10,000) held a demonstration against the local Food Committee and a similar affair took place in Luton. In the first week of February it was reported to the Cabinet that "the number of workers involved in short strikes which are occurring all over the country as protests against the food situation is becoming a matter of serious national importance".[55]

The conjunction of the "food queue" problem with the threat of the Amalgamated Society of Engineers to call a nation-wide strike against Auckland Geddes' proposal to comb-out their industry presented the government with a general crisis of defeatism. The skilled engineers were not widely loved for what easily appeared a special claim to exemption from conscription, but they lessened their isolation from other groups of workers by linking their own grievances to the food question. In Manchester, Woolwich, Birmingham and Coventry, local branches of the ASE allied with railwaymen, transport workers and the lesser skilled in planning protest stoppages; in the West Midlands the general unions regarded unequal food distribution and profiteering as so important as to bring them to support the engineers' opposition to conscription.[56]

The repercussion of working-class discontent with the food situation on the temper of the country's soldiers was even more disturbing for the government. The extent to which anxieties and irritations amongst the civilian population affected the fighting men is powerful confirmation of the magnitude of the crisis. In mid-September 1917, in order to ascertain the extent of war-weariness amongst troops, the Directorate of Secret Intelligence ordered the examination of a large sample of uncensored letters from servicemen. Of these only a negligible proportion contained any expression of complaint or war-weariness. The examiners concluded – somewhat naively – that the troops were very cheerful and determined, and that the love of fighting had eradicated the peace-time habit of grumbling.[57] (They do not seem to have considered the possibility that soldiers' letters home were a demotic literary genre whose conventions ensured a decent solicitude for the feelings of the recipient and a complete disguise of those of the sender.)[58] However, there was evidently a change in the tone of servicemen's mail as the "food question" on the Home Front became acute. In February 1918, the Head Censor at Calais reported to GHQ:[59]

"It is immediately obvious that the effect on men in France is very serious and that their morale has suffered considerably in consequence. It is clear that the question is very universally discussed. Men hear from their relatives at home and see accounts in the papers, but the greatest effect appears to be produced by men returning from leave. A large proportion of the extracts [from censored mail] are either remarks made by such men or comments based on accounts given by them. The result is that the question at present looms larger in the minds of the mass of men than any other; questions as to their own food are, for the time being, in the background, and men suggest, not uncommonly, that rations in the BEF should be reduced to increase the amount at home. A few men are found to treat the matter lightly, but these men are an almost negligible quantity."

The authorities had reason to believe that the danger to morale was even greater than this evidence suggested. They were aware of the central place of the food queue in hundreds of thousands of letters *from* people at home and believed this was giving an exaggerated and depressing picture of conditions on the Home Front. For standing in a food queue was often the only incident of note in a housewife's drab day. The Head Censor found that typically men were replying to their wives and relatives in terms expressive of the social dichotomy between "them" and "us" in which working-class attitudes and values were framed:

> "It is a load off my mind to know that you are lucky enough to get sufficient food. I think the Government will have to do something if it lasts much longer. We out here won't have our wives and children starving, War or no War, those at home have got to see our dependants get sufficient food."

> "Yes dear I do think you have had a hard battle to get food. All the men's wives seem to tell their husbands about the trouble they have to get the foodstuffs. You should think they would come to terms when they see the country in that state. Suppose they don't feel it else they would."

> "I am sorry to hear that things are getting so bad at home, for by what I can read in the papers and a few things from the lads that return home on leave we get a very good insight of what you have to put up with at home, and I do hope things will soon improve. It makes one think it is time this was brought to an end."

We must take on trust that the Censor's sample was representative and remind ourselves that letter-writing home remained a highly conventiona- lized mode and not an unvarnished expression of sentiment. But it would require a truly dedicated scepticism not to see in the evidence from both Fronts a sense that the reciprocity which should have governed relations between "them" and "us" – "fair play" between the classes – had been disrupted.

There are a number of reasons why the general crisis of defeatism of early 1918 did not become more serious for the authorities. The skilled engineers angered other workers by their aristocratic pretensions to a privileged status *vis-à-vis* conscription and the government defused the food crisis by reversing the rise in prices in early 1918, extending rationing and co-opting Labour representatives on to Food Control committees. By its own declaration of war aims, the government was able to isolate the organized working class from the movement for a negotiated peace. By late February, the negotiations at Brest Litovsk – with their clear indication of what a peace with a victorious Germany would be like – led to the beginnings of a revival of "King and Country" patriotism which the onslaught on the Western Front in March completed.

But a further reason, which I am far from claiming was the most important, was the ability of the government to turn to the media of communications to placate and persuade its own citizens, and influence their attitudes and behaviour. The War Office and Ministry of Food responded to the Head Censor's report cited above by arranging for a team of speakers, representing in particular industrial areas such as the Tyne and Clyde, to be sent to France to correct the troops' impressions of conditions at home.[60] That they were officially briefed and in reality government emissaries – representatives of "them" – was kept hidden from the ranks. Literature was prepared and circulated and a film *The Folk Way Back* made in order "to show, pictorially, from actual scenes in this country that the letters did not contain the whole truth as to the situation". But "the root of the problem was to get the people at home to exercise thought and care as to the tenor of their letters to the Front". Simultaneously with the counter-propaganda at the Front, Ministry of Food officials began a press campaign at home. Writers and authors with no official connections with the government were inspired to write articles and paragraphs under the general theme of "Smile Across the Channel". Famous War Correspondents were persuaded to include in their despatches a reminder of the need for sending cheerful letters to the men. Sir George Riddell, the Chairman of the Newspaper Proprietors' Association, circulated on official suggestion a confidential letter to the editors of those weekly papers, such as *Answers*, *Tit-Bits* and *Home Notes* ("which circulate among the people it was desirable to reach in order to get at the root of the trouble") asking them to spread the same message. We should be thoroughly suspicious of any claim that popular attitudes were simply constructed and manipulated through the media, although we must respect the opinion of those whose job it was to know that this swift and efficient campaign achieved its objectives.

This incident leads me to something of a coda for this essay in which I will place the working-class "moral economy" within the realignment of government and public opinion which occurred under the impact of war. Before 1914, the attitudes and values of wage earners were set apart from what contemporaries in the political, and other, elites called "public opinion"; indeed, it is ironic to read that phrase consistently used in such a way as to exclude what the great mass of the population thought. "Public opinion" was the common sense of property owners, professional and salaried workers, the better sort of clerks and the more independent shopkeepers. The one category of wage earners' opinion officially recognized, and politically represented, was "Labour" opinion; the opinion of organized skilled male workers (perhaps a fifth of the male labour force in 1914), and this opinion was expected to confine itself to trade union matters or the affairs of the working-class friendly societies. Even the more sympathetic observers of the urban multitude, "the great unwashed", saw it as a prey to its instincts and irrational drives; individual workers might possess courage and fortitude, but in the aggregate the less skilled poor of the great cities were the "mob", the "herd", the "crowd" – a composite personality without rational opinions. It is highly pertinent that one of these observers, Charles Masterman, seeing a crowd "Up for t'Cup", numbering five times the Boer Force that surrendered in 1902, was prompted to ask whether this "congestion of grey, small people with their facile excitement and their little white faces inflamed [by the artificial interest of the game] whether in a day of trial, similar resources could be drawn from them, of tenacity, courage, and an unwearying devotion to an impersonal ideal" shown by the Boers.[61] He doubted it.

Before 1914, the state distanced itself from "public opinion" whose virtues were that it was self-forming and self-articulating. As a memorandum on the work of the wartime information departments puts it:

> That the state should advertise itself was an idea which occurred to few before [1914] and which, had it been brought to the notice of the general public, would have seemed to them repellent: advertisement, apart from commercial advertisement ... was thought to be the work of the vulgarian; it was also thought useless. Only with the war has the public learnt that there is nothing disgraceful in the state advertising its wares.[62]

After 1914, there were complex changes in the relationship between the state and "public opinion" which we can simplify under four headings: firstly, there was a manifest need to lead "public opinion" and for the state to publicize itself. The first efforts of wartime governments, focused as they were on the gentlemanly literary activities of Wellington House, illustrate the socially narrow notion of "public opinion" operative when the war began. Secondly, there was the need for the surveillance of "public opinion" which resulted, by mid-1917, in the regular and systematic monitoring of industrial workers' attitudes. Thirdly, this surveillance contributed to the emergence of a much more socially inclusive, even populistic notion as to what "public opinion" was. Fourthly, "public opinion" became a definite part of the power of the state in that it entered the moral armoury with which the state belaboured strikers, heavy drinkers, pacifists, profiteers and food hoarders, and became, after the war, the court of moral appeal in the arbitration of major industrial disputes. But the state was not free to forge this moral weapon at will. A congestion of grey, small people had shown tenacity, courage and surprising, if not unwearying devotion in a terrible trial. They had made it known to their governing class that their devotion was conditional on "fair play" on their side; it was an opinion the state could not ignore.

Notes

1. On this point see J.S. Hinton *The First Shop Stewards' Movement* Allen & Unwin, London (1973) p. 30.
2. See "The Sequel to the Engineers' Strike: An Historical Memorandum", 1/10/17, drawn up by the Ministry of Munitions Intelligence and Records Section, copy in P(ublic) R(ecord) O(ffice) LAB 2/254.
3. The memorandum cited above refers to collusion as an "actuality" but is, nonetheless, somewhat ambiguous.
4. The Leaving Certificate was introduced under the Munitions of War Act of July 1915. No-one could employ a workman who within the previous six weeks had been employed on munitions work, unless the man held a certificate granting the consent of his previous employer to his departure. It was the most unpopular feature of an Act widely known as the "Slavery Act", and the refusal of certificates was used by employers to retain workers at rates far less than they could have obtained by moving elsewhere. The leaving certificate was abolished in October 1917.

5. In 1918-19, an estimated 1.43 m. weekly wage earners were paying income tax; almost the same number were assessed for tax, but paid none because of the married man's, and other allowances. See PRO IR 75/185, p. 348 (Papers of the Royal Commission on the Income Tax).

6. The quotation is from the account of wartime film censorship by J. Brooke Wilkinson (of the British Board of Film Censors); typed manuscript, PRO INF 4/2, p. 300.

7. See memo on "British Propaganda during the Great War", 1914–18, INF 4/2.

8. PRO MUN 4/3335 "Notes on Labour Problems in Wartime" (being a copy of a Memorandum which Mr. Garrod took with him to the USA. . . .) 21/4/1917.

9. Devonport to Lloyd George, 17/2/1917; David Lloyd George Papers, F/15/2/3.

10. "The Moral Economy of the English Crowd in the Eighteenth Century", *Past and Present*, **50**, 1971, pp. 76–136.

11. For a contemporary analysis of this fissure see J.A. Hobson "The General Election: A Sociological Interpretation", *Sociological Review*, iii, April 1910.

12. For a study which ably synthesizes the evidence see Standish Meacham *A Life Apart: the English Working Class 1890–1914* Thames & Hudson, London (1977).

13. B.S. Rowntree *Poverty* Macmillan, London (1902 ed.) p. 43; Mrs. Pember Reeves *Round About a £ a Week* G. Bell & Sons, London (1914) pp. 39–40.

14. Stephen Reynolds *et al. Seems So! A Working Class View of Politics* Macmillan, London (1913 ed) p. xix.

15. "The present unrest in the Labour world", PRO CAB 37/107 (70), 25/7/1911.

16. George Bourne *Change in the Village*, Gerald Duckworth & Co. London (1912) p. 70.

17. On this point see the highly perceptive article "Why was there no Marxism in Great Britain?" by Ross McKibbin, *English Historical Review*, April 1984, p. 314.

18. J.W.F. Rowe *Wages in Practice and Theory* Routledge, London (1928) pp. 154–159.

19. See *The History of the Ministry of Munitions* H.M.S.O., London (1922 onwards) vol. 1, part 2, p. 32.

20. "Exceptional Profits due to the war", PRO IR 74/70, 16/3/1915.

21. See W.A. Orton *Labour in Transition* Philip Allan & Co., London (1921) p. 64; *The History of the Ministry of Munitions*, vol 1, part 2, p. 55.

22. See C.J. Wrigley *David Lloyd George and the British Labour Movement* Harvester, Brighton (1976) pp. 122–128 and R. Page Arnot *South Wales Miners: A History of the South Wales Miners' Federation 1914–1926* George Allen & Unwin, London (1975) p. 25–26.

23. *Report of the Commission of Enquiry into Industrial Unrest: Wales and Monmouthshire*, P(arliamentary) P(apers) 1917–18, Cd 8668, p. 22, p. 28.

24. Gosling's address is given in *The Times*, 5/9/1916.

25. Mr. Ridley, speaking at the 18th Annual Conference of the Railway Clerks' Association; see *The Railway Clerk*, July 1915.

26. G.R. Askwith *Industrial Problems and Disputes* John Murray, London (1920) p. 372.

27. Cd 8666, p. 2.

28. Cd 8664, p. 2.

29. Cd 8667, p. 5–6.

30. J.C. Stamp *Taxation during the War* Humphrey Milford, London (1932) p. 214.

31. *The Economist* 21/2/1920, quoted in W.G. Runciman *Relative Deprivation and Social Justice* Penguin, Harmondsworth (1972 ed.) p. 66.

32. See the Cabinet Report on the Labour situation, 22/10/1919 PRO CAB 24/90, G.T. 8388.

33. See J.A. Dowie "1919–20 is in Need of Attention", *Economic History Review*, 1975 2nd series, vol xviii, no. 3, pp. 429–450 and K.O. Morgan *Consensus and Disunity* Oxford University Press, London (1979) pp. 46–7, p. 167.

34. Report on the Labour situation, 9/7/1919 PRO CAB 24/83 G.T. 7672.

35. Report on the Labour situation, 27/8/1919 PRO CAB 24/87 G.T. 8059.

36. On the Workers' National Committee and the demand for a capital levy, see Royden Harrison "The War Emergency Workers" National Committee, 1914–20, *Essays in Labour History*, vol ii edited by Asa Briggs and John Saville, Macmillan, London (1971) pp. 211–259; J.M. Winter *Socialism and the Challenge of War* Routledge, Kegan Paul, London, (1974) pp. 184–222; W.A. Orton *Labour in Transition* (1921) p. 14–16, p. 108.

37. J.C. Stamp "The Capital Levy: Theoretical and Academic Aspects" in PRO IR 74/48.
38. See Ross McKibbin *The Evolution of the Labour Party, 1910–24* Oxford University Press, London (1974).
39. Royden Harrison, *loc. cit*, p. 222.
40. See the Fortnightly Report on pacificism and revolutionary organizations in the U.K. (no. 24), 21/10/1918 PRO CAB 24/67 G.T. 6079 for observations on workers' chauvinism sent to Basil Thomson by "correspondents all over the country." (Thomson was the Special Branch officer who took over the surveillance of industrial militancy from the Ministry of Munitions in December 1916 and began reporting to the Cabinet on so-called revolutionary organizations in 1917.) For Lloyd George's Newcastle speech see Arno J. Mayer *Politics and Diplomacy of Peacemaking* Weidenfeld & Nicolson, London (1967) p. 156.
41. A point made by Geoffrey Best in a review of E.P. Thompson's *The Making of The English Working Class*; see p. 916 of the Penguin edition Harmondsworth (1968).
42. Notes of evidence submitted to the Commission of Enquiry into Industrial Unrest by Arthur Pugh for the Iron and Steel Trades Confederation. University of Warwick, Modern Record Office, MSS 36, Box 4.
43. Cd 8662, p. 2.
44. On Coventry during the May 1917 engineering strikes, see the memorandum by Mr. Chorley, 9/11/17 in PRO LAB 2/254/ML 2440/37.
45. See the 12th Annual Report of the Thrift and Savings Committee of the London Charity Organisation Society, p. 17.
46. For the rise of Food Vigilance Committees, see the Quarterly Report of the Ministry of Munitions Intelligence and Record Section, 4/8/1917, PRO MUN 5/56 300/108.
47. Minutes of the London Trades Council Executive Meeting, 26/6/1917.
48. There is a detailed account of the meeting in *The Shop Assistant* (Journal of the National Union of Shop Assistants, Warehousemen and Clerks), 11/8/1917.
49. Memorandum on the Prevention of Queues by S.G. Tallents, 19/12/17 in PRO MAF 60/243.
50. *Birmingham Daily Post*, 12/12/17, article on the introduction of the city's rationing scheme.
51. *Birmingham Daily Post*, 5/1/1918, 14/1/1918.
52. *Birmingham Daily Post*, 30/1/1918, Report on the Labour Situation, 6/2/1918 PRO CAB 24/41 G.T. 3545.
53. *History of the Ministry of Munitions*, vol VI, pt i, p. 26.
54. See the *Manchester Guardian*, 17/1/1918; Report on the Labour situation, 23/1/18, PRO CAB 24/40 G.T. 3442.
55. Report on the Labour situation, 6/2/1918, CAB 24/41 G.T. 3545 for this quotation and the Bedford demonstration.
56. Reports on the Labour situation, 9/1/1918 and 16/1/1918, CAB 24/38 G.T. 3293 and CAB 24/39 G.T. 3369.
57. Note on the morale of British troops in France as disclosed by the Censorship, 13/9/1917, CAB 24/26 G.T. 2052.
58. For a brilliant insight into the conventional character of soldiers' letters home see Paul Fussell *The Great War and Modern Memory* Oxford University Press, London (1975) pp. 181–183.
59. The extracts from the Head Censor's report, and from servicemen's letters which follow, are taken from a memorandum on The Effect of Food Queues at home on men at the Front, 16/4/1918, by Sydney Walton, PRO MAF 60/243.
60. For this and what follows in this paragraph, see the Walton memorandum cited above.
61. C.F.G. Masterman *The Condition of England* Methuen, London (1909, 1911 ed.) p. 114.
62. British Propaganda during the Great War, 1914–18, undated memorandum in PRO INF 4/4a.

13

Fuller and the Tanks

TONY TRYTHALL

My subject is J.F.C. Fuller, Major-General, author, devotee of the occult, sometime fascist, shining star of much intellect and perhaps not enough tertiary education, who attempted to make, and in practice as well as in theory did make, a significant contribution to the First World War, to subsequent thought about it and to the development of concepts stemming from it. Even in 1914–18, however, his contribution was primarily, as ever with him, intellectual. No donkey he, or lion either, but rather a bird of prey, eagle or wild hawk, not falcon, for he never belonged to anyone, flashing about the sky and then swooping like a swift arrow on to his pedestrian victims, and off again to soar and swoop some more – an officer who described his seniors as military cows (because their eyes were too close to the ground as they munched the grass) – and survived, well, up to his retiring age and the rank of Major-General.[1]

But in spite of being neither lion nor donkey he certainly fits many of the themes and preoccupations of the papers given at the Sunderland Conference. He was a TA Adjutant in 1908; he, of all critics of the war, thought many of its generals were BFs – especially Haig; he was an unforgettable personality, and his personality was the stimulus for much of his thought and many of his actions; hindsight – the future that lay before the tank – has coloured our judgement of his recommendations in 1918; he was a military historian; he contributed to the literature of war – indeed he published 45 books; he was even, I have learned, related to the conference speaker on the literature of the war, Hugh Cecil, since Boney's mother was Hugh Cecil's great grandmother's sister!

In view of all this richness of relevance it is therefore very necessary to identify very clearly what manner of man he was, where he came from, his provenance as it were, in order to understand his contribution to the war and the subsequent consequences and development of that contribution. He was born on 1 September 1878 in Chichester, the son of an Anglican rector and a French mother, Hugh Cecil's great grandmother's sister, who had been brought up in Germany, in Naundorf near Leipzig. As a boy he was known as Fritz, a name he retained until his first letters home were censored in 1915.

His earliest years were warm and comfortable and partly spent in Switzerland. His environment was the solidity and confidence of the late Victorian middle class, national wealth, imperial glory and religious and moral certainty. Fritz, however, was a clever and rather solitary little boy with a penchant for macabre pen drawings of devils and precocious letters home. He went to Malvern which he disliked, was put in the Army class but after only 2 years at the school was sent to a crammers in London to prepare for the Sandhurst examination. In September 1897 he entered Sandhurst for the privilege of which his father had to pay the considerable fee of £150 a year.

Sandhurst irked Fuller a little and it was at this time that he began to perceive the hypocrisy and foolishness which characterized, in his opinion, so many of his contemporaries. He wrote to his Mother that "the great aim of life is not merely happiness or suffering but a far greater wider and nobler aim namely Development".[2] That development at that time was not the primary aim of the Royal Military College is evidenced by a passage in another letter which Fuller wrote home:

"Once a week for 2 hours at a stretch we sat in a classroom and read the Manual, and when we had exhausted those sections dealing with murder, rape, and indecency, we either destroyed Her Majesty's property with our penknives or twiddled our thumbs. Fortunately our instructor was as deaf as a post, for this enabled us to keep up a running conversation, broken on occasion by a wild Irishman, named Meldon, banging on his desk to make our teacher look up. Then Meldon would solemnly say: 'Please, sir, may I come and kick your bottom?' And our unsuspecting master, not having heard a word, would invariably reply, 'Come to me afterwards, boy; come to me afterwards.'"[3]

After his year at Sandhurst Fuller was commissioned into the Oxford-shire Light Infantry, the 43rd, now part of the Royal Greenjackets, of which he joined the 1st Battalion in Mullingar in what is now Eire. He must have appeared a bit of an odd fish to his fellow subalterns but the Light Infantry has a reputation for greater tolerance than most infantry regiments and Fuller survived in spite of the difficulty he found in living on his pay of £7 15s 8d a month after tax plus a small allowance from his father. He did the normal things a subaltern does but he also began to read widely and his reading included Carlyle, Huxley and Marcus Aurelius. In his *Memoirs*, written 37 years later, he noted that though in 1899 he took no interest in things military "it all appeared to me very ridiculous; yet what did it matter? – we had to fill in time somehow, and what had been good enough for Wellington was good enough for us".[4]

In September the battalion moved to Plymouth and in a letter from there we get a glimpse of Fuller's sharp but not necessarily sound cast of thought:

"The French nation ought to be abolished the more I read about them the more absolutely disgusted I get with their venomous qualities. They literally stink with oily backstair skunkiness ... They have a few good points but I am sorry to say many bad ones as well being gross cowardly and essentially effeminate and always were so in the time of Caesar when in a state of barbaric savagery they even used soap, curious as it may seem. What fine nation could ever spring from a soapy savage? None. What is needed is a good, lousy, stinking, rancid Saxon or Goth, not a hair-combing toe-nail-clipping Gaul."[5]

The rancid Saxons were about to engage the equally rancid Dutch in South Africa. The Oxfordshires forsook red for khaki and knowing "nothing about war, about South Africa, about our eventual enemy, about anything at all which mattered, and upon which our lives might depend"[6] on 22 December 1899 sailed aboard R.M.S. Gaika from Southampton for the Cape where they disembarked on 14 January 1900.

In South Africa Fuller grew up. He moved up to the fighting with his battalion but before he was engaged in it he was sent down the railway line to De Aar to seek out a lost consignment of mess stores and buy up as much whisky as he could find. A letter home posted on this journey gives us a glimpse into his state of mind.

"I really begin (he wrote on February 6th) to wonder what we are fighting for, for this country is quite impossible – for the whole lot is not worth a twopenny d... and unless the Transvaal turns out to be a Paradise flowing with milk and honey I shall really think that the leaders of the English nation are deserving cases for Broadmoor ... I have not been in the army very long but quite long enough to see that nine officers out of every ten, I might say ninety-nine out of every hundred, know no more of military affairs than the man in the moon and do not intend or want to know more ... It is no more a profession than shooting pheasant or hunting foxes ... That we ultimately will win in this war is highly probable, but unless the tactics of our generals change it will be simply through sheer force of numbers ... War as everything else nowadays is reduced to a science ... I think William the Conqueror could teach us a thing or two".[7]

A few days later he began to feel extremely ill. Eventually he was taken to hospital in De Aar where a "twisted gut" was diagnosed. Nothing was done and he got worse. In the end he reached Cape Town where appendicitis was diagnosed and an operation was performed. Recovery was slow and on the 28th he wrote home a letter which contains one of Fuller's most lucid of comments. "Oh", he wrote, "this war is an awful thing. When will it come to an end?"[8] For Fuller it was over for some months. He was sent home to convalesce and did not return to South Africa until November when he rejoined his battalion just south of the Transvaal border. Life was some-times exciting, as when one of the "Black Watch", the native force employed to guard the wires, inadvertently shot another. The victim, John

No 4, had been hit in the forehead and Fuller gave him whisky out of a teapot and stuffed his brains back into his head with the handle of a fork. He wrote to his mother some days later about the incident:

"Any ordinary civilized individual would have fallen down dead at once, but I suppose these semi-savages use their brain so little that it doesn't much matter if they lose a part of it."[9] In due course he became an intelligence officer in charge of seventy unreliable Kaffir scouts and had a most adventurous and unconventional time for the next seven months.

His last action of note took place on May 7th when he was almost caught and shot while engaged in posting up peace proclamations in farms near Bothaville. The reason why he would have been shot had he been captured needs some explanation. Fuller was in the position of a federal agent in the American West using armed Indians to fight the local settlers. He himself agreed that the Boers fought chivalrously and normally the worst that befell prisoners was to be stripped and turned loose on the veldt. However those who armed and led Kaffirs had broken the rules of South African life by undermining white supremacy, and the Boers showed no quarter to either the leaders or the led; similarly, according to Fuller, the Kaffirs showed no quarter to the Boers. One of Fuller's scouts, Simon, was captured, tied to a horse's tail and dragged for some four hundred yards while the Boers shot at him at a distance from a flank ... Fuller discovered his body later, "blown out like that of a dead mule and surrounded by a horrible stench ... hit in many places, certainly through the knee, heart, breast, head and elbow". Just before discovering Simon's body, Fuller saw a notice pencilled on a whitewashed farm wall which read:

"PRAY TO GOD YOU ARE NOT CAUGHT FOR WE WILL SHOOT EVERY ONE OF YOU AS WE DID SIMON AND THE ENGLISH OFFICER TOO WHO LEADS YOU."[10]

In *The Last of the Gentlemen's Wars* he commented: "Though the English was not faultless, for I was still alive, its meaning left the reader (particularly myself) in no doubt. Under this dramatic obituary I wrote one word".[11]

In the end he had to go back to his regiment which he did not enjoy. He had tried to join the Indian Army, but failed and he returned to Chatham with the 43rd. Chatham he thought a sordid town "full of sordid women against whose low animal natures discipline was no more than a paper shield".[12] Late in 1903 he went to India and became fascinated with Indian culture and began to develop his later passion for the mystic and the occult. In India he first corresponded with Aleister Crowley, Beast 666, later Fuller's occult mentor. Enteric fever resulted in his return to England in 1906 where he met Crowley and married Margarethe Auguste Karnatz, generally known as Sonia, beautiful but for Fuller a social disaster that ruled out for the time being further regimental service. In 1907 he became a

Volunteer, later a Territorial Force adjutant in London and at the same time published his first book *The Star in the West – a Critical Essay upon the Works of Aleister Crowley*. It was at this time too that he first became preoccupied with problems of military training and morale and the sight of the second battalion of his own regiment marching along sweating "in full paint" decided him to try for Staff College. He failed the exam in 1912 but passed the next year but by the time he arrived at Camberley he had already published or written "Hints on Training Territorial Infantry", "Training Soldiers for War", "The Mobilization of a Territorial Infantry Battalion", "Notes on the Entrainment of Troops to and from Manoeuvres", "The Revival and Training of Light Infantry in the British Army, 1757–1806", "The Three Flag System of Instructing Infantry in Fire Tactics" and "The Procedure of the Infantry Attack". In the latter articles he forecast that the reappearance of the shield in war, for the artillery, might lead to its general reintroduction.

At Staff College Fuller incurred considerable displeasure for writing a paper called "The Tactics of Penetration: A Counterblast to German Numerical Superiority". The displeasure was occasioned by the fact that Staff College thinking at that time was based on the tactics of envelopment. Fuller believed that technological change – the introduction of quick-firing field guns and machine guns – had made pentration possible. In fact the First World War was to demonstrate that in a mass war in Western Europe the flanks disappeared so envelopment became impossible and penetration essential but also impossible – until technology provided the shields Fuller foresaw or new tactics of fire, movement and infiltration were introduced. He also put forward the view that artillery had become the superior arm and began his lengthy intellectual love affair with the principles of war.

And then on 4 August 1914 war broke out. Fuller was instructed to report to Southampton as an Assistant Embarkation Staff Officer; he should not have written that article although the posting probably saved his life so high were officer casualties in France in the first months of the war. In time he held other staff jobs in England until in July 1915 he was sent to VII Corps HQ near Doullens in France. One of his first thoughts there was that we needed more machine guns, to take on where artillery left off once trenches were taken. He was a Westerner not an Easterner. In February 1916 he was sent to 37 Div as a GS02. He wrote a paper arguing that the capture or retention of ground should be regarded as a means to victory not an end in itself. 37 Div was then broken up to reinforce others on the Somme and Fuller was given another GSO2 post in Third Army HQ. In early August a sapper officer, Captain Townshend, showed Fuller a paper he had written, "The MS in Red Ink" which put forward the idea that all that was needed to win was a few hours penetration five miles deep on a hundred mile front. This reinforced Fuller's view on penetration but there seemed no means of achieving it until on 20th August, Townshend and Fuller saw their first tank at Yvrench – the putative missing tool of penetration, Swinton's brainchild.

For the remainder of 1916 Fuller had nothing to do with tanks but Lt. Col. H.J. Elles was made Colonel commanding the Heavy Branch of the Machine Gun Corps, the embryo Tank Corps, and Fuller became his GSO2 and reported to him at Bermicourt on Boxing Day 1916. Tanks were designed and produced to destroy machine guns, cross wire and trenches, protect their inmates from bullets, and facilitate infantry movement. They were, Swinton [13] specifically stated, the alternative solution to the neutralization of machine guns in order to achieve penetration, the first being artillery bombardment but that, as a counter to machine-guns, was "not at present within our power". Swinton also recommended that the tanks should be saved up and used *en masse* in a surprise assault.

Swinton wrote a paper on tank tactics which was completed in February 1916 but its contents were unknown at Bermicourt in early 1918. Fuller was in fact the architect of the tank tactics of 1917 and of Cambrai although some credit must also be given to Martel and Fuller's own ideas were often altered and distorted by higher authority. In spite of Swinton, tanks had in fact been first used in driblets on the Somme in September 1916. In February 1917 Fuller produced a training note which defined tanks as mobile fortresses intended to escort attacking infantry. In April he was made GSO1. In April, however, he failed to prevent tanks being split up for the Battle of Arras. In June tanks were used at Messines after which Fuller wrote another paper in which he argued that shallow linear fronts could be defeated by a tank – supported infantry advance of a few thousand yards leading to exploitation among the enemy guns and in the rear. As time passed Fuller, and Major General Sir John Capper, the new Administrative Commandant of the Heavy Branch, became more and more concerned that preliminary bombardment destroyed the ground over which tanks had to advance. In spite of that Third Ypres was artillery-prepared. On July 28th the Heavy Branch became the Tank Corps.

Fuller was now engaged at Bermicourt in campaigning for the opening up of a tank battle south of Cambrai. Fuller wanted this to be the first of a series of penetrative tank raids leading to a decisive battle in 1918. He wanted air support and fascines for trench crossing. The raid materialized as the Battle of Cambrai but GHQ attempted to turn it into a decisive battle, without enough tanks, and leading to cavalry exploitation. There was no preliminary bombardment and the tanks achieved an initial penetration of 10,000 yards in less than twelve hours. There was however no cavalry exploitation and the Germans soon regained almost all the ground the tanks had won.

Fuller began another round of thought and concluded that the decisive attack would have to wait until 1919 when 12,000 tanks would be needed.

Tanks meanwhile were strung out by GHQ in a sixty mile cordon in the role of Martello Towers or "savage rabbits". Then on March 21st the Germans themselves, reinforced from the East, and dreading the U.S. build-up, attacked, and without tanks but using artillery and the tactics of infiltration, in a fortnight drove the British Fifth Army back forty miles. This offensive lasted until the summer.

Meanwhile on 24 May, after concluding that the British defeat in March had been brought about by the paralysis of our command, and after a decision had been made to produce 13,000 tanks for 1919 one of them being the Medium D, a 20 m.p.h. machine with a 150–200 mile radius of action, Fuller produced "The Tactics of the Medium D Tank", later called "Strategical Paralysis as the object of the Attack" and "Plan 1919". This was not entirely original, of course, it was in line with some of the ideas of Foch and Wilson, and had similarities with Stephen Foot's "A Mobile Army". It certainly led to Capper's paper "Armoured Striking Force for 1919".

Plan 1919 called for an attack on the German command structure to be achieved by a surprise attack on a ninety mile front. The primary objective would be the area between the German Divisional and Army Headquarters while the area between his front line and his guns would be the secondary objective. In two hours the Medium Ds would reach the primary objectives at top speed. Supply and road centres would be bombed but signal communications would be left alone in order to spread panic. While all this was going on, a tank, infantry and artillery attack would be mounted on the secondary objectives. A pursuit force would follow through to Army Group Headquarters and the German Western GHQ would be bombed. The attack itself would be morcellated i.e. unattacked portions being enveloped.

Undoubtedly something like this would have been attempted in 1919 but there is not time now to detail how far the planning got before a more conventional offensive and the changing balance of forces and resources brought about the Armistice in November. Before that offensive, at Hamel in July, tanks played a decisive role, but during it they were fundamentally only an additional but prominent arm.

So we have in fact a paradox: a set of circumstances creating a problem and calling forth a man with the intellect, drive, originality, detachment (as shown by his occult interests), and experience which could provide a solution to the problem; he does that but his solution is not used and is not necessary. This led to the emergence of two most important questions, on the answers to which must depend our judgement of Fuller as a strategic and radical thinker. First, would Plan 1919 have worked? Second, how original was it? Third what consequences did it ultimately have?

As regards its feasibility my judgement now, almost 10 years after I wrote my biography of Fuller, and taking into account Brian Reid's PhD thesis on "The Development of the Military Thought of Major-General J.F.C. Fuller", is that strategically it would have worked if technologically the instrument, the tank, it required tactically, could have been produced in sufficient time, in sufficient numbers and with sufficient reliability.

As regards originality the concepts of making the enemy's various headquarters the primary objectives, and of using fast armoured fighting vehicles to capture them, together with the absence of artillery preparation, were original.

Finally the third question takes us into the areas of both the subsequent history of armoured warfare and its present problem and future prospects. Plan 1919 was to a considerable degree the launching pad for Fuller's future career both as a soldier and as a military thinker. It confirmed him as a founding father of the Tank Corps but it led him also through the frustration of his reforming crusades in the 1920s to his ultimate relative failure as a career soldier and thence to his dalliance with Mosley and fascism. It led him also to the lecture platform at the RUSI on February 11 1920 and to his remarkable vision that day:

"Let us now become clairvoyant about the future ... I see a fleet operating against a fleet not at sea but on land. My astral form follows one side and I notice that it is in difficulty; it cannot see; there appears an aeroplane and gives it sight ... I see a man in one of the aeroplanes whose head is swollen with the future; he is the C-in-C of the land fleet I am following ... I sniff the air; it seems impure. Is it gas? The Tanks submerge; that is to say, batten down their hatches. The battle begins ... gaps are made ... the fleet moves through. Then I see the old scene re-enacted – the contest between armour, gun – fire and mobility."[14]

Fuller went on a long time in that vein. Curious ships – submarine tank carriers – raced through the Skaggerak and spewed amphibious tanks on to the Warnemunde beaches. And he ended:

"Do not let us now in 1920, only look backwards to 1914. Let us think forwards to 1930, or we shall become pillars of salt in an arid and unproductive wilderness."

It led him also to his RUSI Gold Medal, to his partnership with Liddell Hart, to "The Reformation of War", "The Foundations of the Science of War" and to "Lectures on FSR II" and "Lectures on FSR III". It led him eventually to "Armament and History" and "The Conduct of War". But in the realm of action it can be most cogently argued that "Plan 1919" was the seed from which "Blitzkrieg" or deep armoured pentration, grew – Guderian's and Rommel's campaigns and the later battles in the Arab-Israeli wars are examples. And it is most fascinating, now that some military leaders and thinkers are beginning to question the continued dominance of the tank, and that other thinkers are wondering if conventional deterrence, based on emergent technology and relying on the growing transparency of war and increasing accuracy and effectiveness of artillery, could be substitued for nuclear deterrence, to recall that Fuller first saw artillery as the tool of penetration, because it could become the tool of counter-penetration in the future.

This lecture has been called "Fuller and the Tanks". I cannot close without pointing out that Fuller eventually agreed that once the counter to the tank existed, the aeroplane would become the master weapon. He also foresaw star wars and he even put forward the view that in the end man himself would become an encumbrance on the battlefield. Fuller's preoccupations with tanks in 1917–18, and up until the 50s, was an inevitable result of the times in which he lived. From 1917 until quite recent times the tank has offered many opportunities to the offensive. Perhaps it will offer fewer in the future. After all it was Fuller himself who devised what he called the Law of Military Development and the Constant Tactical Factor. He held that weapons and their quality were of supreme importance in war, that "civilization is environment, and armies must adapt themselves to its changing phases in order to remain fitted for war"[15] (the law) and that "every improvement in weapon-power has aimed at lessening the danger on one side by increasing it on the other. Therefore every improvement in weapons has eventually been met by a counter-improvement which has rendered the improvement obsolete; the evolutionary pendulum of weapon-power, slowly or rapidly, swinging from the offensive to the protective and back again in harmony with the pace of civil progress; each swing in a measurable degree eliminating danger"[16] (the factor).

The First World War itself, with which the Sunderland Conference members were so poignantly involved is itself one of the supreme examples of the painful operation of both the Law and the Factor. Perhaps avoidance of the Third will depend upon how sensibly we observe the requirements of both in our Defence policies today and in the future.

Notes

1. This chapter is largely based on my *Boney Fuller: The Intellectual General 1878–1966*; Cassells, London, 1977.
2. Kings College, London. Fuller Collection 1V/3/4.
3. J.F.C. Fuller, *Memoirs of an Unconventional Soldier*, War Nicholson & Watson, London 1936, pp. 5–6.
4. *Memoirs*, pp. 7–8.
5. Kings, 1V/3/21.
6. *Memoirs* p. 8.
7. Kings 1V/3/26.
8. Kings 1V/3/28.
9. Kings 1V/3/70.
10. J.F.C. Fuller, *The Last of the Gentleman's Wars*, Faber & Faber, London, 1937, p. 252.
11. *Ibid*, p. 252.
12. *Memoirs*, p. 16.
13. E.D. Swinton, *Eyewitness*, Hodder & Stoughton, London 1932, p. 131.
14. RUSI Journal, vol. LXV, pp. 291–293.
15. J.F.C. Fuller, *Armament and History*, Eyre and Spottiswoode, London, p. 32.
16. *Ibid.*, p. 33.

14

The Literary Legacy of the War: the Post-war British War Novel – a Select Bibliography

HUGH CECIL

As Richard Aldington said, in his preference to *Death of a Hero*: "the excuse for a novel is that one can do any damn thing one pleases".[1] Fiction gave British writers who had passed through the searing experience of the First World War an opportunity to express their feelings about it without being limited by libel laws, the Official Secrets Act, by failing memory or their own reluctance to reveal themselves completely. The war offered invaluable "copy" to young men who in the normal run of things would have had little to say about their lives before they were thirty. Even more than is the case today, aspiring and ambitious writers wanted to get into print with a novel; and they stood a better chance of doing so in those days of lower publishing costs.

Is the resulting mass of war fiction really as useful to the historian as personal memoir? Clearly it is not the best way of finding out what actually happened in a campaign or to the author personally; but memoirs, too, have to be treated with circumspection and what a novel can do at least as well as a reminiscence is to describe the sensations of military service in and out of battle – and of the home front as well. What it should be able to do even better is to recreate soldiers' conversations. This is an essential human ingredient in any account of the war. Yet factual memoir seldom contains more than a few exchanged words.

Even so, not many war novels succeed completely in conveying the war atmosphere. Stuart Cloete spoke for himself when he admitted in his autobiography – "no one can describe war".[2] Certainly he failed to do so in his attempt at realistic treatment in *How Young They Died* (1969),[3] a shallow, sensational book. Other war veteran writers have done better than he. But there were none who would really have disagreed with his remark. Paul Fussell – and others before him – have pointed out the inadequacy of available literary forms to do justice to that overwhelming torrent of horror, noise and massed human activity.[4]

Apart from this, two faults mar many First War novels: one is poverty of characterization: it is as though the deafening roar of events reduced the human individuals to insignificance in the authors' minds. Too much rambling detail is another failing: the compulsion for some veterans to include almost every campaign they had been through was clearly a strong one, but it was usually a mistake; there are limits to how much a reader can absorb. Nevertheless, nearly all the novels contain some detail of interest to the historian: even if this does not amount to verifiable evidence, it does at least demonstrate points of view which were current at the time of writing.

For the purpose of introducing this select bibliography of novels describing the experience of the war, I have found it illuminating to separate the books into broad categories; based on what the authors were trying to tell their readers. The desire for fame and fortune or to get the war out of their system may well have been the fundamental reasons why many of them wrote their books. But a great proportion of them had reached some conclusion, genuine or otherwise, about the mighty conflict they had experienced.

First there were novels with a specific social or political message. They began to appear immediately after the war and continued into the thirties. The best is undoubtedly A.P. Herbert's *The Secret Battle* (1919).[5] A brief, harrowing book, it describes how a brave and responsible young officer loses his nerve in battle after intolerable pressures in the fighting line over a long period. He is court-martialled and on the hostile evidence of a brother officer is sentenced and shot for exemplary reasons. The purpose of the book was to draw attention to the injustice of the British Army's very harsh wartime disciplinary code. Herbert himself served with the Royal Naval Division at Gallipoli and the Western Front, was invalided out in 1917 and was called to the bar in 1918. As an officer, he had taken part in a number of courts martial. The book – the beginning of Herbert's long and successful career as a writer and broadcaster – has all the power of an impressive forensic performance. It was influential at the time and continues to be read.[6]

Oliver Onions' *Peace in Our Time* (1923)[7] is dedicated to "the Lads of the Village" and the book tells the story of what has happened to some of them. Its purpose is to make people realize the plight of demobilized ex-servicemen. Onions had an established reputation as the author of novels with a social message well before the Great War. He was over 40 when hostilities began and though he served briefly in France, he took no part in the fighting. Formerly a socialist, he described himself by 1923 as a "Tory with a conscience". *Peace in Our Time* tells the story of Kenneth Chacey, a dashing young man with wartime field rank and a D.S.O. who is made to feel that at 26 his past is the most important thing about him. He finds that he and large numbers of his desperate, footloose fellow ex-officers are an embarrassment and scandal to older people with their roots in the pre-war period and a mystery to the really young who have grown up since. They dabble in dubious commercial ventures, gamble, try their hand at poultry farming or live off rich, elderly ladies.

Onions argues the case of the veterans persuasively: they are entitled to gratitude – just because their haloes have slipped a little it is not to be supposed that they have lost all sense of honour. They need more help than government assisted emigration policies or the British Legion can give them. As in most of his books, the facts are drawn from observation and carefully checked. Historically, therefore, this is invaluable. The tone of the book is jocose and ironical. Far more bitter and impassioned is Peter Deane's tragic tale *The Victors* (1925)[8] – which also describes the miseries of a demobilized officer and makes the same point in melodramatic fashion.

Like Onions, Sir Philip Gibbs, another author with a message, already had a high reputation as a writer before the war. A leading Fleet Street journalist, he became one of the five accredited correspondents with the Allied forces and is generally regarded as the best British reporter at the front. Like Onions too, and like his own brother, Arthur Hamilton Gibbs, Philip Gibbs tackled social and political problems in his novels. *Back to Life* (1920) was a plea for international peace and brotherhood – a message he was to repeat in his other writings, though by the time he wrote *Blood Relations* (1935) his optimism had begun to wear thin. *The Middle of the Road* (1923)[9] was an early anti-war tract, making much of the dislocation, unhappiness and monotony. Considering that the war had made him a figure of national importance, his books show a creditable sensitivity and independence where one might have expected complacency. As literature they are respectworthy rather than distinguished, lacking the vitality of the other works I have mentioned.

By contrast, my second category consists of war novels written purely for entertainment. These include Oliver Maddox Hueffer's *Cousins German* (1930)[10], F.O. Mann's *Grope Carries On*[11] (1932) – the funniest novel of the war – and a large number of spy thrillers.[12] One of the best in this group is Philip Macdonald's tale of the Mesopotamia campaign, *Patrol* (1927).[13] Macdonald served in a cavalry regiment in Mesopotamia. After the war he wrote successful detective stories and, later, screenplays for Hollywood films. It was no surprise to find that *Patrol*, which is fast-moving, tough and dramatic, was made into a movie. It tells the story of a horse patrol who lose their way in the desert. They come upon a small oasis, from which, during the night, the horses are stolen by Arabs. The patrol is stuck there, facing, without prospect of relief, two of the worst menaces of the Mesopotamia campaign – a waterless wilderness and a murderous thieving native population. One by one, the soldiers' nerves collapse; one by one, they are killed off. Only the sergeant survives, to die a hero's death destroying his foes as they close in on him. Besides being an excellent psychological thriller, it illustrates vividly the strain of desert fighting; and provides, at the back, a very useful glossary of Mesopotamia campaign terms. Authors like Macdonald, though they make no important statements about the meaning of war, cannot be dismissed as historically worthless; they write from direct experience.

In my third category come those works whose principal message is a celebration of English values or patriotic virtue. Few post-war novelists made this their main theme, even those whose outlook verged on the chauvinistic. It may be significant that all three mentioned here were non-combatants with the forces – padres and RAMC. They were cast – perhaps to their embarrassment – in the role of observers and also moral judges. But this cannot be the whole explanation.

The patriotic novel which made by far the greatest impact, Ernest Raymond's *Tell England* (1922)[14], was published only 3 years after the end of the war and before the fashion had really swung towards the unillusioned.

Ernest Raymond was born in 1888, the illegitimate son of a retired Major-General and of a woman he was brought up to believe was his aunt. He was reared by her sister. The miseries of his childhood drove him to succeed as a writer and its mysteries endowed him with a sense of drama which is present in all his best works. After several years as a school teacher he trained for the priesthood and in 1915 joined the army chaplain's service. He was at Gallipoli, leaving with the forces at Cape Helles at the time of the evacuation. He served in Sinai from 1916–17, and was briefly at 3rd Ypres. He volunteered for Mesopotamia service and went subsequently to South Russia with Dunsterforce. *Tell England* – the MS. of which was nearly left behind at Baku – was a composite of his schoolteaching and Gallipoli experiences. The book can still appeal – though perhaps only the very young can enjoy in an innocent way its sentimental atmosphere. Very readable, it remained in print until the mid-1960s. Its huge success at the time of publication showed that the British public still had a taste for mawkish public school tales about beautiful youths, though more sophisticated reviewers like Rose Macaulay found it nauseous, as Raymond himself good-humouredly admitted in his memoir.[15]

The patriotic message of this book – that glorious young lads from the public schools gave their lives for England – is throughout intertwined with a religious one. Padre Monty, the boys' spiritual mentor when they go out to the Dardanelles, stresses the importance of making their confessions before battle and going into action "white". The struggle between Muslim Turk and Christian British is described as a "crusade" – a view which had been widely adopted by the press and caused embarrassment to the authorities who had to consider Indian and Arab feelings. Raymond summed up England's future as being inseparable from her religious development:

"England's past is holy; her future is unwritten. But Idealism is mightily abroad among those who shall make the England that is to be. And all that remains for the preacher to say is this: nothing but Christianity will ever gather in that harvest of spiritual ideals which alone will make good our prodigal outlay . . .

... only by turning your sufferings into the seeds of God-like things will you make their memory beautiful." (1922 edn. p. 317).

It is a curious irony that by the time all this was published Raymond had lost his faith and withdrawn from the Church. In 1930 he produced a second war book, *The Jesting Army*, which followed his own experience more closely, though it included a section on the March 1918 retreat which he never witnessed. The book was part of a long-planned trilogy on English life. The characterization is poor and clumsy, the dialogue unreal and the dramatic power of *Tell England* is lacking, despite some harrowing episodes – one of them reminiscent of *The Secret Battle*. Far too much is crammed in, without variation of tempo. On the other hand the book is valuable as an historical source – particularly on the Sinai campaign. Raymond's message is that the indestructible cheerfulness of the soldiers personifies England herself; they, in their millions, "had written for ever", as he puts it, "that her heart was humorous and kind" (1930 edn. p. 448).

Another writer who made a large fortune as the author of sentimental fiction and who, like Raymond, owed his reputation to his appeal to patriotic gratitude after the war was Warwick Deeping.[16]

Deeping had trained as a doctor before the war, but after a year in a country practice began a career writing romantic medieval historical novels. At 38 he joined the RAMC and served in Gallipoli, Egypt, France and Belgium. *Sorrell and Son*, his story of a demobilized war hero – an officer and a gentleman – forced to work as a hotel porter to support his son, appeared in 1925 and was a runaway success. The author's obsession with class in part accounts for this success and is of some historical interest. The book's readability is largely due to the good old device of submitting the hero to a series of hurdles and humiliations which he has to overcome. Deeping used this technique to effect in his much better and more informative war novel *No Hero-This* (1936). Here there is a little plot. Deeping takes the reader through the campaigns that he himself exper-ienced and keeps the excitement up by making his doctor protagonist the victim of a succession of sadistic military jacks-in-office. He is keen to dispose of any illusions about the elevating nature of army life in wartime. Deeping was near middle age and had enjoyed some worldly success before he joined up: he was disinclined to be submissive to authority. His message is partly an individualist one: what makes the war bearable or unbearable is particular men: "Men who will fight like hell under a man they like and respect", he makes one of his characters say, "will chuck up and panic under some savage little cad." (1936 edn. p. 107). Deeping's anti-socialism comes out as strongly in this work as in *Sorrell and Son* – which is probably one reason why George Orwell dismissed his works as "garbage"; though Orwell might well have been expected to sympathize with Deeping's denunciations of the dangers of a large state bureaucracy – military or otherwise – where second-rate men could climb into positions of power which they would abuse. Deeping's patriotism comes over equally strongly – however stupifying and wasteful the war may have been, the cause has been a just one: "We have managed to save Europe from military damnation", he concludes (p. 308).[17]

Edward Thompson's *Lament for Adonis* (1932)[18] while it issues from a cleverer and more sophisticated mind than those of either Raymond or Deeping, is, too, unashamedly sentimental about English youth. It is set in Palestine during the last months of the war. Much of it is a hymn of praise to Britain's better educational institutions and to the courage and cheerfulness of the British army. The "Adonis" of the story is Warren Remfry – supposed to typify the English public school product at its finest – flippant and arrogant, but generous, brave, honourable and athletic. He has a romantic affair with an American girl, becomes engaged to her, is spirited off to France with his battalion and killed.

Though Thompson emphasizes the mess and tedium of war and the inhuman relentlessness of its organization, he celebrates its warriors. He most emphatically proclaims its power to draw out the best in them. "Those who imagine that war brings degradation only know nothing of the thing they presume to discuss." (1932 edn. p. 16). He speaks without any particular enthusiasm about the reasons for Britain's original involvement in the war; but he thinks it splendid that so many young men gave themselves gladly and carelessly in the struggle.

Thompson served as a padre in Mesopotamia and Palestine with the 2nd Leicesters and was awarded the M.C.

A Methodist, he worked as an educational missionary in Bengal before and after the war. He was a poet, a writer and later an academic; he passionately supported the cause of Indian independence. He belongs to a strong English radical tradition both puritan (in its original sense) and romantic. His works show a vigorous intellect and a sense of natural beauty; they radiate life and human sympathy; their tone is far from mild; it is often sharp and satirical.

A similar variety and complexity of views is to be seen also in the next category – the authors who set out to describe the part played by the war in the development of the individual fighting man. Wilfred Ewart's highly successful *Way of Revelation* (1921)[19] tells a story of how the war reveals true worth.

Ewart's protagonist, Sir Adrian Knoyle, suffers agonies at the front because of the infidelity of his beautiful, frivolous fiancée, Lady Rosemary

Meynell; he survives suicidal states of depression through the courageous example of his friend and commanding officer and the sympathetic letters of the friend's noble-hearted widow. The climax of the book comes at the Victory Ball, two weeks after the Armistice, when his faithless love dies in his arms from a drug overdose, to the strains of *God Save the King* (an incident inspired by the real case of the actress Billie Carleton, whose sordid death shortly after the ball caused a national scandal).[20] Cruel as Knoyle's wartime ordeal has been, it is intimated that the real losers have not been those who have suffered through accepting sacrifice but those who have put snobbish materialism or sensational novelty above their common duty.

The book is packed with clichés. It belongs to a genre of aristocratic society romance which was nearing the end of its popularity even by 1921.[21] But it would be unfair to Ewart to dismiss it as insincere. An examination of his manuscript shows that he agonized over it. His publishers wanted many changes, including the alteration of the death scene at the end , which they considered squalid. His repeated revisions (no less than 4) of the last two chapters demonstrate that he had great difficulties in conveying what he wanted to say.[22] His battle scenes are unmoving. Possibly he shrank from reliving them. A shy, stiff-mannered young man, he was also uncomfortable describing Society events. He was at his best portraying the front on a quiet night or the beauty of the countryside behind the lines. He was drawn towards natural life; he is reputed to have had a strange power over wild birds – one reason why Henry Williamson, another war writer who was also a naturalist, felt an affinity with him and praised his work.[23]

Ewart's many corrections also suggest that he was uncertain about his own conclusions. His war experience had left him unhappy. With the help of his cousin, the Earl of Ruthven, he had joined the Scots Guards in 1914 at the age of 22; he was wounded at Neuve Chapelle, rose to the rank of Captain, and in 1918 returned to England, a victim of concussion and shell-shock. He tried like so many of his generation, to make sense of what had happened to him. But, to the end, he remained undecided about how he should finish the book. Certainly this sentimental and humourless work seems unconvincing now. He evidently wanted more time for reflection. In fact he had little left. A promising post-war career as a journalist was cut short when he was killed at the age of thirty by a stray bullet from the gun of a merrymaker during a New Year's Eve fiesta in Mexico City.

Also concerned with the theme of personal development through the war was Gilbert Frankau's *Peter Jackson, Cigar Merchant* (1919).[24] As with Ewart's book, its actual conclusion does not carry conviction – for a very solid reason – it is based on a fantasy, not an experience. Peter Jackson (like Frankau himself, of Jewish extraction, Old Etonian, a trader in cigars, and unsatisfactorily married with two daughters) joins up in 1914. This action makes his wife fall in love with him. Unaware of her new feelings, Jackson proves himself (like Frankau) a very competent officer in the Royal Field Artillery; he takes part in the Somme battle and eventually suffers from shell-shock. It takes him many months to recover or indeed to face up to the nature of his condition. Jackson (like Frankau) cannot at first reconcile a psychological affliction of this kind with the tough insouciant character which he imagines himself to be. All this is interesting and well told. The end, however, is glib: humbled by his ordeal, Jackson begins at last to see his wife with new eyes. They have an idyllic honeymoon camping on the banks of the Thames. The next morning, Mrs. Jackson emerges "like a nymph in the dawn" and prays aloud that she may be allowed to bear him a son. Family bliss is thereby assured. It is true that Gilbert Frankau himself badly wanted a son. It is less true that he wished to remain in a state of faithful conubiality. Fast and flamboyant living alternating with rigorous obsessive literary work were more in his line. By 1924 he was divorced. The book's happy ending, which doubtless had some wishful thinking behind it at the time it was first imagined, also had a sound commercial motivation. According to his daughter Pamela he dismissed the "highbrow success" of his verse novel *One of Us* in 1912, with the words: "*This* isn't what I want. I'm going to write a book that sells a hundred thousand copies". *Peter Jackson* reached that target and started him on a career as a best selling novelist with his eyes firmly fixed on public taste.[25]

Another novel that achieved a huge popular success was Robert Keable's *Simon Called Peter* (1921).[26] This also dealt with war as an agent in personal fulfilment. An Anglican missionary in Africa from 1912 and a compulsive writer since childhood, Keable came over to France in 1917 at the age of thirty as a chaplain with the South African forces. Already disenchanted with the Church, he had a crisis of faith on the Western Front, the substance of which he explained in *Simon Called Peter*, in an effort to get his indignation off his chest. The novel was not autobiographical but drew on actual memories. It made his fortune. He wrote nine more books before his death in 1927. A move to Tahiti failed to save his health which was worsened by overwork. His worldly success was remarkable, though brief: by 1925, *Simon Called Peter* had sold 286,000 copies; the sales of five novels that followed had reached, by the same date, over half a million. 15 years later Keable's name was already almost forgotten.

Simon Called Peter tells the story of a promising and ambitious young London clergyman who joins the army as a padre. The happy courageous spirit of the soldiers whom he meets at Caudebec, Abbeville and Dieppe and the apparent inseparability of their virtues from their habits of blasphemy and fornication persuade him that there is more to life than the genteel Christianity in which he has hitherto believed. He falls violently in love with Julie Gamelyn, a South African nurse who represents all the generous, earthy, liberated sexuality which orthodox religion seems to forbid. Later, however, his faith in Christ is handed back to him with reinforced vigour, largely through his friendship with a prostitute.

Julie sees that he is in the grip of a mighty call and that whatever he may say, she will never mean as much to him as that. So, after some appetizing though unexplicit love scenes, she leaves him. The story is continued in *Recompense* (1925). The plot itself strikes a number of false notes: Keable never recovered his faith, and according to his dedication, he never met a Julie either. Like *Peter Jackson*, *Simon Called Peter* credited the war with healing powers which had no basis in its author's experience. Keable seems to have wished for the return of his faith; at any rate the book's ending has a daydream quality of a kind which evidently appealed to a large public. He has been described as an attractive but divided personality, life-loving, sympathetic and boyish on the one hand, conscience-ridden and austere on the other.[27]

From an historian's point of view the book is worth studying. It handles well the difficulties of a padre in that period; it is one of the books which would really have gained from much freer use of "four-letter words" – unthinkable, of course, at the time; it is precisely that free and easy usage in army circles which presented the Church at the front with many of its difficulties.[28] The soldiers' chats about religion, morality, sex and gambling which fill Keable's book provides excellent illustrations of this aspect of First World War experience.

The hugely successful popular novelist, A.S.M. Hutchinson,[29] also cast the war in the role of redeemer and revealer. Hutchinson was in France with the Royal Engineers. In *If Winter Comes* (which appeared in 1921 and remained in print into the 1950s) he makes the war part of a purgatorial process which brings the hero eventually to bliss in the arms of a high-born lady. It is a device to arouse the masochistic instincts of the public before satisfying their snobbery. *One Increasing Purpose* tells the tale of a man who gains, during the war, a sense of religious mission, through asking the question "Why am I spared?" This was not uncommon and Hutchinson himself seems to have felt something of the kind, which he turned to profit.

There were other, less popular, works which also explored the subject of personal enlightenment through the war. The best things about Kenneth Ingram's *Out of Darkness* (1927)[30] are the author's fictionalized memories of the work of an anti-aircraft battery. Its "revealed" message – that courage and devotion to duty will always triumph over heartless carnage and mean-minded intolerance – is absolutely sincere, but the plot is fantastic and it is clumsily told. Patrick Miller's *The Natural Man* (1924)[31] is original and disturbing; it describes a cold, ambitious, intelligent subaltern in the RFA who is determined to test himself in action. He comes out of the war with an enhanced belief in his own powers and in the need to rely on himself alone. His almost sexual passion for danger and his dark semi-mystical brooding on the military life are not agreeable; but it is quite incomprehensible why a prize was awarded for the book, which has since sunk into near-oblivion.

The strangest book about personal revelation and the war is Olaf Stapledon's *Last Men in London* (1932).[32] Stapledon was an unorthodox socialist thinker who wrote and lectured on scientific and philosophical subjects. Born in 1886, and public school and Oxford educated, he had already begun to live by teaching when the war broke out. An avowed pacifist, he served from 1916 with the Friends' Ambulance Brigade. He is best remembered for his work of science fiction: *Last and First Men* – which speculates on the evolutionary development of men in forthcoming millenia. It is a work of powerful imagination which attracted the admiration of, among others, Sir Winston Churchill. *Last Men in London* is a sequel. It examines the twentieth century as it appears to a very advanced type of humanity who are able to travel back in time, into the minds of selected human specimens and to analyse the progress they are making. Stapledon tries to isolate and draw attention to those elements in the human outlook of his day which represent the next step forward for mankind, the supranational, non-tribal, non-possessive instincts and the moments of greater self-awareness. The book includes a memorable and ironical picture of the Friends' Ambulance Brigade in action and the curious situation of being neither quite a soldier nor quite a pacifist; neither military nor free from military discipline.

It is in consequence of a disaster which takes place while the protagonist, Paul, is with the Brigade, that Stapledon faces the reader with what to *him* is the most baffling question that arises from the war. Paul watches a young fellow ambulanceman die before his eyes. Then he sees "beyond this one dead boy, the countless hosts of the prematurely dead, not the dead of your [this] war only, but of all ages, the whole massed horror of young and vital spirits snuffed out before their time. Paul's mind reeled and collapsed; but not before he had glimpsed in all this horror a brilliant, an insupportable, an inhuman beauty." (1932 edn. pp. 214–5). "How", Paul asks, "can things be so wrong, so meaningless, so filthy; and yet also so right, so overwhelmingly significant, so exquisite?" (p. 225).

The answer comes to him after the war; his conclusion is this: every human being is an instrument which is playing a part in a great music which is the spirit. It is our duty to play harmoniously to the limit of our excellence and to appreciate the best of other people's efforts. We must not dishonour the music; but even if we do so by our actions, the music is not thereby sullied; pain indeed, is essential to the music's grandeur and inseparable from wholeness; "without Satan, with God only", writes Stapledon, "how poor a music". (p. 249). High mysteries indeed. Other writers, including Ernest Raymond,[33] asked similar questions. Whether they would have been satisfied with Stapledon's reply, one may never know. At any rate here one sees the novel about the war as a vehicle of profound speculation on the meaning of that extraordinary event.

Clearly the theme of the war offering some kind of personal salvation was enormously popular and this had nothing to do with the truthfulness of the author's message. Most of these highly successful books came out within 4 years of the end of the war. Some went on being read for a long time thereafter – but after the early 1920s only a few new books in the same genre appeared, less popular and more serious.

By the end of the decade more writers seemed ready to talk in a direct way about their feelings in wartime; many adopted an openly anti-war stance, especially following the appearance of Remarque's *All Quiet on the Western Front* (1929) and the deaths of some of the leading British generals. A flood of books on the war was unleashed. Some novelists were simply preoccupied with presenting their impressions, not necessarily in an autobiographical form, but as accurately in detail and atmosphere as they could manage. I do not count these among the disenchanted school though they are frequently critical of the High Command and readers may draw what pacifist conclusions they wish from their works. Not surprisingly, this category includes some of the best novels of the war, since the main object is fidelity to feelings and experience. The outstanding work is Frederic Manning's *The Middle Parts of Fortune* (1929),[34] later, *Her Privates We*, which has finally appeared in an unexpurgated (1977) edition with its original title restored. It now contains all the swear words which give complete authenticity to its skilfully reproduced conversations. The story, which occupies a short period of time, during the prolonged battle of the Somme in 1916, is tightly controlled and has none of the monotony which is the failing of so many books of its kind. The author was a cultivated Australian who was an established figure in the English literary world by 1914, when he was in his thirty-second year. He served, by his own choice, as a private throughout the war, in the 7th King's Shropshire Light Infantry. The novel served as a vehicle for his views on the conflict and for expressing the outlook of the working-class private soldiers whom he knew.

Enough has been written in this book for there to be little to add here. Its great merit lies in the author's detachment. He is able to look at his subject dispassionately and unhysterically. For him the war is a terrible fact of life which one is powerless to withstand. The plot is grim and tragic; but the qualities of steadfastness and loyalty to comrades are not undervalued – indeed they are held to be a sacred duty. It is a generous-hearted book and, at times, a humorous one. There is a memorable moment of farce when a nice young corporal's words of praise to his elderly *billetrix* "*Cushy avec Mademoiselle*" are interpreted as "*Coucher avec Mademoiselle*", and a storm of outraged Gallic fury follows.[35] Though the characters in the book do not really stand out in one's memory, their conversations are convincingly real in a way that is true of very few other novels of the Great War.

Less accomplished, but also very effective, is Charles R. Benstead's *Retreat* (1930)[36] – an acount of a padre breaking down mentally and physically during the Ludendorff offensive in March–April 1918. It is one of the most harrowing fictional accounts of the war. The priest is a victim of his own hypersensitivity and selfishness – but also of the good hearted indifference of the officers in the battery to which he is attached. Bent on survival in a moment of great crisis, they have no time to help him cope with his nervousness or sympathize with his difficulties in fulfilling his duties. Inadvertently, they humiliate him, and the wretched man, who never actually undergoes the extreme dangers faced by his comrades, gives up completely and eventually dies of the effects of his ordeal. *Retreat* is an intense, violent book; but Benstead, a prolific writer, chiefly on naval matters in later years, cannot quite enlist the sympathy of the reader for the unhappy Padre Warne, who is too inadequate to be a real figure of tragedy. The portrait is a cruel one, reminiscent of H.G. Wells' raving curate in the *War of the Worlds*.

In conveying the chaos and pitilessness of war, Benstead's book is highly effective. There is a very exciting account of the rescue of guns from under the noses of the Germans; and the narrative is helped by a battle map in the endpaper. Benstead's feelings about the General Staff at this time are mixed, if not muddled, but he comes out clearly against Lloyd George and in favour of General Gough and the Fifth Army. The message is not anti-religious as such. On the other hand, the Church of England is criticized for letting men like Warne be its representatives.

Richard Blaker's *Medal Without Bar* (1930)[37] is a seemingly endless account of one man's war in the Royal Field Artillery. Blaker based the book – his seventh novel – on his own experiences in France, Egypt and Palestine. He tells a drab, sometimes horrific tale of endurance, comradeship and anxiety. The leading character is in his late thirties – Blaker's age when he wrote the book; his increasing nervousness, particularly about premature shell explosions, is described as one man after another in his battery is killed. He worries also about his wife, his firm and his son – who joins the RAF. All this invites comparison with Frankau's *Peter Jackson*; it is a more authentic account, but less readable. Some failure in the author's imagination prevents it coming fully to life. Apart from some comic batmen, the personalities are not vivid, though painted with affection – even the youthful charm of the subaltern Reynolds, whose death is the central tragedy, comes over but faintly. Though there is criticism of individual divisional generals, this is hardly a rebel's book. The strongest message is the enriching and unique experience of the brotherhood in arms, beside which even happy married life seems insipid.[38]

Between these realistic accounts and the classic novels of disenchantment, there is an intermediate category – fiction which is clearly anti-war, but whose tone is elegiac rather then embittered. Two novels, both by Edward Thompson, are of this type.

In Araby Orion (1930)[39] is a poetical and poignant story of a soldier being left to die in the Palestine wilderness during the spring of 1918. Corporal Bateman is a portrait, drawn from the life, of Lance Corporal Henry Osborn, 2/16th London Regiment whose death tormented Thompson for many years afterwards. Like the original, Bateman is a kind of saintly puritan mystic – in his last moments of total loneliness he actually sees the face of Christ. For the others who have had to abandon him, there is no such transcendent moment of comfort. One officer is able, in an ambush, to wreak an Achilles-like vengeance on their foes. But the machine of war, inhuman and relentless, takes them further and further away from their friend:

> Through the long dusk they moved, borne despairingly downwards and backward, through the riot of white and crimson cistus and creamy broom and beneath cliffs where the blue, spider-eyed hyssop seemed to watch them. Always, in never-ending avenue, towered the red hollyhocks, a nightmare of mocking brightness. (1930 edn. pp. 82–3)

These Men Thy Friends (1927)[40] is about the Mesopotamia campaign from shortly after the final Turkish surrender of Kut to the days following the British capture of Baghdad. Thompson describes memorably the conditions of that war theatre – first the travel up the sluggish river Tigris, then the inhospitable desert, the sandflies and the sinister menace of a hostile native people; he evokes the ancientness of the land of Nebucadnezzar and of Xenophon's Anabasis. The scenery offers no relief from tedium:

> "If this narrative is dreary", he writes, "the Chronicler is succeeding in making the reader realise the Mesopotamia war as it was." (2nd edn., 1933, p. 45).

It is indeed much more a chronicle than a novel – a critical one, presenting a non-official version of a campaign that in its early stages was mismanaged and all the time was wasteful. It is a tale of generous, heroic men wantonly thrown away. The disparaging views of the leadership which he voices through his principal characters are ones which he claimed often to have heard at the front. He even introduces real friends of his, like Edmund Candler, the official "eyewitness" with the Mesopotamia forces, to support his case with their comments. Like all of Thompson's writings it has a richness, humour and life which make it less dispiriting though no less sad than its more embittered brothers in fiction and memoir.

Ronald Gurner's *Pass Guard at Ypres* (1929)[41] tells the story of Freddy Mann, the cheerful, harmless, baby-faced son of a shopkeeper. Most of the story seems like a classic tale of disenchantment: Man loses faith in his country's cause; his nerves fray; finally he is killed. At the very end, however, we are told that all these losses are part of the complete self-sacrifice that a soldier had to be prepared to make at that time. This was, Gurner told a colleague: "My answer to *All Quiet on the Western Front*". The book contains detail of historical interest – for example, a sympathetic account of General Victor Couper, the commander of the 14th Division.[42] There was in Gurner's writing "the sombre note that gives the chord its power". *Pass Guard* is a wistful little work, like a sad, shadowy dream, but not nearly as tragic as Gurner's own tale. Gurner was clever, powerfully-built and ambitious. Decorated with the M.C., but wounded and shell-shocked, he left the army (8th Rifle Brigade and Cyclists' Corps) and returned to his peacetime occupation as a schoolmaster. He held a number of headmasterships and became a leading educational writer before being appointed, in 1927, Master of Whitgift School. It is plain, however, that the war cast a shadow over a psychological temperament which, it has been suggested, was in any case of the manic depressive type. A novel he wrote in 1931, *Reconstruction* is about a successful school teacher who cannot forget the war, and who is so determined to make the younger generation face the lessons of the past that he sacrifices family and happiness in an effort to achieve a change of attitude. There was at least an *element* of self-portraiture in this tale. The energetic domineering Gurner became increasingly the target of criticism at Whitgift. This had more to do with personal jealousy, his peremptory style, his eccentricities of speech and his reputation for unreliability than with his usually sensible and constructive innovations. The war wound gave him continual pain; mysterious and terrible anxieties haunted him. He became depressed and unstable during his last year at the school (1939) and, finally, killed himself.

Disenchanted anti-war fiction flourished in the late 1920s and early thirties. It took two principal forms. The first was direct expression of anger at the folly and humbug. A striking example is an early one, A. Gristwood's volume *The Somme including also The Coward* (1927).[43] The first paragraph of *The Somme* sets the dramatic tone: "Before the world grew mad, the Somme was a placid stream of Picardy, flowing gently through a broad and winding valley northwards to the English Channel . . . and then came 1914 and the pestilence." A futile action takes place in which the central character is wounded. Both in and out of the line he behaves selfishly and unheroically. *The Coward* is about a man who wounds himself to escape from the war during the March 1918 Retreat, and gets away with it. He is haunted, however, by fear of discovery. The point is that both men are more perceptive than most about the true nature of the war; who therefore can condemn their behaviour? The volume is introduced by H.G. Wells. He invites every schoolboy with a taste for soldiering "to read and ponder" the book. The influence of Wells is, in fact, strong. The self-pitying, callous, clever main characters remind one of those in Wells' fiction – in the *Invisible Man*, for example. There is the same sympathy for the moral outlaw, the same contempt for the stupid. This clear affinity with a literary model raises doubts about the authenticity of the writer's feelings. Both stories are undeniably readable and disturbing.

The most notorious work in this vein is Richard Aldington's *Death of a Hero* (1929).[44] A spiteful, arrogant, badly-assembled book full of unhappy rage, it nonetheless contains scenes of life at the Front which match anything written. It is well enough known not to need much further comment; Aldington served in the infantry from 1916, when he was twenty-four. Later demobilized with shell-shock, he found it impossible to adjust to civilian life and retired to a cottage in Berkshire. His recovery took 8 years. Before the war he had been an accomplished poet in the vanguard of London literary life. By 1929 he felt acutely that he had been left behind. Though the bitterness he poured out in many of his books was morally unimpressive, he could be generous in his judgements and was a champion of any war writing he regarded as faithful to experience.

Siegfried Sassoon, M.C., in the Sherston trilogy[45] adopts a milder manner than Aldington, though passionate indignation seethes behind it. The book is intended as an explanation of why he came to denounce the war. The case is presented in a muddled but emotionally appealing way. There is more refinement in it and also more humour. He certainly does not come across here or in his autobiography, or in his recently published diaries as "a horrid man" to use C.S. Lewis's unfair description;[46] as egoistic, perhaps, but also romantic, tender-hearted and heroic. The trilogy – which is not quite autobiographical – has been rightly praised for its literary quality; the first volume, *The Memoirs of A Fox-Hunting Man* is best. The trilogy drags at the end and peters out into excerpts from his war diaries. It is less rewarding for the historian than his war poetry and memoirs and Aldington has the edge on him in describing the atmosphere of battle.

The best novel of "disenchantment" seen through intelligent eyes is W.M. Yeates' account of the RFC/RAF at War – *Winged Victory*.[47] Yeates was at Colfe's Grammar School, Lewisham, with another war writer, Henry Williamson. He clocked up 248 flying hours in Sopwith Camels and was shot down twice. The book began, as an idea, after he had been invalided out in 1918 and was published in 1934. By that time he was dying of the effects of T.B. aggravated by war strain. Henry Williamson had helped him with the last parts of his book. It sold less than 1000 copies. Later in the Second World War it was eagerly sought after by pilots as the only account of service flying life that was truthful and unidealized.

It is difficult to tell whether all the views expressed in the pilots' mess room conversations are those of Yeates in his later life or are intended to reproduce accurately the feelings and ideas of 21-year-olds. Probably there is little distinction; Yeates seems to have been irrepressibly rebellious and youthful to the end. At any rate he gives an exhilarating picture of lively intellectual exchange – speculative talk about reforming the world, sincere and passionate, but light-hearted. Authority, old conventions, morality, religion, generals, big business, and landlords are all knocked on the head.

There is a hectic desperate spirit behind this talk – the clash between bright hope and fear of extinction. There are many reflections on death. *Winged Victory* is chiefly an account of the extraordinary strain of six months of air combat on the Western Front; of friendship crashing in flames, of talks that were never finished. Nobody interested in the history of air warfare can afford to pass it by: the problems of handling Sopwith Camels and the dangers of ground attack missions are explained with clarity and close detail in its pages. The last sentences of this tough, cheeky, vital, unhappy book sound the keynote – a kind of *riposte* to Ernest Raymond's *Jesting Army*.

> This was England. Wandering lanes, hedged and ditched; casual opulent beauty: trees heavy with fulfilment. It was his native land. He did not care. (Mayflower paperback edn. St. Albans, 1974, p. 447)

There were also many authors of "disenchanted" novels who denounced the war ironically. They presented their case by telling stories of innocents in arms – usually very stupid – who became sacrificial victims. The best of these is George Blake's *Path of Glory* (1929).[48] The setting is Scotland and Cape Helles, where Blake himself, a chronicler in fiction of Scottish life after the war, saw service as an officer. Its leading characters, members of a Scots territorial battalion recruited on the Clyde, are likeable and credible. Col. Macaulay, a primitive, simple Highlander, joins up because of his passion for the bagpipes. He never understands what is happening to him. He puts up with hardship, cruelty, deceit and danger. The one thing he cannot bear is the thought that his best friend has gone into battle without him and been killed. He loses his own life searching for the body, without realizing that his friend has survived the action. The picture of the war is irredeemably black; but the courage and humanity of the soldiers is not called in question; the effect is therefore all the more poignant.

Sharply contrasting is the most degraded fictional picture of the Great War ever written by a combatant on the British side – Liam O'Flaherty's *The Return of the Brute* (1929)[49] – a tale of superstitious emotional Irish Guardsmen grumbling and hating in the mud of Arras during the spring of 1917. The principal character is another innocent – a giant clod of an Irish peasant, a sort of Woyzeck of the bogs, who eventually goes mad, kills the NCO and runs in front of the enemy machine guns. Of the rest of the section, one freezes to death, one drowns in mud and another is fatally lacerated while defaecating. Only one of them dies like a hero. O'Flaherty, who served in the Irish Guards during the war, made his name as the author of romantic evocations of life in the Aran islands. *The Return of the Brute* has been described as his worst book, but it undoubtedly has a monstrous vigour.

This is lacking in Anthony Bertram's cheaply ironical *The Sword Falls* (1929)[50] another book about an innocent at war: Albert Robinson, a blameless solicitor's clerk is robbed of everything by the war – a Zeppelin bombs his home and shell-shocks his wife who later dies; his son is shot as a coward; his daughter marries an Australian soldier and leaves England. But Albert keeps cheerful, in spite of it all. Bertram served valiantly in both wars. He was also a distinguished art critic who did much to promote Paul Nash. In *The Sword Falls* he was operating below intellectual capacity.

Not unlike it, but superior in execution, is Henry Williamson's *Patriot's Progress*.[51] It is the story of a humble "Everyman at War" figure, John Bullock, who joins up full of innocent patriotic fervour and is worn down, maimed and spat out by the war machine; he ends up an uncomplaining and useless cripple. The book has high literary quality but Williamson came to think afterwards that it had failed to express his real feelings. When he wrote his later sequence of war novels in the 1950s he did not draw any inspiration from it: "I found it mannered to the anti-staff period of the infantryman's war of 1915–1917. I wanted to write balanced novels; the staff also had their problems."[52]

Williamson served right through the Great War. He was in action first with the 1/5 London Rifle Brigade, in November 1914, and later held a commission in the Bedfordshire Regiment. He witnessed the Christmas truce of 1914 and his realization that the Germans shared a common humanity with the Allied side awakened him to a sense of the futility of the struggle. Paradoxically, as he admitted later, he enjoyed the war. It overshadowed the rest of his life. He made an outstanding success with novels of animal life based on a meticulous study of wild nature. But he came back repeatedly to the war; he hoped, like Sassoon, to change men's minds; and like Sassoon his humane feelings were stronger than his powers of rational analysis. Not all political idiots are on the left. Williamson believed that Sir Oswald Mosley's British Union of Fascists offered the way forward to European brotherhood, to the spirit of front line comradeship and to a better future for British agriculture – all of which things were dear to Williamson's heart. By backing this wrong horse most loyally he cut himself off from a large potentially sympathetic audience. His non-political nature works continue to sell, but his great masterpiece, *A Chronicle of Ancient Sunlight*, has had a rougher ride and has several times gone out of print. This fifteen volume work covering English life from the 1880s to the 1950s is based largely on his life and expresses, in places, his unrepentant fascist views. Discussion of this properly belongs to the last section of this essay.

Williamson died in 1977. He was a strange, vulnerable, mesmeric personality, full of whimsical humour, loved by his friends, but touchy and quarrelsome. Observers saw in him something of the feral quality of the creatures he studied. He was a romantic egoist, but a human one, with an acute naturalist's eye which makes his account of life at the Front more detailed and convincing than any.[53]

The last category of war fiction to be included in this bibliographical survey is that describing the major changes in society which accompanied the war. These are some works which look at regional effects of the war, like George Blake's *The Valiant Heart* (1939)[54] – on wartime industrial middle-class life in the Clyde basin; others examine social questions, like Vera Brittain's *Honourable Estate* (1936)[55] – on changes in the position of women during that period.

The more ambitious works include some of the finest war novels written. One of these, R.H. Mottram's *Spanish Farm Trilogy*,[56] consists of three interconnected tales of the Western Front: *The Spanish Farm* (1924) shows the war through the eyes of a young French farmer's daughter, the shrewd, handsome Madeleine Vanderlynden. In *Sixty-Four, Ninety-Four!* (1925) she becomes a subsidiary, though important, character in the war career of Lieutenant Skene. Both fade into the background in *The Crime at Vander-lynden's* (1926); here, Mottram's third central figure, Lieutenant Dormer, tries to sort out a compensation claim for the destruction of the family shrine by a British soldier on M. Vanderlynden's farm. The Vanderlyn-dens want money; the French government, who have made it a *cause célèbre*, want punishment. But the soldier can never be traced. It is a satirical and humorous tale; the message, however, is serious – the real crime is the war; the desecration of the shrine is only symbolic of a general desecration. Mottram loathed the war not only for its physical destructive-ness but for its interruption of the process of civilized and constructive life. The war taught decent men to kill, to thieve, to drink hard, to fornicate and to waste time; the complex inherited and acquired moral disciplines of their civilian lives were undermined.

What Mottram has written, is not, as his mentor John Galsworthy has observed, exactly a novel, nor exactly a chronicle.[57] It is a kind of reflective history of the whole Western Front war in fictional form. It is based on his own service experience which lasted for the duration. He first saw action after Loos, as an officer in the 9th Battalion, The Norfolk Regiment. His skill in French enabled him later to work as an interpreter, handling the difficulties which arose between the army and the local population. The tone of the trilogy is low key, detached, charitable, unemotional, dignified. It is his best work. There is very little about the fighting in it, for what really interested Mottram was the whole world of the Western Front rather than how its worst dangers affected him; in any case his liaison work took him for much of the time out of actual combat. He always talked of himself as an observer of life.

His meditations were mostly historical. Britain's phenomenal nine-teenth-century success and later loss of momentum fascinated him. The war he saw as only one factor in the change. Not that Mottram, an old fashioned Liberal with a Unitarian background, was opposed to change as such, provided it was ordered and evolutionary. He had great faith in Britain's regenerative powers through her industrious, dutiful, unshowy professional classes. The history of his home city, Norwich, and its surroundings, dominated his interests. Born above Gurney's Bank in 1884, he was an employee there, following a family tradition from before the war, until 1927. The success of the *Spanish Farm* – which received the Hawthornden prize – persuaded him finally that he could live by his writing; but he stayed on in Norwich and made its provincial world the object of his creative attention.[58] By the end of his long life – he died in 1971 – he was known as "Mr. Norwich". It is no surprise to learn, from those who remember him, that he was much like his own character, Lieutenant Skene – kindly, reliable, gentlemanly and self-effacing.[59]

Though Ford Madox Ford, another important novelist commenting on his times cannot be described in quite the same terms, friends spoke of his broad-mindedness, sensitivity and imaginative perception – qualities which were applied with genius to his great four volume work, *Parade's End* (with *Last Post*)[60] which was published between 1924 and 1928. It is fictionalized social history of the decade which spanned the war. The characters – particularly the compelling central figure, Christopher Tietjens – are the most valid in all First World War fiction and it is their vitality, with Ford's absorbing comments on the war itself, which are its greatest strength. Ford's intentions were ambitious – "the obviation of all future wars"; and he sought to analyse the major changes in British society and to demonstrate what attitudes, already senescent, had been rendered meaningless by the great upheaval.

After a punishing ordeal in the trenches, Tietjens, an honourable, quixotic, flamboyant quintessential English gentleman, turns his back on the rotten ruling class society which he has long in his heart rejected. His misery is very largely caused by the rumours surrounding his relations with his evil wife and his thwarted passion for a young woman school teacher at home. He is made a kind of lightning conductor for the social unhappiness of his period and of the war in particular. There is little about the physical horrors and a great deal about the psychological damage war inflicts. Ford felt that this was the only way in which it could be comprehensibly described; the rest, for him, was incommunicable.

An important figure in the world of letters – the founding editor of the *English Review* and the author of several novels, including a brilliant "advanced" one, *The Good Soldier* (1915) – Ford entered the army as an elderly (and overweight) subaltern in the Welch Regiment in August 1915. He saw service in France and Flanders from the late summer to early in the following year – with an interval; but he had been badly gassed and shell-shocked and did not return there, though he remained in the army for the rest of the war. The effects of gas contributed to his death in 1939.

Though the character of Tietjens is based, allegedly, on that of Arthur Marwood, with whom he founded the *English Review*, there is much of Ford in his eccentric hero. Ford, like Tietjens, was fat, self-assertive and sexually passionate. Both had strong physical personalities. Like Tietjens, Ford found himself frequently the object of hostile criticism. In both cases this was partly because of misplaced generosity or fear of unpleasantness. Ford was more egotistical and more of a fantasist than his hero. He quarrelled with many lovers and collaborators during his life. However, he was frequently more sinned against than sinner. *Parade's End* is not the work of an embittered man; its message is positive. The chief criticism that might be raised about its merits is that his picture of the English ruling class is a tribute to his imagination rather than to his social perception.

Robert Briffault's two lengthy books *Europa* (1936) and *Europa in Limbo* (1937)[61] are even more ambitious in their scope. Briffault was born in 1876, the naturalized son of a French ex-diplomat who had settled in England. He was educated largely in Florence and obtained a degree in medicine when he was only eighteen. As an officer in the 5th Yorks and Lancs, he fought in Gallipoli and on the Western Front and was awarded the M.C. and bar. He was disabled for active service by gas injuries. After the war, he specialized in anthropology. In the 1930s he became a communist and began writing novels. He moved to Paris, where he stayed during the Second World War when he was interned by the Nazis. Afterwards he continued to write until his death in 1948.

The two *Europa* volumes drew partly from his experiences in the early part of his life. Their character lists are far too long and their philosophical arguments go on for pages. To compensate, they are full of bizarre and sensational erotic passages. At certain points, indeed, the publishers insisted on excisions from the text, leaving long rows of dots in their place. Clearly the public of the time must have enjoyed them, for the first volume sold over 200,000 copies in a year.

Briffault set out to demonstrate the worthlessness of the old ruling classes of Europe before the war. With such leaders and with its countries in the grip of predatory financiers, it was inevitable, Briffault argues, that the war should have occurred. The war itself he treats as a kind of evil farce, kept going to serve international oil interest. The scenes at the Front are recounted with savage and fantastic humour. For example, at one point, the biggest coward in the battalion gets so drunk that when he is prodded over the top by his companions, he takes a machine-gun post single-handed and is given the V.C. Briffault sets out to debunk: several pages are devoted to explaining why Nurse Cavell deserved to be shot; others to the defence of conscientious objectors. All this is exhilarating. Unfortunately when he moves the action to the birth pangs of Soviet Russia, the book begins to read like a Bolshevist tract. His sense of humour fails completely at the end in a scene when the hero, Julian Bern, and an upper-class young English woman decide to mate, so that their child can enjoy a splendid communist future.

The last fictional account of war and society to be examined here is Henry Williamson's *Chronicle of Ancient Sunlight* (1951–1969). The leading themes of this mighty *oeuvre* are the stunting effects of city life, Victorian morality and Liberal capitalism; the socially liberating, but devastating impact of the war on individuals; and the hopes of international peace and agricultural revival in the interwar years. Five volumes are devoted to the war period.[62] If we count also the volumes dealing with the adjustment to peacetime conditions, this is by far the longest British fictional account of the war. There is a case for saying that it is the best, though it is uneven. Because of its length, Williamson is able to devote a generous space to each campaign and build up tension in a masterly fashion. He achieves this without monotony by varying the tempo and shifting action backward and forward from the fighting to the home front, keeping each episode short. He is as full of detail as Mottram or Blaker but his language is far more striking and imaginative. Williamson's protagonist comes over strongly – a wild, nervous, self-hating youth, maddening and foolish, yet responsive and full of curiosity. Whether you like him or not, he is not a cardboard figure.

Williamson's ear for conversation varies; it is usually good, but sometimes an uncharacteristic note comes in, fussily didactic, when the author begins to hold forth on certain pet obsessions. But he is very skilled at picking up a regional turn of phrase, and one of the most impressive things about the Chronicle is the way he conveys the fact of *all England* being at war – in every locality, occupation and class.

Finally he comes closer to describing the sensations of fear and the awesome nature of battle convincingly than any of the other novelists, and that, surely, is the supreme test. Richard Aldington stated that these scenes in Williamson's Chronicle were "absolutely accurate in every particular".[63]

There are not many First World War British novels which have so deservedly earned their place in literature. Less than a dozen of the works mentioned in this essay are more interesting to read than the average memoir or outshine the best fiction of the Second World War. Nor have the best authors earned the greatest sales. "Optimistic" British war novels on the whole have fared better than disenchanted ones, particularly in the early twenties – the peak period for First War best-seller fiction. The real vogue for disillusioned accounts of the war only began in the later end of that decade. Even so, "optimistic" sentiments persisted and, with them, indignation at the derogatory descriptions of the British soldier which were becoming common currency: "Martin was not one of the minority of neurotics who have furnished war novelists with their officer heroes, nor of the majority of crude (yet vaguely unhappy) beasts who are now supposed to have composed the rank and file of the warring armies," wrote Edward

Thompson in 1932.[64] The disenchanted writers need further analysis; as well as the influence of literary example at the time it would be interesting to find out how many of them experienced their real disenchantment *after* the war, rather than *during* it, and how many owed their feelings to exceptional suffering or to serving in low-morale battalions.[65]

The excellence of Williamson's *Chronicle* suggests that slow gestation produced the best works. Certainly nothing coming out straight after the war, except *The Secret Battle*, has great merit. On the other hand, one of the last war novels by a veteran to be published, Stuart Cloete's *How Young They Died*, is among the worst.[66] All in all, the war produced few first-rate works of fiction. It is not of course an author's "copy" but the quality of the mind interpreting the experience which really counts. Such quality is at a premium in any period. The novel was an act form developed to describe a relatively stable kind of existence. It proved difficult for less original talents to adapt it to chaos and violence on a hitherto unimagined scale.

Notes

General: *Dictionary of National Biography; The Times; Twentieth Century Authors: A Biographical Dictionary* ed. Stanley J. Kunitz and Howard Haycraft, Wilson, New York 1942, and First Supplement, Wilson, New York 1955; *Who Was Who.*

1. Richard Aldington: *Death of a Hero*, Chatto & Windus, 2nd edn. London 1930 p. IX. See also R.H. Mottram: "A Personal Record", in *Three Personal Records of the War*, Scholartis Press, London 1929, p. 4.
2. Stuart Cloete, *A Victorian Son: An Autobiography 1897–1922*, Collins, London 1972, p. 290.
3. Stuart Cloete: *How Young They Died*, Collins, London 1969.
4. See Paul Fussell: *The Great War and Modern Memory*, O.U.P. Oxford 1975 and Walter Benjamin: *Illuminations*, ed. Hannah Arendt, Jonathan Cape, London 1970.
5. Alan Patrick Herbert (1890–1971): *The Secret Battle*, Methuen, London 1919.
6. Less effective on anatomy of courage is Terence Mahon: *Cold Feet*, Chapman & Hall, London 1929, about an officer condemned to death for cowardice whose nerve has been broken, at school, before the war.
7. George Oliver Onions (1873–1961), novelist and former war artist: *Peace in Our Time*, Chapman & Hall, London 1923. *The New Moon; a romance of reconstruction*, Hodder & Stoughton, London 1918.
8. Peter Deane: *The Victors*, Constable, London 1925.
9. Philip Hamilton Gibbs (1877–1962), journalist and novelist, Balkan War correspondent 1912; Knighted 1920; *Back to Life*, Heinemann, London 1920; *The Middle of the Road*, Hutchinson, London 1923; *Blood Relations*, Hutchinson, London 1935.
10. Oliver Madox Hueffer, younger brother of Ford Madox Hueffer (Ford); Officer in 8th Btn. East Surrey Regt.: *Cousins German*, Ernest Benn, London 1930.
11. Francis Oscar Mann, O.B.E. (1885–1935). Educ. Oxford (1st Class Hons. History), Ministry of Munitions 1915–18, Ministry of Labour 1919–22, Board of Education before War and 1922–35: *Grope Carries On*, Faber and Faber, London 1932.
12. In same genre is Bernard Newman (1897–1968): *The Cavalry went Through*, Victor Gollancz, London 1930 – war veteran's speculations about an alternative military ending to the war.
13. Philip Macdonald: *Patrol*, Collins, London 1927. Filmed as *The Lost Patrol* (U.S. 1934) dir. John Ford, starring Victor MacLagan and Boris Karloff.
14. Ernest Raymond (1888–1974) novelist, educ. St. Paul's London: *Tell England*, Cassell, London 1922. Also on war: *The Jesting Army*, Cassell, London 1930.

15. Ernest Raymond, *The Story of My Days: An Autobiography 1888–1922*, Cassell, London 1968, pp. 182–183.

16. George Warwick Deeping (1877–1950), novelist, educ. Merchant Taylors and Trinity Cambridge: *Sorrell and Son*, Cassell, London 1925; *No Hero – This*, Cassell, London 1936; *Seven Men Came Back*, Cassell, London 1934; *Mr. Gurney and Mr. Slade*, Cassell, London 1944.

17. *No Hero – This* can be compared with Gerald O'Donovan's *How They Did It*, Methuen, London 1920, an intensely patriotic attack on Britain's wartime bureaucracy.

18. Edward John Thompson (1886–1946) Father of Prof. E.P. Thompson: *Lament for Adonis*, Ernest Benn, London 1932. Also on war: novels – *These Men Thy Friends*, London 1927 (q.v.) and *In Araby Orion*, Ernest Benn, London 1930 (q.v.); and – *Mesopotamian Verses*, Epworth Press, London 1918; *Crusaders' Coast*, Ernest Benn, London 1929. *The Leicestershires beyond Baghdad*, Epworth Press, London 1919.

19. Wilfred Herbert Gore Ewart (1892–1922), writer, grandson of 4th Earl of Arran: *Way of Revelation*, Putnam's, London 1921; also on war, posthumously: *When Armageddon Came: Studies in Peace and War*, Rich & Cowan, London 1933; *Scots Guard: Reminiscences of the European War*, Rich & Cowan, London 1934. *Love and Strife* (novel), Richards, London 1936. See *Times* Obituary, 5 Jan. 1923, and Stephen Graham, *Life and Last Words of Wilfred Ewart*, Putnam's, London 1924.

20. See *Times* 20 Nov., 4 Dec., 14 Dec., 21 Dec. 1918.

21. Another novelist who wrote – with some popular success – novels with a similar setting was Hon. Herbert Asquith (1881–1947), R.F.A. 1914–18, Captain; son of the Prime Minister: *Young Orland* and *Roon*, Hutchinson, London 1927 and 1929; these are far better than *Way of Revelation* in describing the war and English upper-class society, but have less intensity; like it, they are very romantic. See also Herbert Asquith: *Moments of Memory*, Hutchinson, London 1937 and *The Volunteer and other poems*, Sidgwick and Jackson, London 1917.

22. Imperial War Museum: Doc. 75/29/1. C. Huntingdon, Putmans, to Capt. W. Ewart, 17 Oct. 1921; and MS of *Way of Revelation*.

23. Henry Williamson: "Tribute to V.M. Yeates" in V.M. Yeates, *Winged Victory*, 3rd edn., Jonathan Cape, London 1961.

24. Gilbert Frankau (1884–1952) poet, novelist, ultra-patriot; commissioned in 9th Btn. East Surrey Regiment, Oct. 1914; transf. to R.F.A. 1915 (107th Brigade); brigade adjutant; fought Loos, Ypres, Somme. Staff Capt. for Special Duties (Propaganda Films) Italy, 1916; shell shock Oct. 1916; invalided out, 1918; married three times: *Peter Jackson, Cigar Merchant* (first appeared serialized in *Land and Water* 1919), 1st pub. as a book Hutchinson, London 1920. Other novels drawing on war experience include: *Martin Make-believe*, Hutchinson, London 1930, and *Three Englishmen*, Hutchinson, London 1935. War Poetry: *The Guns*, Chatto & Windus, London 1916; *The City of Fear and Other Poems*, Chatto & Windus, London 1917; *The Judgement of Valhalla*, Chatto & Windus, London 1918; memoir – *Gilbert Frankau's Self Portrait: a novel of his own life*, Hutchinson, London 1939; see Pamela Frankau: *Pen to Paper*, Heinemann, London 1961.

25. Pamela Frankau: *Pen to Paper*, pp. 180–186.

26. Robert Keable (1887–1927); educ. Whitgift School, Magdalene College, Cambridge; 1st Class Hons., History; ordained Anglican priest 1911: *Simon Called Peter*, Hurst and Blackett, London 1921. *Recompense* (sequel), Hurst and Blackett, London 1925.

27. Kunitz, *op. cit.* is misleading; see *The Whitgiftian*, 1927; and Whitgift School Archives.

28. See for example: Neville Stuart Talbot: *Thoughts on Religion at the Front*, Macmillan, London 1917.

29. Arthur Stuart-Monteith Hutchinson (1880–1971). Son of General H.D. Hutchinson. Trained as doctor; journalist in Fleet Street editor of *Daily Graphic*; wrote three novels before the war; in 1914–18 war served in France with Royal Engineers and 3rd Canadian Tunnelling Corps; also on Headquarters Staff of 10th Corps after Armistice: *If Winter Comes*, Hodder & Stoughton, London 1921; *One Increasing Purpose*, Hodder & Stoughton, London 1925.

30. Archibald Kenneth Ingram (1882–1965), novelist, journalist, lawyer, and commentator on religious, sexual and political matters. Educ. Charterhouse. Served in France

1915–18, Lieut. R.F.A., despatches. Contributor of special literary work for W.O., 1916–18. *Out of Darkness*, Chatto & Windus, London 1927.

31. Patrick Miller: the pseudonym of George Gordon MacFarlane, author: *The Natural Man*, Grant Richards, London 1924.

32. William Olav Stapledon (1886–1950). Educ. Abbotsholme and Balliol, Oxon. School teacher, shipping clerk and lecturer before 1914. Served with Friends' ambulance brigade from 1916: *Last Men in London*, Methuen, London 1932.

33. *The Jesting Army*, pp. 369–70.

34. Frederic Manning (1882–1935). Pseud. Private 19022: *The Middle Parts of Fortune*, 1st edn. 2 vols., Piazza Press, London 1929; 2nd edn.: *Her Privates We*, Peter Davies, London 1930; 1943 edn., under author's name, *Her Privates We*, Peter Davies, London; 1964 edn., with intro. by Edmund Blunden, Peter Davies, London; 1977 edn. also under author's name: *The Middle Parts of Fortune*, Peter Davies, London.

35. Manning, *Middle Parts* (1977 edn.) pp. 104–5.

36. Captain Charles R. Benstead (1896–1980) author, Bursar of St. Catherine's College, Cambridge: *Retreat, a story of 1918*, Methuen, London 1930; 2nd edn., *The Fifth Army Fell Back*, Mellifont Library, London 1937.

37. Richard Blaker (1893–1940); born India; educ. Queen's College, Oxford. R.F.A. 1914–18; career as novelist after demobilization; died aged 46 from effects of gas poisoning. *Medal Without Bar*, Hodder & Stoughton, London 1930.

38. Another novel in the same genre is V.W.W.S. Purcell: *The Other Side of No-Man's Land*, J.M. Dent, London 1929. Purcell was in 4th Yorkshires (Green Howards); captured at Craonelle, 27 May 1918 and imprisoned at Dänhohn until after the armistice, it gives an unconventional and amusing picture of life as a prisoner-of-war.

39. See note 18.

40. See note 18.

41. Stanley Ronald Kershaw Gurner (1890–1939) school teacher, novelist; educ. Merchant Taylors, St. John's College, Oxford. 1st Class Hons. Mods.; taught Haileybury, Clifton, Marlborough; M.C. & despatches, Major, 1917; Gen. Staff, Intelligence (W.O.), 1918; Head Master, Strand School, London, 1920–26, King Edward VII School, Sheffield, 1926–1927; Master of Whitgift School, 1928–1939; wrote an educational and social topics: *Pass Guard at Ypres*, J.M. Dent, London 1930; *Reconstruction*, J.M. Dent London 1931; *War's Echo* [Poems], T. Fisher Unwin, London 1917; see Frederick Percy: *The History of Whitgift School*, Batsford, London 1976; and Ronald Gurner: *I Chose Teaching*, J.M. Dent, London 1937.

42. *Pass Guard at Ypres*, p. 127. "The worst that could be said against General Vicke as a soldier was that he was too attached to his men." *The Bitter End*, J.M. Dent, London 1928, by John Brophy (1899–1965) deals also with loss of innocence, and, like Gurner, sees salvation in duty and sacrifice.

43. See for example, Corrie Denison [Eric Partridge], "From Two Angles" in *A Martial Medley* by Conal O'Riordain and others, Eric Partridge, London 1931, p. 80.

44. Edward Godfree ("Richard") Aldington (1892–1962) man of letters; educ. Dover Coll. & Univ. Coll. London; sec. to Ford Madox Ford 1914; lit. ed. of *Egoist* 1913; volunteered, 1914, but service did not begin till 1916—private, Royal Sussex Regt.; Lieut. & acting capt., France, Flanders; left England 1928: *Death of a Hero*, Chatto & Windus, London 1929; war poems: *Images of War*, C.W. Beaumont, London 1919; war stories: *Roads to Glory*, Chatto & Windus, London 1930.

45. Siegfried Loraine Sassoon (1886–1967), poet; educ. Marlborough & Clare Coll., Camb.; enlisted as trooper Sussex Yeomanry, 1915 commissioned in the Royal Welch Fusiliers. M.C., unsuccessfully recommended for V.C.; wounded 1917; attacked conduct of war; pronounced a shell-shock case; served in Palestine & France 1918: wounded in head July 1918: *Memoirs of a Fox Hunting Man, Memoirs of an Infantry Officer, Sherston's Progress*, Faber & Faber, London 1928, 1930, 1936; pub. as *The Complete Memoirs of George Sherston*, Faber & Faber, London 1937; memoir: *Siegfried's Journey*, Faber & Faber, London 1945; poems: *The Old Huntsman and Other Poems, Counter Attack and Other Poems*, Heinemann, London 1917, 1918. *Siegfried Sassoon's Diaries 1915–18*, ed. Rupert Hart-Davis, Faber & Faber, London 1983.

46. C.S. Lewis to Arthur Greeves, 6 Oct. 1918, letter, in *They Stand Together: The Letters of C.S. Lewis to Arthur Greeves, 1914–63*, ed. Walter Hooper, Collins, London 1979, p. 232.

47. Victor Maslyn Yeates (1896–1934), private, Inns of Court O.T.C. Feb. 1916; 2nd lieut.; Flying Officer R.A.F. from 1 April 1918: *Winged Victory*, 1st edn. Jonathan Cape, London, 1934. See note 23.

48. George Blake (1893–1961), journalist and novelist; born Greenock, on Clyde; wounded Gallipoli; *The Path of Glory*, Constable, London 1929.

49. Liam O'Flaherty (1897–1984) Irish Guards 1915–18. Shell-shocked Langemarck Sept. 1917: *The Return of the Brute*, Mandrake Press, London 1929.

50. Anthony Bertram (1897–1978); author, lecturer and editor. Educ. Douai Abbey, Pembroke Coll., Oxford; served army 1915–19 (wounded) and 1940–44 (Legion of Honour & Croix de Guerre). *The Sword Falls*, Geo. Allen & Unwin, London 1929.

51. Henry Williamson (1895–1977): *The Patriot's Progess: Being the Vicissitudes of Private John Bullock* related by Henry Williamson and drawn by William Kermode, Geoffrey Bles, London 1930.

52. *The Patriot's Progress* 2nd edn., Macdonald and Jane's, London, 1968, p. 196.

53. See: Ed. Brocard Sewell: *Henry Williamson, The Man and his Works: A Symposium*, Tabb House, Padstow, 1980. The bibliography on pp. 80–82 contains errors which are corrected in these notes.

54. See note 48. George Blake: *The Valiant Heart*, Collins, London 1939. Also see Lewis Grassic Gibbon [James Leslie Mitchell], *Sunset Song*, Jarrolds, London 1932, on Kincardineshire in the war; and Pamela Hinkson: *The Ladies Road*, Victor Gollancz, London 1932, on wartime Ireland and England.

55. Vera Brittain (1896–1970), writer, VAD 1915–18. Educ. St. Monica's Kingswood & Somerville, Oxf.; *Honourable Estate*, Victor Gollancz, London 1936; intended as part of a general survey of English life in the early twentieth century which includes *Testament of Youth: An Autobiographical Study of the Years 1900–1925*, Victor Gollancz, London 1933.

56. Ralph Hale Mottram (1883–1971), poet, novelist, historian: *The Spanish Farm Trilogy*, pub. as single volume with three short stories, Chatto and Windus, London 1927. *The Spanish Farm* (1924) sold over 100,000 copies within three years of publication and is in print at the time of writing. See also by R.H. Mottram: *Ten Years Ago*, London 1927; "A Personal Record" in *Three Personal Records of the War*, London 1929; *Europa's Beast*, London 1930; *The Menin Gate*, 1932, *The Window Seat or Life Observed*, London 1954.

57. See preface to *The Spanish Farm Trilogy*, p. X.

58. For example, *Our Mr. Dormer*, London 1927 (novel).

59. I am indebted to Mr. Philip Hepworth M.A., F.L.A., F.R.S.A., for a most helpful account and for the bibliography of Mottram's writings which he prepared for Norwich City Library.

60. Ford Madox Ford (Hueffer) (1873–1939), man of letters: *Some Do Not, No More Parades, A Man Could Stand Up, Last Post*, Duckworth, London 1924, 1925, 1926, 1928; see: Ford Madox Ford: *It Was the Nightingale*, Heinemann, London 1934 (memoir); and Douglas Goldring: *The Last Pre-Raphaelite: A Record of the Life and Writings of Ford Madox Ford*, Macdonald, London 1948.

61. Robert Briffault (1876–1948): *Europa: A Novel of the Days of Ignorance*; *Europa in Limbo*, Robert Hale, London 1936, 1937.

62. Henry Williamson; *How Dear is Life, A Fox under My Cloak, The Golden Virgin, Love and the Loveless, A Test to Destruction*, Macdonald, London 1954, 1955, 1957, 1958, 1960 and revised edns: *How Dear, Fox, Test*, Hamilton & Co. London 1963, 1963, 1964.

63. ed. B. Sewell: Henry Williamson: the Man, the Writings, p. 36.

64. Edward Thompson: *Lament for Adonis*, p. 179.

65. Research into this question is in progress. The reverse is certainly suggested by the case of the novelist and broadcaster Major Christopher Stone D.S.O., M.C. (1882–1965) who advocated a revival of wartime battalion paternalism as a solution to postwar ills; his battalion, 22nd Royal Fusiliers, was one of the strongest in morale and most enlightened; see: *Valley of Indecision*, Collins, London 1920 and *Flying Buttresses*, A.M. Philpot, London 1927. See G.D. Sheffield: *The Effect of War Service on the 22nd Royal Fusiliers (Kensington) 1914–18, with Special Reference to Morale, Discipline and the Officer/Man Relationship*, ch. 5 – unpub. M.A. Thesis, University of Leeds, School of History, 1984.

66. See note 3; Stuart Cloete (1897–1976), best-selling novelist; gazetted 2nd lieut.

K.O.Y.L.I., 1914; commanded company in Ypres Salient. Wounded in lung on Somme; rejoined B.E.F. 1918; wounded very severely St. Leger; put on retired list after 5 years: *How Young They Died*, a collection of clichés about war and psychology with all the wartime sexual adventures the author wanted but never had, is greatly inferior, in evoking the war, to Cloete's memoir, *A Victorian Son*.

About the Authors

Dr. Ian Beckett is in the Department of War Studies and International Affairs at the Royal Military Academy, Sandhurst. He is a Fellow of the Royal Historical Society and has published *Rifleman Form* (1982 Ogilby Trust) and *Politicians and Defence* (Manchester University Press 1981). He and Keith Simpson are co-authors of *A Nation in Arms, a Social Study of the British Army in the First World War*, (Manchester University Press 1985).

Dr. Hugh Cecil is at the School of History, University of Leeds. Dr. Cecil's D.Phil. thesis at Oxford was on the subject of Lord Robert Cecil and the post-war Peace Settlement. Among his published articles there is one on Henry Williamson's novels set in the Great War. Some years ago he was a Harkness visiting Fellow to the U.S.A. and he is currently editing a volume of essays on Robert, Third Marquis of Salisbury and writing a life of the literary critic Sir Desmond MacCarthy.

John Grigg, the writer and historian, was an exhibitioner at New College, Oxford where he was awarded the Gladstone Memorial Prize. In the Second World War he served in the Grenadier Guards and has followed this with a distinguished career as an Editor and columnist in journalism. He has been a Parliamentary candidate, is a Fellow of the Royal Society of Literature and has written a series of historical works, most notably two on the earlier stages of Lloyd George's life. The last volume was published in 1985 and takes the story to the eve of Lloyd George's War Ministry. There will be two further volumes. In 1980 he had two books published: *1943 The Victory That Never Was* (Eyre Methuen) and *Nancy Astor: Portrait of a Pioneer* (Sidgwick and Jackson) and he has had notable achievements in television with programmes on Nancy Astor, Lloyd George and the 1918 Armistice.

Peter Liddle of the Department of History and Geography at Sunderland Polytechnic is a Fellow of the Royal Historical Society and his 1914–18 archives are a centre for the preservation and study of material relating to all aspects of personal experience in the Great War. He has published a number of books and articles on the First World War, most recently *Gallipoli: Pens, Pencils and Cameras at War* (Brasseys 1985). *The Sailor's War 1914–18*, the first of a trilogy on service experience (Blandford 1985) and is awaiting publication of *1916: Aspects of Conflict* (Michael Russell).

Dr. Mike Pattison of Barry College of Further Education successfully submitted a thesis on *the Munitions Inventions Department* for his doctorate and has published an article in the Social Studies of Science Journal.

Dr. Brian Porter was until 1985 Senior Lecturer in the Department of International Politics at the University College of Wales, Aberystwyth and is now Honorary Lecturer in International Relations at the University of Kent. Brian Porter's university education was at the London School of Economics and he has held lecturing posts in the American College in Tours and at the University of Khartoum. In 1967 he was Acting Vice Consul in the Sultanate of Muscat and Oman. Dr. Porter is a Fellow of the Royal Historical Society and has published *Britain and the Rise of Communist China* (O.U.P. 1967), the *Aberystwyth Papers: International Politics 1919–69* (O.U.P. 1972) and contributed to the *The Reason of States* (Allen & Unwin 1978) and *The Community of States* (Allen & Unwin 1982).

Keith Simpson of the Department of War Studies and International Affairs at the Royal Miltary Academy, Sandhurst is the author of *The Old Contemptibles* (George Allen & Unwin 1981). His new book in collaboration with Dr. Beckett is entitled *A Nation in Arms, a Social Study of the British Army in the First World War* (Manchester University Press 1985).

Dr. Malcolm Smith is in the Department of History at the University of Wales, St. David's University College, Lampeter. Dr. Smith studied at Lancaster University and has published *British Air Strategy between the Wars* (O.U.P. 1984) and numerous articles on British history in the twentieth century, mostly on strategic matters. His book *Elite and Mass Culture* (Croom Helm) will be published in 1985.

Dr. David Sweet,M.A., Ph.D. is a lecturer in the History Department at the University of Durham. He contributed three chapters to the Cambridge University Press volume edited by Professor F.H. Hinsley, *British Foreign Policy Under Sir Edward Grey.* He has published articles on British involvement in the Baltic in the nineteenth and twentieth centuries and is currently engaged on a research project relating to the British Parliament in the first decades of the twentieth century.

John Terraine who studied history at Keble College, Oxford has outstanding achievements to his name as a military historian, both as an author and as a T.V. producer and scriptwriter of epic documentaries. His books, particularly *Douglas Haig, the Educated Soldier*; *To Win a War*; *The Smoke and the Fire* and *White Heat, the New Warfare 1914–18* have been massively influential in challenging the received wisdom of public understanding of the Great War. His most recent book is a history of the Royal Air Force in the Second World War. John Terraine is President of the flourishing Western Front Association and has the further distinction of having been awarded the Royal United Services Institution Chesney Gold Medal.

Major-General Tony Trythall retired as Director of Army Education in April 1984. He is the author of *Boney Fuller: the Intellectual General 1878–1966* and has published articles in the *RUSI Journal*, the *Army Quarterly* and the *Journal of Contemporary History*. He was made C.B. in 1983 and is now Managing Director of Brassey's Defence Publishers.

Dr. Bernard Waites has been a member of the Arts Faculty at the Open University since 1972, his research work on the impact of the First World War on class structure having been under the direction of Professor Arthur Marwick. He has been closely concerned with history course development at the Open University and has published articles for the Journal of Contemporary History, Literature and History and the Journal of the Scottish Labour History Society.

Colin S. White is Deputy Director of The Royal Naval Museum, Portsmouth. He has published a number of articles and two books on the Royal Navy in the nineteenth century, *The End of the Sailing Navy* (Mason 1980) and *Victorian Heyday* (Mason 1983).